Praise for *Team Le*

"The need to build strong leadership teams is a recurring theme in articles and books about leadership, yet there is plenty of evidence of dysfunctional teams due to authoritarian leaders, lack of trust, power asymmetries, and marginalization of individuals who are not perceived as 'team players.' This book will help community college leaders build teams that reflect the diverse racial, ethnic, and experiential backgrounds of community college students. Community colleges face political, financial, and social environments that require complex and creative thinking. The contributors to *Team Leadership in Community Colleges* share research and experiential knowledge to help leaders build teams based on differences rather than sameness."—*Estela Mara Bensimon*, *Dean's Professor in Educational Equity; and Director, Center for Urban Education, Rossier School of Education at the University of Southern California*

"Boggs and McPhail have assembled an all-star troupe of experts from within and outside our community college sector. The chapters present a thorough and exhaustive examination of the power and purpose of leadership at all levels. Leadership is a team sport—Boggs and McPhail have been both practitioners and champions in the field. They know firsthand the power of leadership and its role in advancing a culture of success necessary for our students to achieve their hopes and dreams. This book should serve as a guiding narrative for anyone privileged to play a leadership role in community colleges.—*J. Noah Brown*, *President and CEO, Association of Community College Trustees*

"The timeliness of this publication cannot be overstated. Developing strong, competent leaders—at every level—is one of the most pressing challenges facing community colleges today. Equally important is the book's emphasis on building high-functioning leadership teams, which can reduce divisiveness, unify mission, and advance institutional success. The contributors go well beyond theory to offer strategic, experience-based guidance, from board rooms to classrooms."—*Walter G. Bumphus*, *President and CEO, American Association of Community Colleges*

"*Team Leadership in Community Colleges* is a practical, thought-provoking book for practitioners, policy makers, leaders, and aspiring leaders. Edited by highly respected community college practitioner-scholars, George R. Boggs and Christine Johnson McPhail, this book includes chapters that collectively offer seasoned advice, counsel, and ideas about diverse topics such as coaching and leading, gender differences, working with an existing team, effective midlevel leadership teams, workforce development and teams, teaming and the learning college, succession planning, cultural shifts and urban colleges, multicollege leadership teams, governing board and CEO issues, and transformational leadership. This unique book should be on the bookshelf of all community college leaders, aspiring leaders, and policy makers."—**Deborah L. Floyd**, *Professor of Higher Education, Educational Leadership & Research Methodology, Florida Atlantic University*

"*Team Leadership in Community Colleges* is a practical, well-researched, and engaging work for practitioners, scholars, and policymakers interested in the future of higher education and the role of collaborative and inclusive leadership. Employing case studies and empirical examples throughout, successful community college leaders from multiple perspectives and disparate campus environments offer thoughtful reviews and evidence-based approaches to team leadership in the community college setting. I strongly recommend this important and timely book."—**Larry Galizio**, *President/CEO, Community College League of California*

"George R. Boggs and Christine Johnson McPhail make an immeasurable contribution to the future of community colleges by focusing on the critical importance of leadership and teams. Positions at the top of community colleges are turning over rapidly due to retirements and the growing challenges to those in charge, from the board to the CEO and other team members. This book is a valuable blueprint for preparing current and future leaders. Every new president should receive this book on taking office—as should trustees and vice presidents, deans, and department chairs. It not only serves as an excellent textbook for higher education doctoral programs but also can be the 'survival manual' for effective governance, leadership, and vision."— **Barbara Gellman-Danley**, *President, Higher Learning Commission*

"In today's community college, we are reminded on a daily basis that student success is enhanced when each member of the team contributes in an open and candid manner to the conversations at hand. The contributors to a new book, *Team Leadership in Community Colleges*, share their experiences and proffer that individual and collective success are fostered by understanding the rules of organizational decision-making including a respect for the process, the team, and the development of leadership models that effectively guide us through complex choices."—**Rufus Glasper**, *President and CEO, League for Innovation, Chancellor Emeritus, Maricopa Community Colleges*

"Another terrific book on community college leadership by George R. Boggs and Christine Johnson McPhail—two former community college presidents who really know their stuff. *Team Leadership in Community Colleges* focuses on the all-important role of team-building in leadership: how to put together a great team, how to interact with various team members, and—best of all—how to get that team across the goal line when it comes to carrying out an agenda for positive change. Since all college presidents have to work within a team structure—whether they like it or not—this book is a must-read for anyone who is currently a president or who aspires to be. Because, in the end, leaders are only as good as the teams they lead."—***Rob Jenkins***, *Author of the* Chronicle of Higher Education's *community college column and Associate Professor of English at Georgia State University's Perimeter College.*

"Flagship community colleges are run by effective leadership teams, and no one knows more about such teams than George R. Boggs and Christine Johnson McPhail. In their new book, Boggs and McPhail have assembled the most experienced and knowledgeable scholars of this generation to address the key issues regarding how to select, engage, challenge, coach, collaborate with, and reward members of effective leadership teams."—***Terry O'Banion***, *President and CEO Emeritus, League for Innovation in the Community College*

"*Team Leadership in Community Colleges* is a must-read for community college trustees, presidents, senior administrators, faculty, students, and members of the community. We know that leadership is the key variable in identifying or predicting the success of any organization. However, in a collegiate institution, the term *team leadership* takes on a new and most important meaning. Colleges are in fact collegial, collaborative, and cooperative. It takes agreement with the values and mission of the college as well as commitment to these goals and the provision of quality service to the college's community. This new book provides living examples of teamship and team commitment in current community college settings. The authors are experienced and valued community colleges and bring successful leadership experience to their chapters."—***John E. Roueche***, *President, Roueche Graduate Center, National American University; and Sid W. Richardson Regents Chair Emeritus, the University of Texas at Austin*

"This book serves as a guide to all potential and current leaders in community colleges who recognize that their vision and goals will not be realized unless they build a team to assist in their achievement. Whether the team is inherited or developed, it is imperative that certain insights must be considered for it to coalesce. I highly recommend this book be included as part of the toolbox of all community college leaders."—**Belle S. Wheelan**, *President, Commission on Colleges, Southern Association of Colleges and Schools*

"The stakes for community colleges have never been higher. The public trust in our colleges is substantial but being threatened. The critics are gaining traction, often without adequate knowledge. Funding sources are uneven and subject to political forces. The expectations of students and employers are becoming more precise, more diverse, less patient. All of these demands flow across a leader's desk, prompting in me a deep admiration for those courageous enough to shoulder the task. This volume is a gift to them—the CEOs, the trustees, the key administrators of the great American innovation known as the community college."—**Richard Winn**, *President, Accrediting Commission for Community and Junior Colleges*

"Successful institutions understand the importance of teamwork. Astute leaders who foster high-performing organizations do not guide, direct, and/ or lead independent of others but rise as a result of aligned, complementary leadership teams. Boggs and McPhail have edited a rich volume that has thoughtfully examined the complexity of community college organizations and how critical team leadership is in advancing the institutional mission. The text provides chapters from leading scholar-practitioners that span the nuances of informal and formal team building, the diversity of teams, to mid-level and executive leadership opportunities and challenges across settings. *Team Leadership in Community Colleges* offers readers the advantages and navigating teams toward transformative change."—**Eboni M. Zamani-Gallaher**, *Professor/Associate Head, Department of Education Policy, Organization & Leadership, College of Education, Associate Dean, Graduate College, Director, Office of Community College Research and Leadership, University of Illinois*

TEAM LEADERSHIP IN COMMUNITY COLLEGES

TEAM LEADERSHIP IN COMMUNITY COLLEGES

Edited by George R. Boggs and
Christine Johnson McPhail

Foreword by Eloy Ortiz Oakley

STERLING, VIRGINIA

Published by Stylus Publishing, LLC.
22883 Quicksilver Drive
Sterling, Virginia 20166-2019

Library of Congress Cataloging-in-Publication Data
Names: Boggs, George R., editor. | McPhail, Christine Johnson, editor.
Title: Team leadership in community colleges / edited by George R. Boggs, Christine Johnson McPhail ; foreword by Eloy Ortiz Oakley.
Description: First edition. | Sterling, Virginia : Stylus, 2019. | Includes bibliographical references and index. | Summary: "This edited collection is the first book to address the topic of how leaders work with teams to manage and transform community colleges. There is a need to develop better leadership teams in order to administer community colleges effectively and to improve these organizations, whether it be an individual campus, multi-college system or state-wide organization. Edited by two long-time leaders in the field, the book includes contributions from many other experienced leaders and scholars of community colleges"-- Provided by publisher.
Identifiers: LCCN 2019040794 (print) | LCCN 2019040795 (ebook) | ISBN 9781620368862 (cloth) | ISBN 9781620368879 (paperback) | ISBN 9781620368886 (library networkable e-edition) | ISBN 9781620368893 (consumer e-edition)
Subjects: LCSH: Community colleges--Administration. | School management teams.
Classification: LCC LB2328 .T36 2019 (print) | LCC LB2328 (ebook) | DDC 378.1/01--dc23
LC record available at https://lccn.loc.gov/2019040794
LC ebook record available at https://lccn.loc.gov/2019040795

13-digit ISBN: 978-1-62036-886-2 (cloth)
13-digit ISBN: 978-1-62036-887-9 (paperback)
13-digit ISBN: 978-1-62036-888-6 (library networkable e-edition)
13-digit ISBN: 978-1-62036-889-3 (consumer e-edition)

Printed in the United States of America

All first editions printed on acid-free paper
that meets the American National Standards Institute
Z39-48 Standard.

Bulk Purchases

Quantity discounts are available for use in workshops and for staff development.

Call 1-800-232-0223

First Edition, 2020

We dedicate this book to educators, policymakers, and leaders at every level in America's community colleges. As the American Association of Community Colleges' (2012) 21st-Century Commission on the Future of Community Colleges reported, the connection between education and American prosperity is direct and powerful; a highly educated population is fundamental to economic growth and a vibrant democracy. Today's community colleges are key to meeting the education and training challenges faced by the nation. America's 1,103 community colleges enroll 12 million students, including the students who are most at risk for not completing their programs.

We also dedicate this book to community college students. We thank every single one of them for the decision to pursue higher education at community colleges. Without the students who enroll, community colleges would not have been possible or survived. Although community colleges educate the largest number of undergraduates in the United States, the colleges are the least well-funded institutions of higher education. If community colleges are to be successful in their efforts to improve access to education, increase student success rates, and close achievement gaps, they will need competent leaders to navigate these challenges at every level—executive leadership, midlevel leadership, faculty, and staff. However, the leaders cannot be successful alone; they will need to develop, coach, and lead dedicated and competent teams. We dedicate this book to these leaders and the students they serve.

Reference

American Association of Community Colleges. (2012). *Reclaiming the American dream: A report from the 21st-Century Commission on the Future of Community Colleges.* Washington DC: Author.

CONTENTS

FOREWORD

I t is safe to say that as educators we live in interesting times. As leaders in education, we live in extraordinary times. Globalization, artificial intelligence, automation, and machine learning have affected our world in profound ways and significantly sped up the pace of technological change. America can no longer maintain a competitive advantage with only a handful of privileged or lucky people obtaining a quality postsecondary credential. Today, it is an economic imperative for more Americans, regardless of socioeconomic status or pedigree, to obtain a credential. With this new reality our community colleges have an opportunity to once again step in as a great equalizer. Community colleges have a long history of service, providing access to higher education and training to those who would not otherwise have it, thereby democratizing American higher education. The American community college has always had a mission to make education available to the many, not just the few, and to ensure that the benefits and obligations of education represent a democratic opportunity.

In today's environment, for higher education institutions to be the equalizer that America needs, education leaders have to take on some tough challenges. As opinion polls across the nation show, Americans are losing faith in the college degree and are questioning the value of a higher education. Americans are also amassing huge amounts of debt to obtain a college degree. Few who enter higher education institutions, especially students of color, complete a degree, and adult learners are finding it increasingly difficult to go back to college in a traditional college setting. Social justice organizations have rightly put higher education on their civil rights agenda. In response, more and more higher education institutions, public and private, are challenging the traditional higher education paradigm. The education landscape is changing rapidly. The way we have traditionally taught and the way we have measured learning using specific metrics and credentials are no longer accepted as givens. Universities like Arizona State University, Southern New Hampshire University, and Western Governors University are offering new opportunities for learners. For-profit organizations such as Udacity, edX, and Coursera are rewriting the rules that define a college credential. And in 2019 California community colleges launched a fully tech-enabled, competency-based platform aimed at providing education and training to working adults.

With all this change, how do higher education leaders seize opportunities to position their institutions as leaders not laggards? I would argue that we can achieve this forward-thinking position by building teams of leaders.

The editors of this book, George R. Boggs and Christine Johnson McPhail, have compiled a series of examples and experiences from some of our nation's top community college leaders. The editors and the chapter contributors are leaders who understand the importance of building and sustaining effective leadership teams. No longer can a college president or chancellor lead an institution from the ivory tower. Effective institutions intentionally develop and nurture leaders at all levels of the organization who can work together, adapt, form new teams, and organize external forces. This book contains powerful and contemporary examples of building effective leadership teams and gives readers insights on the complexities of leadership teams as living organisms. The contributors share information about how community college leaders are engaging and developing their teams to meet the workplace demands in their communities every day.

In my own experiences, I can attest to the importance of leadership teams. As president of Long Beach City College and now chancellor of California Community Colleges, I have had two impactful experiences that shaped my thinking. First was the creation of the Long Beach College Promise, a multifaceted, organic, and seamless partnership among very large and complex organizations. The Long Beach Unified School District; Long Beach City College; California State University, Long Beach; the City of Long Beach; and the business and philanthropic communities of greater Long Beach came together to create the promise to provide a quality and affordable higher education to every member of the greater Long Beach community. In the early days of the promise, my fellow education leaders, Christopher Steinhauser and F. King Alexander, and I formed leadership teams across the entire spectrum of the promise. We recognized that although it was important for the top leaders to model the promise, it would not expand and lay roots unless the faculty, staff, and community members also modeled leadership. The results were amazing. The promise not only measurably improved the lives of students in Long Beach but also set off a series of events that supported the launch of President Barack Obama's America's College Promise. Indeed, it has supported the growth of college promise initiatives throughout the country. Today my own state celebrates the California College Promise, which would not have happened if it weren't for nurturing local, state, and national leadership teams.

My second experience was in early 2017 when Jerry Brown, California's governor, invited me to discuss the possibility of creating a new online college. After several meetings, we landed on the idea of creating a new, fully tech-enabled and scalable online college that would focus solely on services for adult learners in the workplace. To say that this proposal had opposition would be an understatement. Before I could proceed with the development of the online college, I had to build a strong internal leadership team capable of fending off the opposition and, more important, creating internal and external partnerships that organized a universe of supporters who were willing to advocate for the new college. Drawing talent from all walks of life including social justice organizations, the Brown administration, and leaders in the former Obama administration, I was able to pull together a resilient, adaptive, and motivated leadership team, which was able to organize a number of external leadership teams from the social justice community, organized labor, and business. These teams helped lawmakers understand the importance of this new venture and created awareness and support for the proposal across the state. Building, expanding, and nurturing these teams were critical components of succesfully passing the legislation that enabled the creation of the California Online College. Going forward, strong leadership teams will bring to fruition the benefits of the new college.

The experiences and viewpoints of the contributors to this book provide useful tools and insights that will assist today's higher education leaders. Our nation's community colleges are in the unique position of taking America's education and workforce preparation challenges and using them to create a new paradigm for higher education in our country that is about inclusion not exclusion and supports diversity and prosperity. In summary, this volume examines the underlying principles that guide effective leadership, in particular the skills of leadership teams that are responsible for the day-to-day work. Leading community colleges is not easy, and it requires courageous and coordinated leadership teams. Our community colleges were designed for this moment in history, and it is my hope that leaders throughout higher education will use this book to develop and strengthen their leadership teams to usher in the changes necessary to make quality, meaningful, and affordable higher education available to all Americans.

Eloy Ortiz Oakley, Chancellor
California Community Colleges

Community colleges are complex and dynamic organizations, and their progress and success depend on the functioning of teams of people working together. Many interrelated teams are needed in any college or college system, from the chief executive officer and governing board team to the executive leadership team to midlevel administrative teams to participatory governance committees to divisions and departments and many others. The most successful colleges and college systems focus on the effectiveness of their teams, how aligned they are with the mission and vision, the diversity of viewpoints team members bring to discussions and recommendations, the effectiveness of communication channels, how inclusive and mutually supportive team members are, and what the opportunities are for succession planning and professional development.

The chapters on team leadership provide readers with information about team member selection, development, communication, and evaluation. The chapter contributors, who are among the most respected scholars and practitioners in the community college movement, address questions such as the following: What should a leader do to communicate expectations for team behavior and performance? How should a new leader assess an existing college leadership team? Do men and women behave and perform differently on teams? What can a college president or chancellor do to develop a midlevel leadership team? How can a leader develop a team to focus on relationships with industry to improve college workforce programs? What can a leader do to unite a team behind a strategic plan to make the college more learning centered? How can succession planning develop leadership teams that can pull a college out of crisis? How might a leadership team be different in an urban college setting or in a multicollege setting? How can a leadership team of the chief executive officer (CEO) and the governing board be developed and strengthened? How can leadership teams transform an institution?

In chapter 1 George R. Boggs updates and expands on his earlier writing about the importance of modeling leader behavior, team member selection, team diversity, communicating clear expectations, team member development and evaluation, and coaching and leading. The importance of leader ethics and virtues and how leaders can be effective in an environment of participatory governance are addressed.

Pamela L. Eddy, Catherine Hartman, and Eric Liu report in chapter 2 on the findings of their 2015 and 2016 national survey to determine the influence of gender in team leadership. Their research documents the differences in how men and women in leadership positions define *leadership* and the language they use to describe it. In general, they found that the language female leaders used was more inclusive and collaborative than that of their male counterparts. However, they also were able to document a shift over time for all community college leaders to a more expansive definition of *leadership* that includes roles for others instead of relying solely on positional authority. The chapter provides information about how the ways men and women define *leadership* influence the ways they see teams functioning, which should be useful for improving the effectiveness of leadership teams.

In chapter 3 Eugene Giovannini relies on his experience after being selected as the new chancellor of the Tarrant County Community College to provide valuable advice about how a new leader can assess an existing leadership team. Giovannini takes the reader through a discussion about knowing oneself as a leader, getting to know the organization, and getting to know the new team.

Kimberly Beatty discusses the role of the CEO in developing the college's midlevel leadership team in chapter 4. Beatty makes the case that the team and its development must be aligned with the college mission and vision. She discusses how the American Association of Community Colleges leadership competencies can be used as a model for the design of a create-your-own development program. A case study is provided.

In chapter 5 James Jacobs writes about his experience building leadership teams for workforce development. Jacobs used team-building concepts to transform the college culture, unite the separate credit and noncredit divisions of the college, develop meaningful partnerships with employers, and heal divisions between the occupational and academic transfer areas. Team concepts and open communications won him the cooperation of employee unions and enabled the college to respond to the increased student demand that resulted from the severe economic recession that began in 2007. Jacobs's chapter provides lessons for leaders who want to bring about cultural change and heal divisions in a college and between a college and its community.

In chapter 6 Irving Pressley McPhail discusses how teams can develop and implement a strategic plan. McPhail uses his experience in bringing together three separate colleges as the first chancellor at the Community College of Baltimore County to illustrate out how a strategic plan focused on student learning and a goal to close achievement gaps can give a college direction and bring its members together. The strategic plan's six components of learning support, learning college, infusing technology, management excellence, embracing diversity, and building community form a model that can guide strategic planning at other colleges.

In chapter 7 Russell Lowery-Hart describes how leadership team development and succession planning enabled Amarillo College to overcome a severe financial crisis while building trust and transforming the college culture. His story provides important lessons about how critical it is for college leaders to build diverse, collaborative, and competent leadership teams, pay attention to student voices, define college values, and make succession planning a priority. The chapter gives readers a blueprint for institutional transformation through succession planning and team development.

In chapter 8 Curtis L. Ivery and Gunder A. Myron discuss urban community colleges, the history of their development, and how they serve a unique population. Ivery and Myron examine the use of cross-functional teams that include faculty, staff, students, and others to work on complex, difficult, and future-shaping redesign efforts such as an enterprise-level redesign initiative to improve student success and completion. Projects at several urban community college districts are discussed as examples.

In chapter 9 Shouan Pan discusses the evolution of multiunit community college districts and the interplay between organizational culture and structure. Pan discusses the risks of fragmented systems and the competencies that are important for leadership teams in a multicollege or multicampus institution. He provides recommendations for high-performing multicollege leadership teams.

In chapter 10, Bill McGinnis, Samia Yaqub, and George R. Boggs discuss the importance of the CEO and governing board team and how to develop and strengthen it. Boards of trustees, whether their members are appointed or elected, are responsible for the governance and oversight of community colleges, but they depend on CEOs (college presidents, superintendents, or chancellors) to administer the colleges and districts. To lead and govern effectively, the relationship between a board and its CEO must be strong. Developing and maintaining an effective CEO-board team requires purposeful actions. The contributors provide advice to boards about how to select, orient, and support a CEO. Tips are provided about communications, incentives, and rewards along with warnings about potential pitfalls. McGinnis, Yaqub, and Boggs provide a thoughtful commentary and useful steps for CEOs and trustees who want to develop and maintain an effective governance and leadership team.

In chapter 11 Christine Johnson McPhail addresses the important topic of institutional transformation at a time when the government, accrediting agencies, and foundations are challenging colleges to improve student success rates and to close achievement gaps. The need for change was highlighted by the 21st-Century Commission of the American Association of Community Colleges (2012). McPhail discusses the sequence of strategies that leaders must undertake to engage their teams in the work of transformation to improve the outcomes of institutions. She provides a case study highlighting the transformational change at Anne Arundel Community College. The results of the college's team-based strategic planning process illustrate the concrete payoff of college-wide engagement in the strategic planning process.

In the concluding chapter 12, Christine Johnson McPhail and George R. Boggs reflect on the lessons offered by the contributors, discuss common threads, and look to the future of community colleges to make the point that effective team leadership will be increasingly critical to success.

Team Leadership in Community Colleges is designed to be a helpful resource for leaders, faculty, and policymakers. The editors and contributors hope it will be used in graduate programs, leadership development institutes, and individual leadership development programs. It does not have to be read sequentially; we encourage readers to highlight and bookmark sections as needed. Although the chapters are designed to help leaders and their teams, graduate school faculty should find the book useful as a resource for training aspiring leaders.

George R. Boggs and Christine Johnson McPhail

Reference

American Association of Community Colleges. (2012). *Reclaiming the American Dream: A report from the 21st-Century Commission on the Future of Community Colleges.* Washington DC: American Association of Community Colleges.

ACKNOWLEDGMENTS

We thank our spouses, Ann Boggs and Irving Pressley McPhail, for their support and understanding. We also acknowledge the significant work of our chapter contributors. The insights they share about leadership teams are a valuable resource for leaders at all levels in America's community colleges.

LEADER AND
TEAM EXPECTATIONS

George R. Boggs

olleges are complex and dynamic organizations characterized by nearly constant interactions among individuals and groups of people. The interactions can be positive or negative, and sometimes they can be disruptive. Interactions are affected by campus climate, but over time they can shape the climate and the culture of an organization. Leaders have a significant influence over organizational interactions through their own behavior and through the expectations they communicate to the members of their executive leadership team.

The top college administrator can have a variety of titles; for clarity, in this chapter I refer to this leader as the college chief executive officer (CEO). This chapter focuses primarily on the college executive leadership team (i.e., the team of administrators who report directly to the CEO) but many of the principles also apply to other college teams. For any team to be effective, the leader's communications and expectations must be clear, and they must be aligned with the leader's own behavior and actions. People pay attention to what leaders do perhaps even more than to what they say, so leaders need to model the behavior they expect from others.

If leaders expect team members to be reliable, fair, and compassionate, for example, they must exhibit those qualities. If they want these qualities to permeate the organization, leaders must hold team members accountable to these expectations. Ideally, college administrators should exercise judgment that is fair, dispassionate, consistent, and equitable, and they should be honest and reliable in all they say and do. Actions and decisions should be well thought out and in alignment with the institution's mission and values. Confidences should be kept, but in today's collegial environment, college business must be transparent, and records need to be accessible. Leaders should not assume that these values will be pervasive without their consistent attention to expectations of team members.

Modeling

Because those at the top set the tone for the entire institution, it is critical for community college leaders to set an example of integrity, fairness, openness, and consideration. It is not sufficient for a college CEO to be strong, well connected, and intelligent; a successful leader must also be ethical (Wallin, 2007). As the leaders of the executive team, college CEOs in particular must model ethical and fair behavior, and they must communicate this expectation to their leadership team.

Ethical values are tested frequently, especially for those in positions of influence. For that reason, it is important for leaders to think seriously about ethical values before they are faced with difficult and ambiguous dilemmas that are all too common. Leaders should thoughtfully develop their own personal code of ethics that guides their behavior and decision-making before discussing ethical expectations with their teams.

Haden and Jenkins (2015) describe nine virtues that they believe leaders must have to be exceptional: Humility, honesty, courage, perseverance, hope, charity, balance, wisdom, and justice. Most people have experienced leadership that is lacking one or more of these virtues. Leaders who have big egos and do not give credit to others, who are dishonest, who lack the courage to deal with difficult issues, and who blame others for problems rather than addressing them are all too common. Their behavior negatively affects the organizations they are supposed to lead.

Values and virtues are reflected in not only how leaders interact with people but also how they confront wrongdoing. When the leader becomes aware of a behavior or a practice that can be classified as bullying or harassment or that unfairly or inappropriately discriminates against students or employees because of their gender, race, religion, or sexual preference, the leader must take corrective action. College processes must be fair to all concerned, and unacceptable behaviors or practices cannot be tolerated.

Modeling positive virtues is important for everyone but especially for leaders and leadership teams. Leaders are human and sometimes make mistakes. Sometimes plans do not work out the way they were intended. Leaders who exhibit positive virtues can survive difficulties and still be effective. Although leaders are not expected to know everything, they must inspire trust and give people the confidence that the college leadership will do what is right for the organization and its people.

Participatory Governance and Leadership

Today's community college leaders need to be inclusive and collegial in their leadership styles. Authoritarian leaders may have been needed when colleges were founded, but to be successful in today's environment, leaders must involve people in the decisions and plans that will affect them. Most commonly, colleges involve stakeholders through internal participatory or shared governance committees.

Participatory governance committees bring together representatives of the college's constituent groups. They provide an avenue for an administrator to obtain valuable advice from those who are most knowledgeable about specific aspects of the college or district while also providing an opportunity for employees and students to have a say in recommendations that will affect them. Recommendations for changes in policies and procedures or new policies and procedures are best brought before a governance committee before being forwarded to the CEO or the board for action. Involving governance committees prior to seeking board approval also demonstrates to the trustees that the leadership team values stakeholders' opinions.

Generally governance committees are made up of a specific number of representatives either appointed or nominated by the constituent groups. Employee unions as collective bargaining groups with special legal status are not usually considered constituent groups for the purpose of participatory governance. Leaders should be careful not to confuse a leadership team and a participatory governance committee. Leaders who add constituency group membership to an executive leadership team in an attempt to appear to be collegial will limit the effectiveness of the team. The membership of a leadership team should be defined by the administrators who report to the leader, perhaps augmented by additional administrators who have significant responsibilities.

The Executive Leadership Team

College CEOs should not take a loyal and effective administrative team for granted. It is often assumed that college administrators should work to satisfy the CEO and not the reverse. However, it can be a significant mistake for a leader to ignore the needs and development of administrators, especially those who form the executive leadership team.

College CEOs are in vulnerable positions. They are dependent on others to give them advice and to represent them accurately to faculty, staff, students, and the community. Moreover, they cannot lead their colleges singlehandedly. They must depend on teams of competent and dedicated executive administrators. In many ways, the success of the CEO depends on the effectiveness of the executive leadership team.

In addition to being the executive team leader, the college CEO is also the team coach. Just as an athletic team coach does not make the plays, leaders should not be solving all the problems or doing the jobs of the administrators who report to them. Instead, the leaders should facilitate the problem-solving work of the team members and help them to see the advantages and disadvantages of alternate courses of action.

Continuing the sports analogy, Acebo (1994) found college executive teams to be more like basketball teams than baseball or football teams. In baseball, coaches give directions to players through complex signals. Batters are told whether they should take a pitch, bunt, or swing away. Base runners are told whether to stay put or try to steal a base. In football, the quarterback huddles with the players before the next play pattern. However, in basketball, the plays move too quickly for the coach to give frequent direction to the team, so the team must be able to function without precise direction by the coach.

In an organization as complex as a college, not every decision can be made in team meetings. The team members must be able to function on their own, but the decisions must be coordinated in much the same way as the plays of a basketball team. That means the members must share a common mission and values, and expectations must be clear. Just as basketball teams practice plays, college leadership teams should discuss scenarios and situations and how values and virtues can guide behavior.

Team Diversity

Sharing a common mission and values does not mean that teams should not be diverse. In fact, healthy teams have members who have different perspectives and knowledge sets. Teams with members of different ethnicities, genders, backgrounds, and so on are stronger teams. Diversity in ways of thinking is also important for a team. The most vital teams are made up of members who bring a range of skills, abilities, and talents to their assignments.

There are several methods for assessing leadership styles or ways of approaching issues that can be helpful to leadership teams. Assessing the leadership styles of team members can help them know how to best relate to one another. The four frames of leadership introduced by Bolman and Deal (2013) can provide valuable insights into how leaders act and how they approach issues. The frames define leaders according to strengths in structure, human resources, politics, and symbolism.

Structural leaders emphasize rationality, analysis, logic, facts, and data. They are likely to believe in the importance of a clear organizational structure and well-developed management systems. Human resource leaders emphasize the institution's people. They believe in the importance of coaching, participation, teamwork, motivation, and good interpersonal skills. Political leaders believe that managers live in a world of conflict and scarce resources. They emphasize the importance of building alliances, networks, and coalitions to secure the outcome they desire. Symbolic leaders believe in the importance of vision and inspiration and make use of symbols and stories in ways that give people hope and meaning.

Although it may not be very likely to find one leader who is well balanced in these four frames, it is possible to achieve balance and depth of styles in a team. These complementary skills and leadership orientations will help the team to view situations and challenges from a variety of perspectives. The quality of the team decisions should be better, and the advice to the leader should be more complete.

Selecting Team Members

The process of selecting its members is critically important to the effectiveness of the leadership team. Most often, a new college CEO inherits a college leadership team, and it is usually wise to try to develop the existing team rather than immediately change it. However, over time, a leader will be given opportunities to replace team members or perhaps add to the team.

Mandel (2013) makes the case for the importance of hiring the right people to be on a leadership team. He believes that with the right people on the team, smart strategy, strong culture, and perfect execution tend to follow. In contrast, when mediocre people are on the team, strategy and culture are negatively affected, and perfect execution is unlikely. Mandel says that too many leaders fail to make the commitment needed to build a team with only the best people. More often, he says, organizations compromise.

Among the most critical decisions a college CEO makes is assembling executive team members. Most leaders welcome the chance to hire their own team members, even though a search committee often does most of the applicant screening, and a board of trustees actually does the hiring. Still, it is important for the college leader either to make the final decision or to make a recommendation to the board.

Even before the selection process starts, the college CEO should meet with the search committee, which should include representatives from the executive leadership team, to discuss the qualities sought in the new administrator (Boggs, 1995). This is the time to think about the skills, talents, expertise, and perspective needed, to not merely do the job but add depth and balance to the team. Teams can be made more effective by hiring leaders who have diverse and complementary sets of styles and talents. The executive team should also be diverse in gender and ethnicity. It is important for the administration of a college to reflect the diversity of the student body and the community. Hiring decisions provide the opportunity to balance the team.

When selecting new team members it is most important for the skills and talents of the prospective new team member to match the needs of the team and the college. The successful candidate must have values that are compatible with those of the team and the team leader. The philosophy of the candidate must agree with the culture of the college. A college CEO should use all available means to determine whether a good fit exists before recommending a new executive leadership team member for employment. The cost of making a bad hiring decision is high for the college and the candidate (Boggs, 1995).

The CEO should develop interview questions that not only measure knowledge and experience but also probe beliefs, philosophy, style, and values. Mandel (2013) advises leaders to look for the following, in order of priority:

- Intellectual firepower
- Values
- Passion
- Work ethic
- Experience (p. 5)

Checking references is important, but it is usually most instructive to interview the references face-to-face during a site visit at the candidate's current institution. The college CEO can schedule particular people for reference interviews. For example, it is usually helpful to talk to the candidate's supervisor and to employees the candidate supervises. Colleagues of the candidate can also provide valuable information. Employee union and faculty senate representatives provide a valuable perspective of the candidate's style and human relation skills. It is wise to remember that doing the right thing is not always popular, so it is sometimes necessary to find the basis for any negative comments that are picked up in a site visit or reference check.

When the college CEO makes a recommendation for employment of a new executive team member, it should be done with the confidence that can come only from a thorough evaluation of the finalists. The leader must be convinced that the recommended candidate is the best available person to meet the needs of the college and to add needed diversity, depth, and balance to the team. Without the necessary match, the best solution is to extend or reopen the search.

CEOs can also be on the lookout for people already at the college who have the potential for leadership. Succession planning, leadership development, and mentoring programs give college leaders the opportunity to develop their own leadership teams. These programs can also improve trust levels at the college as they provide a venue for employees to learn together and to understand how everyone contributes to the success of the college.

Occasionally, it may be necessary to remove someone from the team and reassign that person to other responsibilities or even to terminate employment. According to Mandel (2013), leaders have to do what most people find difficult, that is, removing those who can't do the job well enough and who resist efforts to improve. Ousting a team member is one of the most difficult decisions for a college CEO to make, and it should not be considered lightly. Such a change should be contemplated only when a team member behaves unethically, is unable or unwilling to perform job responsibilities, is disruptive to the operation of the team, or does not respond adequately to recommendations for improvement. Even then, legal and political consequences should be considered. It is important for the leader to check with legal counsel to be sure that individual rights are protected and that the college will not incur unnecessary legal expenses.

The college CEO must be sure the board of trustees will support the decision to remove an executive team member, and the CEO should prepare the board for a potential period of unrest on the campus, especially if the administrator who is removed is popular with faculty and staff members or with students or in the community. If the team member is reassigned to a different position, the person may very well remain with the institution for some time, so the CEO should show whatever consideration is necessary to ease the transition and to avoid embarrassing the employee. The leader must be careful about what is said publicly about reassignment or employment termination of a team member.

Once the team members are in place, the CEO must clearly define the expectations for members' behavior, evaluate the performance of the team and the individual members, and provide opportunities for professional development and team building. Team members should be complimented for their contributions toward the effectiveness of the team. Corrections should be made in private between the individual team member and supervisor.

Expectations

Rosenthal and Jacobson (1968) conducted an experiment in a public elementary school in 1965, telling teachers that the students who were assigned to them could be expected to be growth spurters, based on the students' test scores. Sure enough, the students demonstrated advanced academic growth during the school year, even though the test was nonexistent and the students designated as spurters were chosen at random. The factor that made the difference in the advancement of the students was that the teachers expected more from them.

Expectations can be powerful motivators for a team, and a lack of clearly communicated expectations often leads to serious problems. The team leader as coach should communicate expectations clearly and often. Leaders should talk about their expectations for honesty, ethical behavior, fairness, legality, respect, courtesy, civility, cooperation, visibility, courage, balance, and scholarship. All of these are important characteristics of sound leadership.

If team members are not honest in their dealings with people, or if their behavior is considered to be unethical, the college leadership will not enjoy the level of trust needed to be effective. College leaders must be honest and data informed to keep a college from being politically divided. Lack of attention to fairness and legality can lead to unnecessary legal challenges and costs for the college. However, the threat of a lawsuit should never keep college leaders from doing what is right.

Leadership team members do not have to be best friends, but they should respect each other and treat each other civilly. Some college CEOs encourage a competitive climate among team members, with the belief that competition will bring out greater effort. However, most leaders want their executive administrators to be on the same team and to realize how interdependent they are. Team members should cooperate and collaborate with each other and be institutional advocates, not just narrow constituency advocates.

It is all too easy today for college administrators to become trapped by their inbox and never leave their office. However, it is important for team members to be visible on campus, in the community, and statewide and nationally. Leaders should schedule time to get out of the office and talk to faculty, staff, and students so they are familiar with current issues and can accurately portray leadership plans and decisions. Attendance at community events is important for the college to maintain community support. Involvement at the state and national levels helps keep leaders informed about emerging issues and provides visibility for the college. CEOs must communicate their expectations for involvement in campus, community, state, and national organizations to all members of the leadership team.

Not all leadership decisions will be popular, but leaders need the courage to do what is right for the institution. Confronting faculty and staff with data that show the need for improvement may not be comfortable, but leaders need the courage to do it and the common sense to engage the faculty and staff to help develop plans to do a better job. Leaders who disparage the college and have all the answers will not get the necessary buy-in from others to accomplish anything. Communicating negative information to a board of trustees takes courage, but boards need to know the truth to address issues before they get out of hand. The team leader should ask the team members to be courageous enough to do what is right for the college and its students, and then the leader needs the courage to support the team members.

College leaders must protect their own health and the health and well-being of their team members. College leadership jobs are stressful and can be all consuming. Team leaders should communicate their expectation for team members to protect their health and fitness and strive for balance in their lives. Leaders need to get ahead of their calendars and block out time for fitness, family, spiritual renewal, and recreation. Unless time for these activities is scheduled, professional activities and commitments will fill the calendar. Leadership team members also should be reminded that they are leading a scholarly institution. It is desirable for them to see themselves as scholars as well as leaders. They can remain engaged in their discipline or perhaps study leadership or ways to improve student learning.

The CEO should also communicate that team members are expected to express their own high expectations to faculty and staff in their areas. These expectations should be in alignment with those of the leadership team and with the mission and goals of the college. Employee evaluations should document progress toward meeting individual and college goals, recognize and commend exemplary achievements, and make necessary recommendations for improvement.

Communication

Although communication among members of the college executive leadership team is not usually as intense as it is for an athletic team during a contest, it is nonetheless just as important for success. The executive team members are, among other things, the eyes and ears of the CEO, who should know, at least in general terms, what the issues, problems, and concerns of the campus community are. The CEO should never be sheltered from the truth, no matter how unpleasant it may be. Similarly, the CEO is obligated to pass along information to team members so they can do their jobs as effectively as possible and to be sure board members are appropriately informed.

Communication at a college takes many forms: oral communication in group or one-on-one meetings, telephone calls, or voicemail or written communications like e-mail, text message, letter, circulation, or memoranda. Each of these forms of communication has its advantage. Letters, memoranda, and published newsletters are more formal and less immediate. Given the high degree of individual responsibility of leadership team members and the many demands on their time, voice mail, text messages, e-mail, and social media have taken on greater importance.

Electronic and voice messages are transmitted immediately and can be read or listened to at the convenience of the recipient, eliminating the problems associated with telephone tag or trying to find the time in a busy day for a meeting. Messages can be sent to one or more team members at the same time. While traveling, team members can stay in touch though a laptop computer, electronic tablet, or cellular telephone.

The CEO must always be aware of the type of communication from team members. If team members seem to be constantly seeking detailed directions, they may be afraid of what might happen if they take a risk and fail. If they constantly bring problems to the leader for solutions, they are inviting the CEO to do their jobs. The leader, of course, cannot afford to accept such an invitation. Instead, the CEO should ask team members to communicate their own ideas for solving problems. The CEO can make suggestions or guide a team member, but if the leader makes all the decisions, the team will not function. The CEO should create an environment in which team members are encouraged to take calculated risks in the process of decision-making.

Team members should also be encouraged to communicate regularly with people outside the executive leadership team. An effective college functions on the flow of accurate information. The executive leadership team is not in competition with other teams at the college. Rather, it is the duty of the executive leadership team to be sure that the various teams and individuals at the college function at their best, and sharing information is essential to that purpose. Communication in the form of handwritten notes is often effective in recognizing the contributions of the college's people.

In the course of their administrative duties, executive team members will have access to information that would otherwise be inaccessible. Although it is the responsibility of administrators to promote open communications, some items must be held in confidence. Team members must develop a good sense of issues that can be communicated and those that must be held in confidence. If any uncertainty arises, team members should check with their supervisor before sharing information. When executive team members communicate, they must be sure what they say is accurate.

The leadership team should also have a clear communication plan in place to addresses crisis situations, especially issues of safety and security. The plan should address how communication will take place and who is responsible for contacting internal constituencies such as department offices, students, and employees as well as external groups such as law enforcement, fire and safety organizations, health and mental health organizations, media, and community organizations. The communications plan should be practiced and incorporated into the way the college does business (Boggs & McPhail, 2016).

Team Meetings

Most of the work of the executive leadership team will occur outside team meetings; however, meetings serve some valuable purposes. They provide the opportunity for group discussion, problem-solving, and planning. Meetings can also coordinate the activities of the team. Meeting together, the executive leadership team can be a powerful advisory body for the college CEO.

Some ground rules are important for using meeting time productively and for enhancing the creative abilities of the team. The CEO should never call the team together merely to share information. Information sharing can be accomplished through much less time-consuming methods such as memoranda, voice mails, e-mails, or text messages. Time is valuable for this important group.

Because the executive leadership team is made up of members with demanding schedules, a regular meeting time should be established. Meetings can always be canceled or rescheduled. Meeting agendas with appropriate backup materials should be distributed enough in advance to allow the members to prepare their thoughts.

The CEO has some important functions to play before discussing critical issues or engaging the team in problem-solving. The team should be clearly told whether the team as a whole will decide the final course of action, or if the CEO will determine it after listening to the discussion at the meeting. Both kinds of decision processes can and should be used, depending on the situation. Recommendations and decisions must be motivated by doing what is right for the college in light of its vision statement, mission, goals, needs, and values. The team can also use Terry O'Banion's (1997) criteria for decisions:

- Does this action improve and expand learning?
- How do we know this action improves and expands learning? (p. 9)

If the decision is to be made by the team, the CEO should indicate whether the decision will be made by consensus of the group or by vote after the case has been presented and discussed. Voting is more efficient, but consensus usually yields more team support for the decision.

The CEO should try to create an environment in which it is permissible for members to react to the leader's preliminary decisions without risk so long as members support the final decision of the team or the CEO. Even so, it is usually wise for the CEO to stay neutral, at least until a decision is about to be made. An early indication of judgment by the leader might inhibit the critical discussion that is necessary for the most informed decisions.

The CEO should try to keep the group on schedule, on task, and focused on the problem at hand. All members of the group, even those who seem most removed from the problem, should be encouraged to participate. No one should be allowed to dominate the discussion. Personal criticism cannot be tolerated, and no attempt should be made to assign blame to any team member.

For the executive team to function appropriately, it is essential for its members to respect their colleagues and behave courteously to one another. That is not to say that conflict or disagreement should not exist. In fact, disagreement is important for proper functioning of the team. When it is openly recognized, conflict can serve to test the merit of ideas against challenges. Conflicting opinions can stimulate other points of view so long as all members feel free to participate. In an effective team, divergent views are respected, disagreement is expected and encouraged, and criticism is constructive. An atmosphere that encourages divergent opinions but still maintains the integrity of the team is the most desirable.

The CEO should encourage members to try to influence the outcomes of discussions if they are professional in doing so. Strong opinions and heated (but civil) discussions are acceptable so long as the members can support, explain, and defend the final decision of the team or the team leader.

Finally, the CEO should bring the meeting to an effective close. Conclusions should be reviewed, assignments for specific team members might have to be made, and time lines might have to be established. In subsequent team meetings, team members should spend some time in self-evaluation. The team should view failures and mistakes as learning opportunities. Success should be acknowledged and celebrated.

Mission, Goals, Outcomes, and Rewards

Perhaps the most basic of the expectations for members of the executive leadership team is to understand and support the college mission. Team members must also share a common vision for the future of the college. The colleges that are the most successful have developed a well-defined mission and a shared vision for the future. Leadership team members should be guided by a statement of values and should be sure that plans, goals, and decisions are aligned with the mission and vision statement.

The college mission statement defines the institution's purpose for being, and the vision statement is a picture of what the institution is striving to be. The values are what the college believes in. The mission and vision statements should emerge from an understanding of the educational and training needs of the communities served by the college. They should clearly lead to the strategic goals that everyone at the institution is committed to achieving.

The mission of the executive leadership team is to ensure the effective and efficient operation of the college, guided by the college's mission, a shared vision for the future, and the expectations of the CEO. The team and its individual members should develop goals each academic year. To develop team goals, an extended meeting or retreat, preferably off campus and away from distractions, should be scheduled. A goal-setting retreat may also include team-building activities. Sometimes having an experienced facilitator conduct the meetings can be helpful; the CEO can then freely participate and observe the functioning of the team without having to be concerned about keeping the group on task.

Team goals must align with the college's mission and vision. They should be realistic but still challenging. Most important, they should be measurable. At the end of the year, measures of team goal attainment can be used to evaluate progress in what is otherwise an unending series of challenges that find their way to the executive leadership team. The process of developing team goals and evaluating progress reinforces the value of the team and the interdependence of its members.

After the team goals have been developed and approved, it is important to share them with the college and external communities. College constituencies should know what the goals are and what their role might be in helping to achieve them. External groups will likely be more inclined to support the college if they know what the college leadership wants to achieve.

Individual team member goals should be developed by the team member with the agreement of his or her supervisor. The goals will likely include important objectives for the area of responsibility of the administrator. Goals should also include areas for development or improvement for the individual team member. Again, the goals must be measurable, and they should be used in the personnel evaluation process.

A team leader should reward and recognize team members for their accomplishments and contributions to the success of the team. Leaders need to remember the adage to praise people in public but criticize them privately. Team goal accomplishments can provide an opportunity for the entire team to celebrate together. The team can recognize individual goal achievement publicly within and outside the team. Personnel evaluations should make note of a team member's goal achievements. Supervisors, however, must recognize that extenuating circumstances often delay goal achievement, especially if the goals are ambitious.

Coaching and Leading

Like the head coach of a football team, the college CEO is held accountable for the success of the team. Head coaches can lose their jobs if they cannot develop winning teams, and so can college leaders. The success of the executive leadership team is not measured in wins and losses but in institutional effectiveness outcomes and goal achievement. The way the team operates is extremely important in establishing a climate for excellence throughout the college.

A successful coach empowers team members to perform well. Team members must be given opportunities for professional growth and development; they need to be recognized publicly for their achievements and for their contributions to the success of the team and the college. Leaders should eliminate barriers to their success whenever possible and encourage team members to be professionally active by attending conferences, making presentations, and writing articles.

College CEOs should be ideal role models and mentors for the members of their executive teams. The CEO is likely to be the most experienced leader on the team and draw on a variety of past experiences to help and advise team members. CEOs can help team members plan careers and provide them with the opportunities to gain experience that will enable them to move into higher levels of leadership. CEOs usually speak with pride about the colleagues who formerly worked for them and are now leading their own teams.

Colleges can sometimes be hostile places. The leader must visibly support team members when they are unfairly criticized and when they come under fire for doing what is right for the institution. Doing the right thing can be unpopular. On the other hand, when a team member needs correction, the conversation should be held in private. The CEO can often help by offering advice to team members, clearly distinguishing between advice and directives.

Leaders must let team members do their jobs without detailed supervision or direction. Even when the task is done in a different way from how the leader would have done it, or if the decision is not exactly the same one the leader would have made, team members need this latitude. If the actions and decisions of team members do not place the college in financial or legal jeopardy and are not in disagreement with the institutional mission, vision, and team goals, and if the team member is meeting expectations for behavior set by the CEO, the team member should be allowed to do the assigned job without unnecessary interference. This confidence in team members is essential for the successful operation of the executive leadership team. Of course the leader should be informed and ready to step in if necessary to protect the college and its people, but this intervention should happen rarely.

In addition to responsibilities as coach, the CEO is also the leader of the team and the chief executive of the college. As team leader, the CEO must create an environment in which team members feel free to convey difficult and sensitive information to the leader, offer the leader advice, and even disagree respectfully within the confines of a meeting. The leader should not discourage open debate in meetings and must not shoot the messenger who brings uncomfortable news. Once a decision is made, however, it is important for each administrative team member to support the leader and the decision. This dual responsibility of being coach and team leader at once can be difficult, requiring continuous efforts by the CEO to be sure members know whether the CEO is acting as coach or as team leader. Executive teams are most successful if the members know each other and their leader well enough to interpret actions and statements accurately.

The leader must be aware of any behavior that undermines the effectiveness of the team. For example, some team members may have been trained by prior experience to try to lay the blame for a problem on someone rather than try to solve the problem or determine how to prevent the problem from recurring. Teams that focus on placing blame will destroy the trust and morale of the team. The leader must guide the team to problem solve rather than to assign blame.

Warding off unfavorable information is another behavior that will destroy the effectiveness of the team. No one likes bad news, but team members, including the CEO, cannot isolate themselves from unpleasant information, or they will find it impossible to solve problems before it is too late. Academic publications are full of stories about college leaders who were more interested in protecting the institutional image than in addressing difficult issues. Ignoring problems is never a wise course of action.

Shying away from change is another way to make a team ineffective. Change is difficult for many people, but being open to change is a prerequisite to effective teamwork and a healthy college. It is a good idea for some team members to question suggestions for change so the team can be sure to carefully consider the consequences for the organization. Change and the process for change must be carefully considered. However, leadership teams must not fall into the trap of always favoring the familiar over new ideas.

Ignoring performance problems is yet another way of rendering a team ineffective. Team members know who is performing and who isn't. The CEO must take the initiative and privately confront any team member who is not living up to expectations before lagging individual performance affects the effectiveness of the team.

Conclusion

Acting alone, college leaders simply cannot operate a college and plan for its future. Even the strongest of CEOs cannot have lasting influences on their colleges unless they can change the values and the vision of the institution's people. Extending the college leadership to an effective executive team can make the difference between success and failure for the leader and between excellence and mediocrity for the institution. It is worth the time and effort for college leaders to develop and nurture an effective executive leadership team.

The leader sets the membership and the expectations for operation of the executive leadership team. Complementary styles, skills, and talents improve the health and vitality of the team. Hiring decisions provide opportunities to bring balance and diversity to the team. Membership should include, at a minimum, the executive administrators who report to the CEO. But the executive leadership team is not a governance committee that needs to have broad representation from all constituency groups. Instead, it is an administrative or leadership team, and discussions may include confidential and sensitive issues.

Effective teams must know their purpose and what is expected of them. They must know and use the college mission and vision statements in performing their jobs. They must be able to think and act in ways that are aligned with institutional values and expectations, and they must cooperate across divisional boundaries.

Team members need to set individual and team goals and should be evaluated based on the outcomes. Leaders should recognize team members for their achievements and for their contributions to the team's success. Communications among team members and between the leader and team members must be continuous. Communications to people outside the team should be open but guided by knowledge of what information must be held in confidence and what should be shared.

Executive leadership team members are in very visible positions. What they do and how they do it will be closely observed by members of the campus community. Members should be expected to be honest in their dealings with people. They should find ways to make things happen within the boundaries of high ethical standards. Team members should care about the college's people and let them know they care. They should involve people in their decision-making and planning. Team members should encourage and support innovation while seeking and rewarding good behavior. They need to confront unacceptable behavior appropriately.

Team members must tell the leader what they know and not just what they think the leader wants to hear. They should bring the leader ideas and not just problems. What is best to support and enhance student learning should guide the behavior and decisions of team members. Finally, team members must communicate their own high expectations to the teams they lead.

College CEOs have the responsibility to coach and to lead the executive leadership team. The proper functioning of the team and the development of its individual members should be primary concerns of the leader. In fact, maintaining and developing the team and creating the structure and environment for its successful operation may prove to be the most important and rewarding responsibilities of college leadership.

References

Acebo, S. (1994). A paradigm shift to team leadership in the community college. In G. A. Baker III (Ed.), *A handbook on the community college in America: Its history, mission, and management* (pp. 580–588). Westport, CT: Greenwood Press.

Boggs, G. R. (1995). The president and the executive leadership team. In G. A. Baker III (Ed.), *Team building for quality: Transitions in the American community college* (pp. 63–77). Washington, DC: Community College Press.

Boggs, G. R., & McPhail, C. J. (2016). *Practical leadership in community colleges: Navigating today's challenges.* Hoboken, NJ: Wiley.

Bolman, L. G., & Deal, T. E. (2013). *Reframing organizations: Artistry, choice, and leadership* (5th ed.). San Francisco, CA: Jossey-Bass.

Haden, N. K., & Jenkins, R. (2015). *The 9 virtues of exceptional leaders: Unlocking your leadership potential.* Atlanta, GA: Deeds.

Mandel, M. (2013). *It's all about who you hire, how they lead, and other essential advice from a self-made leader.* San Francisco, CA: Jossey-Bass.

O'Banion, T. (1997). *Creating more learning-centered community colleges.* Chandler, AZ: League for Innovation in the Community College.

Rosenthal, R., & Jacobson, L. (1968). *Pygmalion in the classroom: Teacher expectation and pupils' intellectual development.* New York, NY: Rinehart and Winston.

Wallin, D. (2007). Ethical leadership: The role of the president. In D. Hellmich (Ed.), *Ethical leadership in the community college: Bridging theory and daily practice* (pp. 33–45). Bolton, MA: Anker.

2

GENDER DIFFERENCES IN TEAM LEADERSHIP

Pamela L. Eddy, Catherine Hartman, and Eric Liu

Team leadership has taken on heightened importance given the increasing complexity of leading today's colleges and universities. Kezar and Holcombe (2017) reviewed the literature on shared leadership and noted different terminologies used in the field, for example, *distributed leadership* (Spillane, 2005), *connective leadership* (Lipman-Blumen, 2000), *networked leadership* (Díaz-Gibson, Zaragoza, Daly, Mayayo, & Romaní, 2017), and *collaborative leadership* (Hallinger & Heck, 2010). For the purpose of this chapter, *team leadership* is defined as a process that broadly distributes responsibilities among a group on campus versus relying on a single hierarchical form of leading (Bensimon & Neumann, 1993). Team leadership builds on an interactive process among individuals that involves working up and down the organizational chart and across units (Pearce & Conger, 2003). McPhail (2016) uses the term *matrix* to connote this movement away from hierarchical forms of leadership.

Historically, research on gender differences in leadership suggested that women lead in a more participatory manner relative to men (Bass & Avolio, 1994; Chliwniak, 1997). Yet over time this argument became more nuanced. For example, Eagly and Johnson (1990) conducted a meta-analysis to review gender and leadership style. They concluded that similarities and differences exist between the sexes. Women and men were not different with respect to interpersonally oriented versus task-oriented styles, but Eagly and Johnson found that in experimental and assessment studies, gender stereotypes emerged. A decade later, Eagly and Johannesen-Schmidt (2001) focused on transformational, transactional, and laissez-faire leadership styles between the sexes. Women exceed in transformational leadership, whereas men were more effective in laissez-faire approaches. But, "women's advantage in leadership style may sometimes be counteracted, however, by a reluctance, especially on the part of men, to give women power over others in the workplace" (p. 795). Given these findings, understanding gender roles in team leadership is timely.

Couple the notions of team leadership and gender in the community college context, and different questions emerge. Community colleges have long been described as Democracy's Colleges (Diekhoff, 1950), and their open-access mission provides leaders with a particular context for leadership. Over almost two decades, these institutions have also been undergoing great turnover in leadership positions as leaders retire, creating opportunities for shifts and innovation in leadership approaches (Eddy & VanDerLinden, 2006; Evelyn, 2001; Schults, 2001; Weisman & Vaughan, 2002). Levin (1998) argued that despite the inclusive mission of community colleges, operations are solidly bureaucratic. This orientation could present challenges for leaders seeking more of a team leadership approach.

In contemplating the role of gender in team leadership, community colleges provide a useful site of inquiry given the high percentage of women leading in the sector. One in every 3 community college presidents is a woman (36%) compared with fewer than 1 in 10 (8%) for research universities (Gagliardi, Espinosa, Turk, & Taylor, 2017). Because community colleges are viewed as more open to women leaders relative to other institutional types (Townsend & Twombly, 2007), it is important to understand better the role gender plays in team leadership. The questions at the heart of the study we conducted were

- How do sitting community college leaders define *leadership* with respect to team leadership?
- Does gender influence how leaders use the construct of *team* regarding functions?
- Do leaders operationalize the construct of *team* differently depending on gender?

Team Leadership

Companies and organizations are increasingly advocating for collaborative approaches and leadership among workers to facilitate problem-solving, innovation, and productivity (Kezar & Holcombe, 2017). Collaboration often comes in the form of teamwork, which requires multiple components, including a common goal or objective, defined tasks and roles, and the necessary skill sets to achieve a goal. As Söderhjelm, Björklund, Sandahl, and Bolander-Laksov (2018) noted, "To be regarded as productive, a team should produce more than the sum of what its members produce" (p. 203). Team-centered approaches to work represent a turn from traditional top-down forms of leadership toward those that are horizontal and vertical. This involves a shift from subordinates being led by a single leader toward multiple individuals collaborating with each other to determine the direction of a project. Governance in team leadership models is shared, holding all parties accountable (Lucey, 2002).

In the team leadership model, teams are still subject to external influences, such as a supervisor, but this approach also accounts for peer interactions and influence; thus teams share leadership internally and govern themselves (Kezar & Holcombe, 2017; Pearce & Conger, 2003). Leadership is simultaneously shared and distributed within teams (Yammarino, Salas, Serban, Shirreffs, & Shuffler, 2012). Additionally, structure is more flexible in this model than it is in traditional top-down leadership models (McPhail, 2016). As team members encounter projects and tasks, the role of the leader in teams shifts to the person possessing the most experience and insight for that particular work. Team member expertise and experience is the primary factor used to determine which team member holds leadership during a given project (Kezar & Holcombe, 2017).

Gender plays a significant role in teamwork and team leadership. Researchers began to examine these intersections in the 1970s. Historically, women have been less likely to be in senior administration positions, including dean, vice president, or provost (Wheat & Hill, 2016). Paying attention to women in these roles is particularly important when considering leadership pathways and presidency positions, as 35% of women in college and university presidential positions were either chief academic officer or provost immediately prior to assuming their position as president (Gagliardi et al., 2017). The historical lack of women in presidency pipelines has yielded male-dominant forms of leadership and culture, and stereotypical notions of leadership across gender are pervasive. Traditionally, leadership traits like "task-orientation, aggression, authority, determination, confidence, courage, independence, strength, and vision" (Wheat & Hill, 2016, p. 2) have been associated with male leadership. Women have been noted as practicing "cooperativeness, collaboration of managers and subordinates, lower control for the leader, and problem-solving based on intuition and empathy as well as rationality" (Eagly & Johnson, 1990, p. 233). Women whose actions and leadership do not align with perceived masculine behaviors and traits may not be described by others as competent. Additionally, women who exhibit so-called feminine leadership traits may be perceived as deficient and lacking in strong leadership characteristics (West & Zimmerman, 1987).

Research has revealed that women and men perceive leadership and their roles as leaders differently. In a study of community college leadership, Eddy and VanDerLinden (2006) found that males were more likely to define *leadership* as me centered, meaning that their leadership was necessary to drive others to work and to meet a goal. In the same study, more women than men indicated that their leadership included collaborative elements and building consensus among members. As leadership turnover continues at community colleges, and more women move into leadership positions (Gagliardi et al., 2017), leadership will change. This shift, coupled with increased calls for collaboration, will result in the likely increase of leadership approaches that emphasize sharing of power and participation (Chliwniak, 1997; Eddy & VanDerLinden, 2006; Townsend & Twombly, 2007). This chapter examines how community college leaders define *team leadership* and the influence of gender on the construction of teams.

Project Background

Data for this project were derived from a national survey of community college leaders conducted from 2015 to 2016. College websites were reviewed to identify top-level and midlevel leaders. Leaders' e-mail addresses were obtained from the institutions' or statewide community college associations' directories. A number of leadership groups were included in this manner, such as academic leaders, student affairs leaders, and administrative leaders. This broad-based approach ensured coverage of leadership throughout the institution and along the career ladder. Critically, this participant list provided views of leadership in different positions and illustrated how leadership may operate differently based on position and responsibilities.

The survey instrument consisted of five parts. First, answers to questions determined leaders' career backgrounds and pathways. Second, participants were asked about their educational background and any professional development they participated in. The third portion of the survey focused on the ways the participants learned to lead. Leaders were also asked what tasks associated with their jobs they felt most prepared for and which ones they felt least prepared for. The fourth part of the survey asked about their access to development opportunities, and the final portion of the survey focused on the American Association of Community Colleges leadership competencies. Demographic data were collected to understand better how these variables influenced leadership options and choices. Top-level leaders for this study included the presidents (21%) and vice presidents (27%), and midlevel leaders included academics (26%) and administrative staff (26%). Women responded at higher rates (56%) compared to men (44%).

The data of interest for this chapter focused on how participants defined *leadership*. Areas of differences based on gender were looked for and noted in the findings. We coded the participants' open-ended definitions based on the categories identified by Kezar and Holcombe (2017) and Eddy and VanDerLinden (2006) for elements of shared leadership. Emergent codes were also included, which represented teamwork, inclusiveness, collaboration, and building consensus as well as a code for inspiring followership. The following section describes our framework more fully.

Conceptual Framework

The framework for this study is grounded in Kezar and Holcombe's (2017) findings of shared leadership and Eddy and VanDerLinden's (2006) examinations of community college leadership. Kezar and Holcombe (2017) named the following common elements found in shared leadership:

- A greater number of individuals in leadership than traditional models;
- Leaders and followers are seen as interchangeable;
- Leadership is not based on position or authority;
- Multiple perspectives and expertise are capitalized on for problem-solving, innovation, and change; and
- Collaboration and interactions across the organization are typically emphasized. (p. 3)

The ideas of shared leadership functions, flexible configurations, and leadership that operates vertically and horizontally across the team are important to these concepts. Embedded in these ideals is the ability to inspire followership, to get others to buy into the process and feel like a member of the team.

Eddy and VanDerLinden (2006) examined survey responses from community college administrators nationwide. Using content analysis to query how administrators define leadership, they established emerging codes from their data that examined multiple dimensions of leadership including position, responsibilities, and expertise; initiating and enforcing change; providing vision and shaping direction; expertise and knowledge; being respected as a leader; fulfilling a greater mission, such as that of the college or organization; empowering others; me-centered approaches; collaboration; and influence, power, and authority.

The role of shared responsibility and joint involvement in campus operations are clear takeaways. How leaders conceptualize and describe leadership illustrates how prevalent they consider the team to be. These frameworks formed the basis for coding our data regarding how participants defined *leadership* (Eddy & VanDerLinden, 2006; Kezar & Holcombe, 2017).

Findings From the Field

We found in our coding of our survey data that just under half of the sitting senior and midlevel leaders defined leadership by making some reference to the fact that leadership involved a number of people other than the leader (women = 49%, men = 42%). The change in individuals providing definitions of leadership based solely on position is striking. In an earlier study, Eddy and VanDerLinden (2006) found that 49.2% of men and 45.1% of women defined leadership based on positional responsibilities and being a leader in an area. Notably, a decade later, our survey data showed that thoughts had shifted beyond reliance on leading by authority of position, as only 9% of men and 10% of women defined leading based on position. Here, men and women are aligned in their primary views of defining leadership as involving other people. The question remains, however, in how men and women interpret how others are involved. For example, does including others simply mean having followers marching behind a leader, or does this inclusion mean other forms of team or shared leadership in which followers have active roles?

Four main findings emerged from our survey research. First, the components of team leadership from Kezar and Holcombe (2017) did not have much traction with the participants. The exception was that participants noted they included others when leading. Second, even though several respondents indicated in their definitions of leadership that they involved others, there were differences in how individuals conveyed inclusion. Reliance on so-called real, or traditional, team leadership and nonleader, collective, or shared roles in leading was scant. Some respondents conveyed a sense of power and role hierarchy with comments that essentially stated that they were leading the team, instead of a more collaborative approach to team leadership. Instances of inclusivity and servant leadership still had leaders figuring prominently. The third finding built on this nuance in defining leadership as gendered language was used in the provided definitions. Finally, the largest difference in the definitions of leadership by men and women leaders emerged from the code regarding empowering and advocating for others. Thirty-two percent of men provided definitions that were coded for empowering others compared to 41% of women. A closer look at this code revealed additional differences in meaning.

Defining Leadership

We received a total of 1,000 responses. Seventy-seven percent of those who responded (369 men and 408 women) completed the open-ended survey question that asked how they defined *leadership*. Notably, the responses by women were on average longer than those provided by the men. Because of this tendency for women to be more expansive, there were more opportunities to code a wider range of aspects for how women defined leadership relative to men. Table 2.1 provides a summary of the codes from Kezar and Holcombe's (2017) concepts of shared leadership, Eddy and VanDerLinden's (2006) leadership domains, and emergent codes from our analysis (teamwork, inclusiveness, collaboration, build consensus, inspire followership). The percentage of men and women whose definitions of *leadership* reflected the code topic are also noted.

As observed earlier, the most noted code in our survey analysis was that leading involved other people. For example, a male leader commented that leadership meant "motivating individuals to perform their best within the mission of the department/institution." Being inspirational and motivational was a fairly common response from men; however, another male leader said that leadership was "being able to collaborate with employees and communicate needs. I believe in participatory management." Thus, even though many of the men saw working with others as a means to an end, others viewed leading as more collaborative.

Likewise, women saw the need to inspire others to work toward an end goal but often portrayed this a bit differently. For example, one woman stated that leadership was the "ability to inspire others, individually and collectively, to act in new ways that improve the quality of work/life." The emphasis on the quality of work and life differed from a focus on meeting specific organizational objectives. Another female leader added that leading required "the ability to bring a team to consensus and move forward in a common direction." Another woman offered leadership as "the ability to show a person or group of people the direction in which they should be going and be willing to help them get there." The emphasis is again on the leader defining the direction versus the team participating in providing direction. The point of working with others held different meanings in general for men and women, but this does not hold for every man or every woman respondent.

TABLE 2.1

Summary of Team Codes by Gender Organized by Source of Code

From Kezar and Holcombe (2017)		
Code	**Women (%)**	**Men (%)**
Involves a greater number of individuals	49	42
Leaders and followers interchangeable	3	1
Leadership is not based on position, role, or ability	3	2
Leadership is position, hierarchy, relationship to others	6	7
Multiple perspectives	6	4
Shared leadership functions	2	2
Flexible configurations	0	0
Leadership vertical and horizontal across team	1	1
From Eddy and VanDerLinden (2006)		
Code	**Women**	**Men**
Positional, responsibilities, committees, decision-making, related to job function, experience, leader within area	10	9
Change agent, initiate change, create environment for change	3	6
Provide vision, shape direction	39	35
Ability, knowledge, personal mastery, expertise, frequently asked or consulted because of expertise, other personal traits	38	32
Others see me as a leader, people trust me and respect me	1	5
Fulfilling larger mission of the college, working for the good of the organization	16	16
Me centered, I am successful, I have the ability to make things happen	4	6
Provide resources to others to allow them to do their job, provide access to key resources	9	10

(Continues)

TABLE 2.1 *(Continued)*

Influence, power, role model, authority, control financial resources	21	18
Not a leader, experiencing barriers to being a leader, or too new in the position to be a leader	0	0
Empower others, advocate for others, provide emotional support, mentor, motivate others, set example	41	32
Teamwork, inclusiveness, collaboration, building consensus	19	17
Inspire followership	20	19

It is particularly noteworthy that neither men nor women used specific terms associated with team leadership from Kezar and Holcombe (2017) in their own definitions of *leadership*. With the exception of indicating that leading meant the involvement of a greater number of individuals, leaders referenced Kezar and Holcombe's shared leadership attributes less than 10% of the time. This outcome could mean that leaders make assumptions about what is and is not in their power to change regarding how individuals work together in the organization, such as in flexible configurations. Or it might mean that the language of team leadership has not made it significantly into practice. The fact that so many of the definitions that included involving others focused on the role of motivating or inspiring others to work together for a goal versus motivating others to work on coming up with a shared goal is telling. The meaning behind the idea of what it means to involve others is equally important.

When coding the data using items developed by Eddy and VanDerLinden (2006), little difference was found between men and women in the frequency of the concept of involvement in their definitions of *leadership*. Yet a difference did emerge in the area of empowering others, with women noting this more often (41%) relative to men (32%). This difference is discussed further later.

A few key points were identified with respect to team leadership. First, leaders noted their own competency and expertise as central to their ability to lead (women 38%, men 32%). Clearly, it is important to master leadership concepts to lead others. Second, leadership is about creating a vision and providing a direction for the institution (women 39%, men 35%). One man's response to this question was echoed by others: "The ability to envision a future for the institution and the ability to clear obstacles to that vision." Compare this to one of the responses by a woman in the survey: "Leadership is the ability to develop and present a message and a vision that followers are willing to embrace as their own to move the organization forward." Achieving a goal is important, but here too the process differed. Men's responses indicate that to achieve a goal, traits such as vision and strength are required; it is a leader's responsibility to provide a clear pathway for subordinates to achieve the goals set forth by the leader. Women's responses, however, suggest that leaders must work with coworkers or subordinates to craft a goal and the course of action; it is the team's responsibility as a whole to identify problems and resources associated with achieving the team's goals. Finally, the need to inspire others to follow in order to achieve leader and institutional goals was noted by men and women alike (women 20%, men 19%). Teamwork and collaboration combined was also noted as being equally important (women 19%, men 17%). Especially important in these findings is how little reliance on their position contributed to how individuals defined leadership (women 10%, men 9%). The move to more collaborative constructs of leading represents a change over the past generation of leaders.

I'm Leading the Team

How individuals discussed working with others showed differences among male and female respondents. When conducting a second level of coding on the Kezar and Holcombe (2017) element of involving others, gendered differences emerged. The subcoding examined the following areas: "I get others to do things" versus "I involve others and we get things done together." In this case, 74% of the men used definitions in which they indicated it was their influence and ability that got others to work toward a goal. For example, 1 male leader commented, "Leadership is a personal characteristic which influences others to attain goals and perform tasks they would not normally attempt." In this case, it is the leader's abilities that stand at the forefront of getting others to do things. This concept of inspiring others was summed up by another male leader: "Leadership is having the ability to get others to do what they may not want to do and feel good about it." Another male leader defined *leadership* as "accomplishing tasks through others." In these cases, involving others meant convincing followers to come along to achieve a vision, one that was often crafted by the leader versus being collaboratively created. A scant 8% of the male respondents used the word *team* in their definition of leadership that involved others.

The subcoding of the women leaders painted a different picture—65% of the women defined *leadership* as involving others and felt that they were responsible as leaders to get others involved. A full 35% of the women, compared to 26% of the men, included involvement of others in their definition. As one woman noted, "Leadership is working with those you lead and those you follow to move an area into the best possible version of the future." The notion of "coaching and guiding others in a way that they can achieve their best," as noted by one of the woman leaders, conveyed a different approach relative to holding a singular ability to inspire others. The subtle change in language, which is reviewed in more depth in the next major finding, illustrates how involving others can connote different meanings in what it means to involve others and to work with a team.

The women leaders used the term *team* much more often relative to men. Nearly one out of five women (19%) who indicated an involvement of others in her definition of leadership used the specific word *team* (compared to 8% of the men). The understanding of team was much more expansive for women as well. For example, one of the men who used the term in his definition stated,

> I utilize data-driven decision-making and lots of committee-based analysis of data. I then require my teams to look for a variety of solutions to overcome problems and then we review those solutions and look for pitfalls prior to implementing them.

Another man commented, "A leader is able to draw the best out of his team." This type of commentary illustrates that even when using team-oriented vocabulary, the connotation is still that the leader is involving others more narrowly and much like subordinates. Consider instead some of the comments from the women who used *team* in their definitions. One woman stated that a leader's duty is "to guide an effort or group of people toward committing to and achieving a common goal where the overall goal and the collective efforts of individual team members is greater than an individual's efforts alone." Another woman added, "Leaders give voice to the collective vision that managers can carry out. Leaders support, encourage, and advocate for the team. Leaders find the leadership qualities in all of their managers and employees." These examples underscore how involving others on the team conveys more inclusivity and collaboration than the definitions using team provided by the men.

Overall, the majority of men and women survey respondents used language of involving others that relied most often on the individual leader's ability to inspire and motivate others to follow along. A minority of responses relied on definitions that included more participatory language of inclusive and shared leadership. It is notable, however, that women (35%) more often than men (26%) used more participatory notions of explanation of how they involve others. Further, as previously noted, more women (19%) as opposed to men (8%) used the term *team* in their definitions coded for involving others. On the one hand, these findings might be viewed as discouraging, given that the majority view of involving others is by getting them to do things. On the other hand, the fact that a large minority of definitions included more participatory language is encouraging of emerging conceptions of collaborative and team leadership. Women more often use inclusive and participatory terms in their definitions than men. This finding may signal the beginning of a tipping point in how leadership is explicitly conceptualized in the community college sector. In particular, the increase in the percentage of women leaders, who now represent 36% of all community college leaders (Gagliardi et al., 2017) bodes well for more team-oriented and shared leadership to prevail in community colleges.

He Said, She Said: Gendered Language

Throughout the findings, how men and women defined *leadership* involved different terminology. Gendered discourse often emerges because of socialization throughout one's lifetime, with women and men having different expectations thrust on them based on their gender (West & Zimmerman, 1987). For example, men and women used the verb *direct* in their definitions of leadership, yet differences emerged in meaning based on gender.

A theme in the men's use of *direct* is summed up by one leader who stated the leader is "the individual who is ultimately responsible for the direction in which the department (or organization) moves," which is a more traditional autocratic approach to leadership. This attention to creating a strategic direction was predominantly leadercentric versus collaborative. However, an emerging conception of more collaborative forms of direction was also observed among the male participants with the inclusion of qualifiers such as "facilitating group members," "faculty and staff . . . take ownership in new directions," "empowers everyone to play a role," and "engage people." Thus, even though there were tendencies from the majority of men to lean toward more directive leadership, many men also approach leading from a collaborative standpoint.

Women also spoke about directing others to achieve outcomes, but the language involved a less commanding approach regarding the process. For example, one woman stated leadership requires "the ability to chart the direction of an institution or department and share it with others so that we are all striving for the same thing." Including the phrase *share it* provides a much different connotation of providing direction. Another woman said that leadership was "the ability to bring a team to consensus and move forward in a common direction." The use of subtler language in this case changes the meaning from the leader providing the direction to the leader seeking a common direction informed by multiple stakeholder views that contribute to building consensus. Other tempering terms included *empower, help, facilitate, trust,* and *inclusion.* A summation of women's approach to directing others was aptly provided by one woman who stated that leadership was "walking beside to guide; taking the lead when necessary to protect and direct." Yet, as with men, not all the women spoke in this overtly inclusive manner. Some of these definitions involved terms such as *convincing others, setting the direction,* and *art of direction.*

Overall, women were much more likely to use inclusive language and qualifiers in providing direction compared to men; however, a minority of men also used this same type of inclusive language, an encouraging sign of a possible shift to more collaborative forms of leadership overall. How others in the organization perceived and reacted to the leadership of the study participants is unknown from this research. Other campus members and stakeholders may hold different views of how the leaders are doing in their roles as leaders of the community college compared to the individuals' self-reported perceptions of beliefs in their definitions of leadership. To an extent, the definitions of leadership provided by the participants might be aspirational.

Bringing Others Along

There was nearly a 10% difference in how women (41%) and men (32%) used terms linked to empowering others in their definitions of leadership. As noted previously, a gendered difference in the meaning of involving others and directing others was found. Also, support for continued gender differences in meaning on the coding of empowering, mentoring, and advocating for others was evident. Women more often used terms of support to others relative to men. For example, one woman offered in her definition that leadership is "guiding a group toward a common goal, empowering others to reach their potential, enabling an organization or individuals to strive for something greater than they otherwise would have." Another woman said,

> Leadership is the ability to understand the organization in context, to create vision and optimism, to develop self-leadership among constituents, to manage and plan the deployment of resources to best effect, and to win support from internal and external communities.

These examples show how women wanted to develop others in the institution to meet institutional goals and aid in the development of the individual.

Yet not all women viewed empowerment this way. One stated that leadership is "the ability to lead a group in the direction you want to go and have the people you are leading be glad to do it." This focus on providing direction supports a historic leadercentric perspective, as did the definition provided by another woman, who added that leadership was "the ability to direct effective progress and inspire others to join the movement." Being able to complete a task while still supporting others was viewed as important. Because of the expansive descriptions provided by women relative to men, nuances were possible to discern. For example, one woman stated, "Effective leadership gets the task done while also caring about and supporting the people doing the task." This definition, although task oriented, offers a complementary concept of support. On the whole, women's definitions of empowerment included more supportive language.

Men most often used different terms for empowering others. One male leader said that leadership is about the "ability to remove barriers so people can accomplish the task at hand." Another added that it is about "engaging people to accomplish great things in ways that would not be possible otherwise," with another man saying that it is about "the ability to work with folks to the point where they want to accomplish their tasks versus being forced." Forms of support involved changing systems and processes to remove barriers, serving as a role model, and motivating others to contribute to the overarching institutional mission. These definitions stood in contrast to the type of support noted in the women's definitions.

The notion of being in charge of direction was still evident in the coding for empowering others. Consider the response from one of the male leaders that leadership is "the ability to engage people and direct their activities collaboratively and create a shared vision of the future." The ideal of collaboration or team leadership is present in this definition, yet the qualifier of *direct* reduces the intention of empowering others to do specific tasks versus how others might contribute to the work. Juxtapose this with another man's response of leadership as being "the ability to empower others to do their absolute best," which focuses more on individual agency and potential. The outcome of this type of empowerment is still often linked to production—contributing to the mission, meeting strategic objectives, and so forth.

A traditionally autocratic style of male leadership is now challenged by some of the men in our survey. Being a facilitator was viewed as central for some of the men. The notion of shared leadership was espoused as well; for example, one male leader stated that it is "helping others to find their path to success in a way that engenders positive outcomes for all involved." The complexity of leading was also evident as noted in another man's comment: "Leadership is empowering others to achieve individual, organizational, and common goals. The end goal of leadership is to sustain itself by making new and better leaders." Still another man stated that leadership was "the ability to communicate and collaborate with others exercising a common vision and dream." Thus, even though the bulk of men thought of empowerment more from the standpoint of bringing others along to fulfill the mission or objectives, a number of men spoke from a more inclusive perspective of empowering others for individual fulfillment and focused on the contributions individuals make to the team.

The study investigated other ways gender differences emerged in the definitions that included the concept of empowering and supporting others. A difference was evident in the complexity of the definitions provided that often included several of the other codes in this type of advocacy. For the definitions coded for empowerment, the range of additional codes also evident in the definition was examined, for example, team leadership, involving others, inspiring followership, and so on. See Table 2.2 for a

TABLE 2.2
Frequency of Codes Including Empowerment

Number of Codes	Women (%)	Men (%)
1	2	10
2	22	19
3	28	36
4	25	17
5	13	12
6	7	4
7	1	1
8	1	0
9	1	0

summary of the number of codes linked with the definition of leadership that included the code *empowering*.

The number of codes for the men who noted empowerment in their definition ranged from a single code for empowerment (10%) to seven codes for their leadership definition, including empowerment (1%). The majority of men's definitions included three different codes (36%). Only 2% of the women's definitions included only the code for empowerment, indicating that women's definitions more often included multiple codes. The most codes in one definition for women was nine (1%), with the majority of women having three (28%) or four (25%) codes in their definitions. The longer length of text provided by the women participants provided an opportunity for expanding coding. Even though the frequencies evident for the number of codes (e.g., one to nine for women and one to seven for men) resulted in an expected bell curve, the slope was more pronounced in the men's responses given the noticeable difference among the number of codes emerging in the analysis (recall that three codes represented the biggest average for men at 36%). The bell curve for women represented more of a plateau, with smaller frequencies (e.g., 22%, 28%, 25%) in the number of additional codes linked with empowerment.

As in other findings, there were gender differences between men and women regarding their views of empowering. More women included empowerment and support for others in their definitions than did men. Further, women's discourse regarding empowerment focused more on inclusivity and collaboration compared to men's discourse of empowering others as a means to meet institutional objectives. Similar trends existed in this finding of empowerment, as noted earlier in the theme about including others in leadership. An important caveat is that for both men and women, some leaders did not align with the ascribed gendered approach to empowerment. This integration of perspective provides a fruitful area for further exploration.

Discussion

Despite the outcomes for shared leadership advocated by Kezar and Holcombe (2017), it was significant that definitions in this study of leadership provided by leaders in the field showed little alignment with the categories identified as central to team leadership. The notable exception was that sitting leaders reported that working with others was important to the ability to lead. Yet, as noted in the findings presented in this chapter, how leaders thought about working with others did not necessarily align with concepts of team leadership outlined by Kezar and Holcombe (2017).

Men and women viewed involving others as possessing the ability to get followers "to do things," often to achieve an end goal; however, gendered differences emerged regarding meaning. Men most often focused on structure or policy changes, whereas women paid attention to process. Women's qualifiers in their definitions of leadership were more inclusive and collaborative.

Like Eagly and Johnson's (1990) work, this study found differences and similarities among women and men with respect to their definitions of *leadership* and their conceptions of team leadership. Women were more likely to specifically use the term *team* in their definitions as well as sharing, decision-making, and empowering others to advance their own sense of agency along with meeting the strategic goals of the institution. Indeed, 25 years since Bass and Avolio (1994) argued that women's participatory approaches might make them better managers, we find evidence that in fact women are more participatory in their leadership. Given the structure of this project, whether a participatory approach actually led to more effectiveness remains unknown.

Bensimon and Neumann (1993) argued that presidential teams have three functions, namely (a) utilitarian, getting the work done; (b) expressive, framing problems; and (c) cognitive, thinking collaboratively to find solutions. There were clear tendencies in the participating leaders to focus on getting things done and also inspiring others to follow along. Yet evidence was found of collaborative forms of leading teams. A critical component of team leadership involves team thinking, which "requires individuals to work their minds and express their thinking publicly" (Bensimon & Neumann, 1993, p. 57). At the core of this element is a diversity of perspectives among team members. In thinking about Bensimon and Neumann's notion of teams, it is useful to consider the various roles that members of the team play. For example, one of the women leaders reflected that leadership was "being the head of a team that works together to accomplish a common goal." She perceived her role as bringing others along. Bensimon and Neumann went on to define eight thinking roles for presidential teams that may also apply to partnership roles, which included the following five core roles:

1. definer—frames issues and defines reality
2. analyst—explores and assesses the issues at hand
3. interpreter—translates how others may view decisions outside the group
4. critic—takes on the role of critic and devil's advocate

5. synthesizer—looks broadly at the issues and brings together a summary (Bensimon & Neumann, 1993)

The remaining three supporting roles were disparity monitor, task monitor, and emotional monitor. As evident in the definitions provided in this project, individual leaders served in all of these role capacities but most often saw their role as the individual who would define the circumstances and provide analysis of the current situation. Less evident were the other thinking roles identified by Bensimon and Neumann in the preceding list. Further exploration is required to understand more deeply who on campus is filling these other roles and how leaders are tapping others to provide the necessary thinking elements for the team to function. Investigating leader perceptions of teams tells only half the story.

Gendered language was evident in how men and women described what it means to be a leader. Men provided shorter answers and used more directive language, whereas women provided longer responses and used more qualifiers in their definitions. The long socialization of men and women to gender expectations rewards them for acting the part (Eddy, 2009; West & Zimmerman, 1987). Yet, what was encouraging in this research was the large minority that appeared to counter this trend. Gendered language was clearly evident in the definitions provided, but men were increasingly likely to include inclusivity and collaboration in their definitions, and men and women were less likely to see themselves as leaders solely based on position. This evidence may signal a turning point in how community college leadership is conceptualized and operationalized.

Implications for the Field

The findings from this study have implications for the ways team leadership operates in community colleges. The move away from hierarchical conceptions of leading that rely on solo leadership is clearly happening, given the definitions provided by the research participants. The language of leadership indicated incorporating reliance into a team approach to get important work done on campus. To fully implement team leadership, campus leaders must begin to intentionally conceive the roles for each member and build the structures required to best support the work of the team. First, structures must allow for lateral and vertical forms of work based on a matrix form of organizational functions (McPhail, 2016). Second, campus leaders must clearly recognize the variety of roles that team members have and purposely work to identify who in the college fills these roles previously identified by Bensimon and Neumann (1993). Third and finally, leadership development must occur broadly in the college. Building team leadership requires moving past thinking of leadership as only occurring when a person has a particular title or position. Faculty leaders must be developed, leaders in the middle must be encouraged to take on more of a leadership role, and leading in place should be encouraged.

Given the evidence of the power of team leadership and the positive outcomes associated with participatory types of leadership, it is critical to involve others and to empower campus members. Transformational change happens when truly shared leadership occurs (Kezar & Holcombe, 2017), but different meanings emerge of what it means to work with others in terms of involvement. Traditionally, women have been associated with collaboration and participatory leadership, making them a logical choice in terms of leading the team. But as the research of Eagly and Johannesen-Schmidt (2001) demonstrated, men are often reluctant to give up power to women leaders. Breaking down these historic patterns of power differentials must occur. It is also evident from this study that not all men take a hierarchical view of leadership. Thus, men can also lead teams effectively. What makes teams most effective is including different perspectives and individuals bringing different talents to the table. The gender of the team members matters less; rather, what matters is the frame of mind and commitment of team members regarding expectations of one another and the building of trusting relationships among the collaborators.

When women lead teams they should recognize that gendered expectations exist for how they should lead and that women are often penalized when they act outside these gendered roles (Eagly & Johannesen-Schmidt, 2001; West & Zimmerman, 1987). Recognizing that some men may be reluctant to recognize the power of women leaders can help break down these views. Men are often not penalized for acting outside gender expectations and instead are rewarded for acting in traditionally female collaborative ways (Eddy, 2009). When men lead teams they should be conscious of the language they use to communicate team expectations. Moving away from me-centered or authoritative language is central to success in team leadership (e.g., "Team members, do what I say" versus "Team, let's do this together"). Stakeholders will quickly pick up the intention of what is meant by team leadership based on the language used in practice, and if campus members do not feel empowered or valued, the team will break down. Being conscious of power differentials on campus is important to understanding how teamwork is perceived and fostered. In this era of heightened awareness of harassment and discrimination, all leaders must be conscious of the need to treat others with respect and equity.

Conclusion

We offer three main takeaways from our research on team leadership. First, gender differences exist in how men and women defined *leadership* and the language they used. Women's language was more inclusive, and their definitions relied on process more than that of their male counterparts. Second, overall, working with others and empowering others is nuanced and does not necessarily mean that team leadership is in place. Indeed, with the exception of involving others, little support was found for the elements of shared leadership (Kezar & Holcombe, 2017) among the participants. Third, a shift has occurred over time to more expansive definitions of leadership that include a role for others versus relying solely on positional authority (Eddy & VanDerLinden, 2006).

The increasing complexity of higher education means that reliance on a single leader is no longer tenable (Eddy et al., 2015). As a result, leaders and campus members must determine what is required to engage in team leadership based on collaboration and sharing of leadership functions. Merely stating that collaboration exists is not enough. As evident in this study, there is little evidence to support building flexible organizational configurations or the occurrence of vertical and horizontal levels of leading. To really embrace the ideal of team leadership, organizational structures and policies must change and with them individual roles and expectations. Once these critical building blocks are in place, true leadership collaboration can emerge.

References

Bass, B. M., & Avolio, B. J. (1994). Shatter the glass ceiling: Women may make better managers. *Human Resource Management, 33*(4), 549–560.

Bensimon, E. M., & Neumann, A. (1993). *Redesigning collegiate leadership: Teams and teamwork in higher education.* Baltimore, MD: Johns Hopkins University Press.

Chliwniak, L. (1997). Higher education leadership: Analyzing the gender gap. *ASHE-ERIC Higher Education Report, 25*(4).

Diekhoff, J. (1950). *Democracy's college: Higher education in the local community.* New York, NY: Harper & Brothers.

Díaz-Gibson, J., Zaragoza, M. C., Daly, A. J., Mayayo, J. L., & Romaní, J. R. (2017). Networked leadership in educational collaborative networks. *Educational Management Administration & Leadership, 45*(6), 1040–1059.

Eagly, A. H., & Johannesen-Schmidt, M. C. (2001). The leadership styles of women and men. *Journal of Social Issues, 57*(4), 781–797.

Eagly, A. H., & Johnson, B. T. (1990). Gender and leadership style: A meta-analysis. *Psychological Bulletin, 108*(2), 233–256.

Eddy, P. L. (2009). Leading gracefully: Gendered leadership at community colleges. In D. R. Dean, S. J. Bracken, & J. K. Allen (Eds.), *Women in academic leadership: Professional strategies, personal choices* (Vol. 2, pp. 8–30). Sterling, VA: Stylus.

Eddy, P. L., Sydow, D., Alfred, R., & Garza Mitchell, R. (2015). *Developing tomorrow's leaders: Contexts, consequences, & competencies.* Washington, DC: Rowman & Littlefield.

Eddy, P. L., & VanDerLinden, K. E. (2006). Emerging definitions of leadership in higher education: New visions of leadership or same old "hero" leader? *Community College Review, 34*(1), 5–26.

Evelyn, J. (2001). Community colleges face a crisis of leadership. *Chronicle of Higher Education, 47*(30), A36–A37.

Gagliardi, J. S., Espinosa, L. L., Turk, J. M., & Taylor, M. (2017). *The American College President Study: 2017.* Washington, DC: American Council on Education.

Hallinger, P., & Heck, R. H. (2010). Leadership for learning: Does collaborative leadership make a difference in school improvement? *Educational Management Administration & Leadership, 38*(6), 654–678.

Kezar, A. J., & Holcombe, E. M. (2017). *Shared leadership in higher education.* Washington, DC: American Council on Education.

Levin, J. S. (1998). Making sense of organizational change. *New Directions for Community Colleges, 1998*(102), 43–54.

Lipman-Blumen, J. (2000). *Connective leadership: Managing in a changing world.* London, UK: Oxford University Press.

Lucey, C. A. (2002). Civic engagement, shared governance, and community colleges. *Academe, 88*(4), 27–31.

McPhail, C. J. (2016). From tall to matrix: Redefining organizational structures. *Change: The Magazine of Higher Learning, 48*(4), 55–62.

Pearce, C. L., & Conger, J. A. (2003). All those years ago. In C. L. Pearch & J. A. Conger (Eds.), *Shared leadership: Reframing the hows and whys of leadership* (pp. 1–18). Thousand Oaks, CA: Sage.

Schults, C. (2001). *The critical impact of impending retirements on community college leadership.* Washington, DC: American Association of Community Colleges Press.

Spillane, J. P. (2005). Distributed leadership. *Educational Forum, 69*(2), 143–150.

Söderhjelm, T., Björklund, C., Sandahl, C., & Bolander-Laksov, K. (2018). Academic leadership: management of groups or leadership of teams? A multiple-case study on designing and implementing a team-based development programme for academic leadership. *Studies in Higher Education, 43*(2), 201–216.

Townsend, B. K., & Twombly, S. B. (2007). Accidental equity: The status of women in the community college. *Equity & Excellence in Education, 40*(3), 208–217.

Weisman, I. M., & Vaughan, G. B. (2002). *The community college presidency, 2001.* Washington, DC: American Association of Community Colleges.

West, C., & Zimmerman, D. O. N. H. (1987). Doing gender. *Gender & Society*, *1*(2), 125–151.

Wheat, C. A., & Hill, L. H. (2016). Leadership identities, styles, and practices of women university administrators and presidents. *Research in the Schools*, *23*(2), 1–16.

Yammarino, F. J., Salas, E., Serban, A., Shirreffs, K., & Shuffler, M. L. (2012). Collectivistic leadership approaches: Putting the "we" in leadership science and practice. *Industrial and Organizational Psychology*, *5*(4), 382–402.

3

HOW A NEW LEADER CAN ASSESS AN EXISTING LEADERSHIP TEAM

Eugene Giovannini

New leaders taking the helm at an organization face a multitude of competing priorities that vie for time and attention. In institutions of higher education, times of leadership transition are particularly complicated. New presidents are called on to deal with the by-products of deep-rooted histories and cultures, juggle the expectations of internal and external stakeholders, and navigate complex leadership teams all while trying to position themselves and set the course for their new organization. This centrifuge of competing demands is bewildering and unyielding as new presidents try to figure out where to place their energy and strategic emphasis.

In addition to managing these priorities, many new presidents must make some critical assessments, often in a compressed time frame, to make good decisions for the college. Although many leaders may be inclined to make decisions about their newly inherited leadership team as a priority, they should consider other critical areas to address first to have a solid base of knowledge for future decision-making. Having a firm grasp on one's personal leadership philosophy as well as some essential information about the new institution is paramount to accurately assess the new leadership team.

Although there is no exact blueprint to follow when stepping into a new position, this chapter offers some points for consideration for new leaders in transition who are faced with assessing an existing leadership team.

Know Yourself

The Greek adage "know thyself" could not be more relevant than during times of leadership transition. A new president should use the transition opportunity to conduct an up-to-date personal and leadership inventory prior to stepping into his or her new role.

A leader may choose to engage with a professional coach, enroll in a presidential leadership institute, participate in a 360-degree feedback evaluation, complete personality inventories, or identify a peer mentor (or veteran president) for support prior to and during the transition. No matter what method one chooses, it is important to become familiar with current leadership strengths, weaknesses, and philosophies to create a greater sense of personal awareness. New leaders who have a firm sense of self can communicate their values and principles to their new organizations and leadership teams more authentically.

As a part of this process, a new leader may choose to develop an elevator speech or key personal pillars that describe what guides his or her leadership philosophy. This can serve as an important tool to begin interaction with the organization, because stakeholders frequently want to know what new leaders are going to do and what actions they are going to take very early. Rather than issuing premature and loosely formulated proclamations, new leaders can use the opportunity to talk about what their core values are and how they will use those values to inform what they learn about the college. In the early stages of transition, sharing these perspectives can build more authentic relationships with stakeholders and allow the new leader more time to make more accurate assessments.

A number of advocacy organizations offer programs for new leaders to assess and reacquaint with their core values and connect with peer mentors. New leaders might consider one of the following programs for an appropriate fit:

- American Association of Community Colleges President's Academy Summer Institute and New Presidents' Workshop
- American Council on Education Institute for New Presidents
- Harvard Graduate School of Education Institute for Management and Leadership in Education
- Higher Education Leadership Development for Women
- Aspen Institute Executive Seminar on Leadership, Values, and the Good Society
- American Association of State Colleges and Universities New Presidents Academy

- Chair Academy Mentor Matching
- Association of Community College Trustees Governance Leadership Institute
- Association of Governing Boards Institute for Board Chairs and Presidents
- League for Innovation in the Community College Executive Leadership Institute

Know Your Organization

Getting to know the college's mission, vision, culture, and people at all levels will enable new leaders to assess the state of the college in a way that provides breadth and depth to understanding. It is crucial for the leader to know these kinds of details about the new playing field before stepping into a formal role and making assessments about the organization or its existing leadership team. However, developing an appropriate depth of understanding of the organization and the leadership team takes time.

Bensimon (1989) conducted a study of second-time presidents and found that presidents with prior presidential experience were more likely than those with no presidential experience to become familiar with the institution before making assertions. According to McLaughlin (1996), second-time presidents also approach the acclimation process more systematically and cautiously to make their mark on the institution. Research shows that intelligent change takes time, and existing situations have a host of complicated histories, cultural norms, complexities, and relationships embedded (Sanaghan, Goldstein, & Gaval, 2008).

Drawing from this research, coupled with the thought that times of transition are some of the most vulnerable moments for institutions, new leaders should be encouraged to take their time to learn about the institution. While a new leader will employ his or her own methods for getting to know the organization, a few leadership strategies can be used to fit the transition to most institutions.

Methods for Getting to Know the Organization

A new leader can employ static and active methods to get to know the organization. Historical information, no matter what method is used to gather it, will help the new leader obtain a sense of why things function a certain way.

Most commonly, new presidents ask for a number of hard-copy resources they can peruse to formulate questions and impressions prior to arriving on site at the college. Some examples of information requested include the following:

- strategic plans, current and past;
- financial and audit statements, current and past;
- board minutes and board bylaws;
- departmental briefing materials from each senior leadership team department;
- curricula vitae for leadership team and direct reports;
- biographical information for current and immediate past board of trustee members;
- accreditation reports, current and past; and
- organizational charts.

It is also advantageous for the new leader to spend time with the members of the board of trustees to gain a clear understanding of the board's perceptions and desired direction for the college. This could be accomplished through hosting a special retreat, facilitating one-on-one meetings with board members, or attending an institute specifically designed for presidents and board chairs to establish the focus for their partnership. These president and board chair institutes are offered regularly by organizations such as the Association of Community College Trustees and the Association of Governing Boards.

Doing an informal assessment of the external perception of the institution can also provide new leaders with an important perspective. What the community thinks about the organization the leader will soon helm is a critical piece of information to have when making subsequent assessments. A survey of the college's Web presence and the latest press coverage will give the new leader an idea of how the college promotes itself to outside entities. Some leaders also choose to set informal meetings with chief executive officers of major partner institutions to obtain a sense of how the college is performing in critical partnerships.

Drucker (2004) believes the spirit of an organization is inspired by those at the top and, further, that "the proof of the sincerity and seriousness of a management is [its] uncompromising emphasis on integrity of character" (p. 3). In addition, knowing the mission of the institution—its purpose, values, and goals—is fundamental for a new leader as illustrated in the following from Gaff and Meacham (2006):

> The president (and the administration for which she or he is responsible) and board of trustees must act consistently and repeatedly to assure institutional integrity. They must be certain that their organization does what it says and says what it does. (p. 1)

Most often, this integrity is reflected in a mission statement, which serves as the institution's formal public declaration of its purposes and its vision of excellence (Gaff & Meacham, 2006). The new leader will be able to tell a great deal about the breadth and depth of the work he or she needs to undertake by how clearly these elements are articulated in the college's mission statement.

As mentioned in chapter 1, the mission statement is a cornerstone for decision-making, and its strength is a key indicator of organizational health. If the mission is not clear and does not permeate throughout the institution, the president may have to consider developing new goals or a vision that rallies people around a more distinct focus for the institution. Stewardship of the mission's relevance and efficacy is a key part of institutional leadership, so developing an early understanding of how the organization lives it should be a priority. Of course, this point of view assumes that the mission, regardless of its efficacy, is an engrained part of the organization's culture, which would be politically difficult to modify or change.

Almost every community college mission refers to some element of student access, student success, or serving the needs of the local community. But words strung together in a mission statement do not always accurately instill understanding and purpose for the people it is supposed to inspire. All too often colleges identify target numbers or percentages that everyone rallies around, such as a 2% increase in enrollment, 10% retention goal, or 5% decrease in expenditures. A natural connection between the mission and the numerical outcomes that have been targeted is the expectation. But without an understanding of why these numerical targets are important and relevant, members of the college community work toward a particular outcome without knowing what connects the two. When a new president is faced with this type of circumstance, he or she must be prepared to develop new goals that can provide a focus for why the college pursues what it pursues. When successful, well-articulated goals will provide the reason the college needs to aggressively pursue its outcomes with meaning and purpose.

Examining other organizational health indicators is also critical. A number of things can be considered institutional health indictors, but in general, health indicators give the leader a sense of how well an institution is achieving its mission. The following can be useful indicators of organizational health:

- level of fiscal reserves
- accreditation status
- level of employee satisfaction and turnover
- condition of physical facilities
- stability of institutional governance practices

- degree of diverse funding streams
- status of recent financial audits
- leadership stability

The initial information gathered from institutional health indicators gives leaders a fixed perspective on the current status. But it is critically important for leaders to understand the reason behind the status quo to have a solid foundation for future decision-making by asking questions such as the following:

- What is the gap between actual and potential?
- How does work currently get done? If favorable outcomes are being delivered, are they being delivered at a considerable cost to the institution's fiscal or human resources?
- How does the college solve problems? How do campus or divisional levels work together to find solutions?
- Are there recurring (or foundational) items that never get addressed?
- Are there silos in the organization? If they exist, what steps are needed to overcome or redirect them?
- How do colleagues relate to and work with one another?
- What are the recurring road blocks that the organization encounters?
- How successful (or prevalent) are cross-program collaborations?

How people work with each other in an organization should indicate to new leaders how well an organization is functioning. The information gathered about the organization (i.e., the work), when considered in context with the reasons behind the status quo (i.e., how the work gets done), will give leaders a more holistic understanding of the organization and how it operates. The case scenario in Box 3.1 shows how one president used institutional data to stimulate a series of questions about degree attainment.

Once equipped with some basic information and a well-developed formula of questions for determining why the situation exists, the new president should move toward a better understanding of his or her initial impressions by engaging more actively with internal stakeholders.

Organizing an informal gathering with the new leadership team is a way for members to get to know each other in a more neutral and less pressurized setting. A shared meal can be a useful method of creating open dialogue and can be a more natural venue for sharing the new leader's key pillars or elevator speech. This informal gathering gives the new leader and the existing leadership team an opportunity to learn about each other and their respective values and dispositions without the immediate pressure of discussing current

BOX 3.1
Case Scenario 1

A new community college president was reviewing data, and she noted that the institution consistently produces 20% more associate in arts degrees than its counterpart institutions; however, the college produces a fraction of associate in science degrees compared to its counterparts. The president was immediately prompted to ask the following:

- What does the lower percentage of associate in science degrees tell us about our transfer programs that are focused on science, technology, engineering, and math?
- Does the college have comprehensive and relevant associate in science offerings? What do these offerings reveal about the college's health care programs?

Data discoveries like this should stimulate additional probing about the purpose behind the status quo.

or past performance of their department or the institution. Once this rapport has been established, it is advisable to set up one-on-one meetings with members of the leadership team so the president's initial impressions can be discussed privately in more detail. Each leader will facilitate the first one-on-one meetings differently. However, it may be helpful to focus in greater detail on understanding the team members' leadership values, purposes, connections to their work, and their visions for the future of the work they steward as part of these initial learning opportunities.

New presidents can also conduct listening tours with different groups in the college. Some choose to actively conduct skip-level meetings, which is when a manager's manager meets with employees to discuss department challenges, concerns, and opportunities for growth or advancement (Boulton, 2014). Overall, ways to improve communication is often a focus area for a new president. Consider the following:

> A leader may have a manager with 12 direct reports who reports to a director. A skip-level meeting would involve the director meeting with the 12 direct reports of the manager without the manager being present, in effect, "skipping" a level over them. (Boulton, 2014, p. 1)

Skip-level meetings are effective when appropriately framed, planned, communicated, and timed in such a way that they build trust and open communication in the college. By meeting with members of the college community in an open, authentic, and confidential way, the new leader can get a clearer and accurate picture of the true perspective of the college community and specific points of view of those in certain departments.

Other leaders may choose to have informal chat sessions with a broader subset of members of the organization. Sometimes tagged "Chats With the Chancellor" or "Pizza With the President," these should be strategically cultivated group meetings (by topic, department, division, or some other purposeful grouping) that allow dialogue with the new president. These can be done in smaller forums or larger, more all-call settings. However, in both circumstances, the intent and purpose of the chat should be clear for participants. Planners may consider using a neutral facilitator to help create a safe space for the president and participants to interact authentically so that it does not become an unintended gripe session.

Both methods provide opportunities to gather firsthand perspectives from employees in a variety of positions across the institution. The goal is to encourage discourse, dialogue, and engagement across all levels of leadership and not just rely solely on the perspectives of those closest to the leader to shape his or her perspective.

Culture: The Dark Horse of Leadership Transition

As the information from these initial efforts begin to coalesce, another adage will begin to become abundantly clear to new leaders: Culture eats strategy for breakfast. No matter how clearly and logically a vision is articulated, efforts to implement it can be quickly derailed if unknown cultural elements are at play.

The cultures of higher education institutions have been described as organized anarchies characterized by problematic goals, unclear technology, and fluid participation (Cohen & March, 1974). Assuming the new leader is faced with some derivative of this culture, it is important to understand the reasons why he or she faces certain problems (Sinek, 2009). According to Sanaghan et al. (2008), everyone understands the unspoken reasons why things are done a certain way and what behaviors are rewarded, but rarely does anyone explicitly document and provide references why something is done. New leaders who do not take time to learn the culture can find it to be a stumbling block. Understanding the culture and what contributes to it will allow the leader to better assess individual people and leaders. Box 3.2 shows how the culture of the organization affects decision-making at the college.

Culture drives daily behavior, organizational thinking, and decision-making and is often steeped in institutional history. New presidents should

BOX 3.2
Case Scenario 2

During the first several months of his tenure, a new president could not locate the root cause for the many areas of concern he identified. Despite the fact that the college was in a favorable fiscal position, almost everyone exhibited a persistent poverty mentality, claiming to be a victim of someone else's choices and decisions. Another key problem was that the advancement office was pursuing small grant opportunities that did not add much value to the academic program. In some cases, they cost more in compliance personnel than the face value of the award. There were other equally troubling issues, but he was not able to immediately identify a common thread for why things were like they were.

At his third executive team meeting, he asked a key question, "What is our strategy for accomplishing the things we want to accomplish here at the college?" He was met with blank looks and silence. Those who did answer gave myopic responses based on their individual department work. It became abundantly clear the institution suffered from a strong case of siloed leaders who confused activity with progress. Everyone was doing work and making decisions based on what he or she thought was correct through his or her lens, but no one was making intentional and strategic decisions that were right for the institution as a whole. The president quickly went to work on defining a strategy that could be understood through an institutional lens.

listen and learn from stories and pay close attention to what they reveal about institutional culture (Sanaghan et al., 2008).

Know Your Team

Although the advice for assessing an existing leadership team is last in this chapter, it is not the last thing a leader does in his or her transition. Taking deliberate steps to know oneself, the organization, and the leadership team are not mutually exclusive steps. Rather, information gathering for all three aspects happens simultaneously and contributes to the basis of the new leader's future decisions. The assessment of the new leadership team is discussed last to underscore the importance of having the knowledge of self and the organization before making assumptions about the team. It is important to bring others along with the leader (i.e., get them to follow his or her lead) on the journey. However, the leader must know where he or she wants to go first.

The phrase *leadership team* is emphasized because this is a key concept for new leaders to embrace as they assume their new position. Quite often, members of the leadership team have been with the college for long periods prior to the new president's arrival. They possess key pieces of information and institutional memory that could contribute to or detract from a president's success. The new leader's ability to build trust and show appreciation for that knowledge so that he or she is better positioned for success is crucial. New leaders often overlook the importance of building genuine relationships and meeting the existing leadership team members where they are.

Taking time to better understand the existing leadership team members' personalities, past experiences, and individual professional goals and communication styles will contribute to a more positive and lasting working relationship. It is important to remove personal thoughts, feelings, and biases and to approach every conversation with a willingness to listen and learn. Indeed, no one person serves all the needs of a college student. It takes multiple people and departments to ensure that a student is successful in his or her college journey. The role of college president is no exception to this. It is important to acknowledge that the existing leadership team has to work with the new leader to achieve the college's goals and objectives. Therefore, understanding the team members as individuals and as a group is equally as important as knowing oneself and the institution.

Individual assessments of the members of the existing leadership team can frequently be made in one-on-one meetings and day-to-day interactions. Although each leader will achieve this assessment in his or her own way, Dowdall (2004) noted that two personal qualities are most often desired in new colleagues: the ability to listen and the ability to learn quickly. It is also important for new leaders to ask questions that give insight into team members' sense of purpose and the reason members of the leadership team choose to do the work they do. This connectivity with individual and collective purpose is a key indicator to overall fit with the new leader's philosophy. The degree to which members of the existing leadership team, as well as the new leader, exhibit these qualities and articulate these reasons is a significant sign of how successful the team members will be in participating in a larger group dynamic.

Although a new president may be faced with a number of strong individual performers, the success of an institution is built on the outcomes of the group. For that reason, a new president may also choose to conduct an outside assessment to determine how individual members of the team should work together as a group. According to McCauley and Fick-Cooper (2015), leadership involves far more than the person who holds the leader title. It is a social process that enables individuals to work together as a cohesive group to produce collective results—results they could never achieve working as individuals. Central to the process are the interactions and exchanges between the formal leader and group members, and among group members themselves. The process is influenced by the beliefs and values of the individuals involved, the quality of relationships in the group, formal structures and procedures, and the group's informal routines. To diagnose the source of the problems in this process, one needs to take a whole system rather than an individual leader perspective. (p. 2)

A neutral and objective evaluation of the cohesive group dynamic can be accomplished by interacting with leadership coaches, peer reviewers, or an organizational development firm, and the evaluation can be helpful to the president by identifying what he or she needs to tweak to get the desired results from the team as a group.

No matter what method the president chooses for the neutral assessment, a useful instrument is McCauley and Fick-Cooper's (2015) direction, alignment, and commitment model. Direction measures the extent of widespread agreement in the group on overall goals. Alignment is the degree to which work is coordinated within the group, and commitment is the extent of the existence of a sense of mutual responsibility among the group members. By understanding what the group's strengths and opportunities are in the areas of direction, alignment, and commitment, the leader can make appropriate modifications and provide targeted support to produce better outcomes. The case scenario in Box 3.3 illustrates how one president promotes collaboration among team leaders to solve college-wide problems.

In ideal situations, leadership in place prior to the new president's arrival would have addressed any performance or ineffectiveness issues in the senior leadership team. However, when this is not the case, new presidents are faced with assessing the senior leadership team for its fit under new leadership. No matter how deliberately and methodically a new leader approaches the assessment of an existing leadership team, the information gathered may indicate outlying factors that do not fit into the larger leadership design or that there are necessary efficiencies to be gained by making adjustments. In those cases, leaders must take the information they have gathered and make the difficult decision to make a change in the leadership team.

In some cases, existing team members possess leadership potential that can be developed and coached so that the talent is retained for the benefit of the institution. In other cases, there may be potential, but the functional area of responsibility they oversee may need to be improved right away to do

BOX 3.3
Case Scenario 3

In a review of a data report, the college's leadership team identified a major vulnerability in its recruitment pipeline, a common problem for many institutions. During the monthly one-on-one meetings with the president, each executive floats an innovative solution to the president for approval. The enrollment executive suggests adding more staff to do the recruitment work, the executive for information technology suggests developing a new application aimed at the demographic of students not currently being served, and the faculty suggest adding programs that are more relevant to the curriculum.

All the ideas have merit and are worthy of being explored for efficacy. However, when asked if their departments have collaborated with each other on the feasibility or scalability of solutions, no one is able to indicate any prior discussion with their colleagues about points of intersection. Faced with a significant issue—lack of alignment of potential strategies among the leadership team—the president began to support the advancement of solutions that exhibited cross-functional collaboration, thereby rewarding and reinforcing work from the team that was aligned.

---

what is best for the institution. In these kinds of cases, the leader may not be able to invest the time required to develop the team member because the functional area of responsibility may be the more important priority for the overall health of the institution. These are case-by-case decisions, and new leaders are encouraged to weigh what the right decision is for the institution given the available information at the time.

Lessons Learned

Much of what happens during transition for a new leader cannot be captured by telling a theoretical story. Rather, it is a lived experience best conveyed by sharing lessons learned. Therefore, this chapter closes with a few lived experiences for new leaders to consider.

Assume Nothing: A Double-Edged Sword

Throughout this chapter, new presidents are encouraged not to make early assumptions about the organization and the leadership team. The importance of this cannot be stressed enough. New leaders should not assume what they have been told is substantial enough to be practicable, and they are encouraged to get more (trusted) counsel from many perspectives in many situations. More information will only allow leaders to make better decisions.

But there is another side to assuming nothing. New leaders must not assume that because they see two appropriate sequences, the third will naturally follow (i.e., do not assume that a + b = c). Again, particularly when assessing members of the new leadership team, it is important to confirm that new leaders can independently and consistently string together the expected sequences. To draw from another relevant adage, carefully inspect what you expect.

Everything Is Situational

Hersey and Blanchard (1977) argue that sound and effective leadership is task relevant and situationally based. There is no single style, framework, or model of leadership that will work for all situations and scenarios. In fact, leaders' adaptability and willingness to be flexible and nimble will take them much further. Everything depends on the function or job needing attention and structure (Hersey & Blanchard, 1977), and new presidents will be well served to acknowledge that every situation is different and may require a customized remedy. Just because one approach or inclination worked in a previous role or institution does not mean it will transfer to another situation; what works famously in one situation may fail miserably in others.

The other aspect of situational leadership is making sure that one understands what needs to be accomplished in a particular situation. One college may need an expert in securing alternative funding sources, another college may need someone who is capable of leading major cultural change, and another college may need a person who can respond to both needs. No matter what the case calls for, it is imperative for the new leader to clearly understand (from the board of trustees and other key stakeholders) what is required. Once leaders know the purpose and intention behind what they are being asked to do, they can align an appropriate strategy. Intention and purpose inform strategy.

Emotional Intelligence and Intellectual Humility

New presidents who accept the role while also acknowledging that their success depends on the intellect, perspective, and partnership of others have a leg up. Those who acknowledge the reality of their own levels of emotional intelligence and intellectual humility have an additional leg up. Leaders with strong levels of emotional intelligence exhibit the ability to identify emotions of others and their own, are able to discern feelings and acknowledge them properly, and use emotional insight to facilitate behavior and thinking to achieve goals (Colman, 2008). Those with intellectual humility, for example, demonstrate a consciousness of the limits of knowledge, "including a sensitivity to circumstances in which one's native egocentrism is likely to function self-deceptively; sensitivity to bias, prejudice and limitations of one's viewpoint" (Foundation for Critical Thinking, 2019, p. 1).

Leaders in tune with these personal elements are better positioned to

- remove personal thoughts, feelings, and biases as appropriate;
- demonstrate patience and resist false senses of urgency so they can make fair and accurate assessments;
- understand that the presidency is not about the president as an individual. Instead, understand the presidency is about what the president does for the institution; and
- acknowledge that no one person knows everything and that no one has all the right answers.

As previously mentioned, arriving and making quick and sweeping leadership changes to shore up the team in a way that makes the new leader more comfortable is a natural instinct. Leaders who embrace the values of emotional intelligence and intellectual humility as a part of their leadership philosophy are much more likely to take a measured approach during the critical times of a new presidency. Do the right things for the right reasons, and the right outcomes will happen.

References

Bensimon, E. (1989). *On assuming a college or university presidency*. Washington, DC: American Association of Higher Education.

Boulton, S. (2014). The art of the skip level meeting. Retrieved from https://www.linkedin.com/pulse/art-skip-level-meeting-scott-boulton%2C-chrp-5948801065834024960

Cohen, M. D., & March, J. G. (1974). *Leadership and ambiguity* (2nd ed.). Boston, MA: Harvard Business School Press.

Colman, A. (2008). *A dictionary of psychology* (3rd ed.). New York, NY: Oxford University Press.

Dowdall, J. (2004, December 3). Interim and internal. *The Chronicle of Higher Education*. Retrieved from https://www.chronicle.com/article/InterimInternal/44702

Drucker, P. F. (2004). *The daily Drucker: 366 days of insight and motivation for getting the right things done*. New York, NY: Harper Business.

Foundation for Critical Thinking. (2019). Valuable intellectual traits. Retrieved from http://www.criticalthinking.org/pages/valuable-intellectual-traits/528

Gaff, J., & Meacham, J. (2006). Learning goals in mission statements: Implications for educational leadership. Retrieved from https://www.aacu.org/publications-research/periodicals/learning-goals-mission-statements-implications-educational

Hersey, P., & Blanchard, K. H. (Eds.). (1977). *Management of organizational behavior: Utilizing human resources* (3rd ed.). Englewood Cliffs, NJ: Prentice Hall.

McCauley, C., & Fick-Cooper, L. (2015). *Direction, alignment, commitment: Achieving better results through leadership.* Greensboro, NC: Center for Creative Leadership.

McLaughlin, J. B. (Ed.). (1996). *Leadership transitions: The new college president.* San Francisco, CA: Jossey-Bass.

Sanaghan, P. H., Goldstein, L., & Gaval, K. D. (2008). *Presidential transitions: It's not the position, it's the transition.* Lanham, MD: Rowman & Littlefield.

Sinek, S. (2009). *Start with why: How great leaders inspire everyone to take action.* New York, NY: Portfolio.

4

DEVELOPING MIDLEVEL
LEADERSHIP TEAMS

Kimberly Beatty

A chief executive officer (CEO) of a community college may think the executive leadership team is the most important team to develop at the institution. Although the executive leadership team is essential, the reality is that these leaders are not on the ground dealing with everyday issues. When it comes to getting the work done and executing the mission and vision of the institution, the leadership development focus must also include the college's midlevel leadership.

For this chapter, *midlevel leadership* is defined as the midlevel layer of administration in a community college, whether a multicampus, multicollege, or single campus institution. The members have supervision and budget authority but do not report directly to the CEO. This layer of leadership represents a large group of administrators, but that is precisely the reason developing the midlevel leadership team is so critical.

There are many theories in higher education about developing effective teams. In this chapter, the discussion focuses on the strategy for developing midlevel teams, the competencies needed for midlevel leaders in twenty-first-century community colleges, approaches to developing these leaders through a develop-your-own leadership development program, and how to align the work of the midlevel leadership team with the execution of the vision of the college.

The Leadership Development Strategy

A significant challenge for any community college CEO is developing a shared vision for the college. This vision must be bold and ambitious yet attainable and must drive everything in the institution, including the selection, behaviors, and performance of midlevel leaders. Therefore, the leadership strategy put forward is simple: Align the midlevel leadership team with the vision for the college. Typically, the vision statement describes the desired future of the college and is developed through broad college consultation with stakeholders and approved by the board as a part of the strategic plan. The vision is what the college aspires to be in the future. It is essential for a CEO to develop a leadership team that is in alignment with college values and has the skills necessary to help realize that vision.

At Metropolitan Community College (MCC; Metropolitan Community College, 2017) in Kansas City, where I serve as chancellor, the vision is that "Metropolitan Community College will be a high performing institution that is learning-centered, affordable, and aligned around student success" (p. 2). The key phrases in the vision that guide the development of MCC's midlevel leadership team are *high-performing institution*, *learning-centered*, and *student success*. These primary elements serve as a framework for measuring leadership competencies, professional development, execution of plans, and evaluation of progress.

If the organization is going to realize its potential, the team's decisions and actions must be aligned with the vision. At MCC, aligning the leadership team with the vision of the college is an ongoing process. As the vision at MCC continues to evolve, the team members also evolve in their approach to executing that vision. The fact that an institution and its teams are always evolving is often difficult to sell to a college community. Often college employees want stability, which is too often translated as keeping things the same.

Simply put, keeping things the same does not fit the true mission of community colleges. The strength of community colleges is that they are nimble, flexible, and dynamic. These values are what make the institutions great and capable of meeting the community's needs. These same values must be reflected in the college's vision statement and must guide the leadership teams that are assigned to implement it. Institutional vision evolves, but that does not mean that every time the vision changes, the team members must be changed as well. However, it does mean that ongoing development must be designed to align with the ever evolving college mission and vision. It is important to ensure that everyone in the entire organization understands and shares the vision and that the team development is constantly connected to the vision. Aligning the midlevel team with the vision is a strategy that will help the organization thrive.

Leadership Competencies

The American Association of Community Colleges' (AACC's; American Association of Community Colleges, 2018) *Leadership Competencies for Community College Leaders* is a fully comprehensive document to guide the development of emerging leaders and assist colleges with the selection of employees dedicated to the community college mission, vision, and values. The AACC's three categories of leadership competencies are for emerging leaders, new CEOs in the first three years on the job, and CEOs who have been in their positions for three or more years (American Association of Community Colleges, 2018). For the purpose of the discussion in this chapter, the AACC competency framework for emerging leaders applies to midlevel leaders. Although the AACC does not explicitly define the term *emerging leaders*, a good case can be made for these competencies applying to midlevel leaders because they represent the pipeline for future executive leaders and CEOs.

The AACC separates leadership competencies into five broad categories: organizational strategy, communication, collaboration, fund-raising and finance, and community college advocacy. These competencies serve as the foundation and should be developed and enhanced with the vision of the college in mind (American Association of Community Colleges, 2018). To be clear, aligning the development of midlevel leaders with the vision of the college is the primary goal as the competencies serve as skills that will help the team achieve the vision. Table 4.1 shows the AACC leadership competencies with brief descriptors of each. Later in this section, how a CEO can integrate these competencies into a curriculum is discussed.

When considering these leadership competencies, it is best to think about them in terms of the outcomes that undergird what the CEO hopes to achieve in developing a leadership team. For example, communication is an important skill for anyone in a leadership role, and many aspects of communication should be explored when developing a midlevel leadership team. Consider the following:

- the type and frequency of communication that is necessary between a team leader and team members, supervisors, and other stakeholders
- the style of communication with internal and external stakeholders
- the lines of authority for communication
- the plans for effective communication in a crisis

TABLE 4.1

AACC's Competencies for Emerging Leaders

Organizational Strategy	Institutional Finance, Research Fund-Raising, and Resource Management	Communication	Collaboration	Community College Advocacy
Understand the mission, vision, and goals of the college, and how your role supports them.	Know your unit's budget and monitor it routinely. Notify leadership if the unit's allocated budget and expenditures are not in keeping with the institution's key performance indicators.	Be articulate. Work toward having strong presentation skills.	Understand that there are no lone rangers.	Recognize there are multiple government programs at the state and federal levels that contribute to funding a college's students and programs.
Learn the culture of the institution to effectively perform your duties within the cultural constructs that exist.	Institutional fund-raising is everyone's job. Work with the advancement office to determine where you might be supportive.	Always have a succinct pocket speech that is consistent with the mission and vision.	Know the key stakeholders that are advocates for the institution, and the roles they play in the community.	Recognize there is an interplay of public perception and policymaking that can impact college operations.
Have a forward-looking philosophy and be prepared for change.	Understand the institutional dashboard and how to interpret data to improve the student academic experience.	Know the chain of command for communications.		We all serve as advocates for the college.

(Continues)

TABLE 4.1 (*Continued*)

Organizational Strategy	Institutional Finance, Research Fund-Raising, and Resource Management	Communication	Collaboration	Community College Advocacy
Know your institution's strategies for improving student success and completion.	Understand the importance of time management and planning in your positions.	Be willing to offer a realistic solution to any institutional problem. Be willing to participate in an environment that takes shared responsibility.		
Provide exemplary customer service that makes members of the community feel welcome.	Understand the organizational protocol; if you are unable to resolve conflict, understand how to have it addressed.	Learn the nuances of communications with various internal and external stakeholders. Know when and when not to use appropriate jargon.		
Have an ongoing focus on process improvement for internal and external customers.		Become familiar with what it means to be globally competent, meaning seeking to understand the societal complexities that encompass other points of view and new ways of thinking.		

(*Continues*)

Understand the organizational structure of the college and the function that your unit plays in supporting the institutional goals.		Be familiar with grassroots efforts to organize stakeholders to advocate for the college mission.
Understand the responsibilities of all employees within the organization.		

Note. From American Association of Community Colleges (2018).

The point of this example is to demonstrate that these competencies are overarching. The practical applications that lead to mastery of competencies may differ depending on the institution, its geographic location, institutional culture, and leadership philosophy. This partly explains why develop-your-own programs are so essential to developing midlevel leadership teams.

Develop-Your-Own Program

There are three types of leadership development programs (creating your own leadership development programs, doctoral programs, and leadership institutes), and all can serve as great methods that contribute to the overall growth of an individual's leadership abilities. The remainder of this chapter focuses on the develop-your-own approach, which is the most comprehensive approach because it provides an opportunity for everyone in the entire institution to learn. The other two options for leadership development, although important and valuable, are typically individualized. The develop-your-own approach creates an opportunity for the individual to learn and to learn in a team and allows the institution (with facilitation and a focus on outcomes) to learn and continuously improve. In addition, a develop-your-own program allows an institution to infuse into the training the cultural nuances that may be specific to the college. It cannot be stressed enough how important it is to include the institutional culture in the curriculum of these programs. Many of the challenges midlevel leaders may encounter are shaped by institutional culture.

A develop-your-own program can be designed in a variety of ways, but it should be based on the vision for the college. Following are four potential outcomes for this type of leadership development programing:

1. developing a cadre of leaders for succession planning
2. providing a leadership toolbox for the midlevel leadership team
3. creating an academy-like experience with a beginning and an ending date that may assist an employee to develop broader knowledge about the institution and the students it serves
4. training midlevel leaders to execute specific interventions needed by the college

CEOs should strive to achieve all of these outcomes. All four are needed to create a robust, comprehensive experience for the leadership team. However, the situation may dictate a single focus for leadership development at a particular institution. Implementing a comprehensive development program may take time. In terms of time frame, a year-long program is the most desirable.

A year-long program allows for time for learning and its application to take place. For example, MCC created a two-tier approach for leadership development. The initial programming was one year with a kickoff program and monthly half-day meetings with online engagement between meetings, ending with a culminating ceremony. In the second year of the program, the initial cohort served as ambassadors to the second cohort. In this model, the learning continues for the first cohort and provides continuity. Short, intermittent programming is not effective for long-term impact for individuals or the institution. Professional development in most cases is playing the long game of preparation—it takes a serious investment.

Develop-Your-Own Curriculum

Although the AACC leadership competencies mentioned in the previous section serve as the road map for the leadership training curriculum, the competencies must also align with the vision of the college. The vision-driven curriculum development for leadership development training programs can be approached in several ways. Following are three examples that can be used as guides for developing leadership training:

1. Top-down approach: In this approach, the vision is central to the curriculum, and the senior administration will typically develop the curriculum, perhaps with the help of a consultant.
2. Bottom-up approach: The leadership team is central in this approach, and the expected outcomes of the experience are shaped by the team. This strategy gives participants a sense of ownership of the outcomes.
3. Curriculum-in-a-box approach: There are many existing leadership training programs, and many institutions may take a preexisting curriculum and shape it to meet the needs of the college.

The best approach is often a hybrid of these three. CEOs must remain focused on the overarching goal and be willing to recognize there are experts in the institution, and people know what they want and need. Therefore, the bottom-up approach is a good starting point for curriculum development. It is advisable to remain flexible when designing the leadership development program. It's okay not to have a solidified plan when the program is launched—in fact, the participants may appreciate the opportunity to be involved in developing the curriculum.

The curriculum should have a strong internal component that is focused on operations, and the college experts in those areas (i.e., budgeting, payroll, human resources) are the best trainers to facilitate these sessions. The program convener needs only to ensure that internal presenters understand the need to go beyond providing an elementary overview of payroll, for example; in this case, their role is to help the participants understand how payroll is managed correctly.

Conveners of develop-your-own programs may start with a plan but can allow flexibility to modify it based on input provided from the participants. The initial input can be solicited in a number of ways. First, when selecting participants, the convener can include a request for feedback on program topics with the acceptance letter. Second, the facilitator can kick off the meeting with a framework that builds in a session that solicits input on the topics or modules for the curriculum for future sessions. There should be some flexibility in the curriculum to allow modifications to occur naturally.

Although the bottom-up approach is good, one cannot forget the overarching strategy: Align the training curriculum with the vision for the college. The accountability for ensuring that the common good of the institution is realized rests with the CEO. Typically, the CEO will engage the executive leadership team in recommending components of the curriculum and a discussion of the value of midlevel leadership training. However, the CEO is responsible for ensuring that the development program is designed in a way that participants fully understand where the college is headed in the future. To ensure the continued alignment of the program with the vision of the college, the CEO must be engaged even if an external consultant is used to conduct the training.

Knowledgeable consultants can be an important resource for a CEO when developing midlevel training programs. At one community college in California, the CEO wanted to strengthen the brand of the college. At this institution, internal stakeholders did not understand their role when interacting with the media. During the leadership development training, an external expert in media relations was brought in to address communication competencies. The consultant used role-play scenarios for training midlevel managers on ways to interact with the media. This nonthreatening approach was well received by the participants.

External consultants can also be employed to facilitate a curriculum-in-a-box approach. There are wonderful existing models of leadership development that could be incorporated into a comprehensive, robust program. However, a model that is entirely externally developed is usually the least effective approach to a leadership development program because it defeats the key aspect of developing your own. If a CEO chooses to use a curriculum-in-a-box, there is very little adaptation of it to the vision and culture of the college. However, if the CEO chooses to take a hybrid approach to a preexisting curriculum by incorporating the vision and culture of the institution, there could be some benefits. Usually internal experts can teach or facilitate the delivery of the curriculum. Each approach has its benefits, and every CEO needs to do what works best for the institution.

Implementation

There is no cookie-cutter approach to implementing a leadership development program. However, the following best practices can lead to successful program implementation:

- Understand the culture of the institution and evaluate the existing leadership gaps. Despite the best of intentions, the culture of an institution can inadvertently cause problems when implementing a leadership development program. However, institutional transformation cannot take place without the development and continual improvement of a college's midlevel leadership team. Today's expectations for leaders are different from past expectations; priorities must shift to accountability and improving student success (American Association of Community Colleges, 2018).
- Assess what is needed. Consider the following questions when assessing the need and implementation design of a develop-your-own leadership development program:
  - Who needs to participate?
  - How aligned is the leadership team with the vision?
  - Has the vision been thoroughly communicated?
  - What are the expected outcomes?
  - Is the institution ready to take this step?
  - Will participation be required or voluntary?
- Use the answers from this assessment to help frame the curriculum for the leadership development program.
- Build process improvement into the training.

Developing midlevel leadership teams is not an event that happens once and then is allowed to grow stagnant over time. Effective leaders will take advantage of opportunities for process improvement from the beginning to the end of the program. Program leaders are encouraged to conduct program evaluations after each session. A short evaluation can gather much information. For example, consider the following questions for participants:

- Did you leave this session knowing more than you understood about [insert topic] than when you entered?
- Will this information help you in your role at the institution?
- If there was one thing you could change about today's session, what would that be?
- Did today's session suggest the importance of a topic that is currently not included in upcoming sessions? If so, please list your ideas for consideration.

This short evaluation and a brief e-mail or discussion about what was learned from the feedback will let the participants know that their perspective is appreciated. In addition to short evaluations, monthly evaluations can be conducted and compiled, leading to a master comprehensive evaluation at the end of the program. The monthly evaluation coupled with the end-of-program evaluation should provide valuable information to improve the program in future cycles. CEOs or their designees must be open to the need for improvement of programs based on the feedback from these evaluations. Curriculum designers rarely get the program right on the first try. Every group is different, and every institution is different. If this is a program that will be repeated at the institution, the feedback will be invaluable to the process improvement aspect of the program.

Although there are consulting firms that develop leadership training programs for colleges, CEOs should use them as an external behind-the-scenes adviser to guide the process or assist with developing the curriculum, not necessarily as the face of the program. The CEO and members of the senior leadership need to own the program as much as possible.

Making It Happen: Execution and Accountability

The midlevel leadership team members must view themselves as vital contributors to the direction of the college. As previously mentioned, the vision of the college should inform the curriculum for the midlevel leadership development program. After the completion of a build-your-own leadership development program, the focus for training can shift to implementation, which may involve policy and procedural changes. One change in leadership development training might be to add the AACC's leadership competencies as a component of the midlevel managers' job descriptions and evaluation process for the leadership team and its members (American Association of Community Colleges, 2018). The AACC competencies can be used to develop training programs to assist colleges with the selection of employees dedicated to the community college mission, vision, and values.

Team members can also be evaluated based on the degree of goal accomplishment and demonstration of leadership competencies. Establishing accountability measures and implementing effective evaluations are areas that many community colleges get wrong. In too many cases, leaders do not hold all midlevel leaders accountable for the outcomes or key performance indicators in the strategic plan. Building your own programs can help supervisors think about how the key performance indicators are linked to the individual manager's role and how they should be measured in the evaluation process.

If a strategic plan lists the key performance indicators of improving college completion and closing achievement gaps, these measures can be linked to the administrator's evaluation process using leadership competencies as the foundation but also including expectations for the midlevel manager. For example, for the communication competency, a goal may be for a dean to have two meetings per month to share completion data with faculty and staff with the expectation there would be a discussion on what each party can do to affect or change the data reviewed. This simple communication approach can lead to creating a culture of evidence and accountability that gets the entire institution talking about completion. Building in accountability is not hard, but it should be aligned with the vision. Aligning everything with the institution's vision is key to the success of developing the team and moving from strategy development to execution of the vision.

Case Study: Restructuring to Align With the Vision

This case study illustrates how an initial round of midlevel leadership development training was required at a large community college system in Texas. At the governing board's direction, institutional transformation began immediately after the new CEO's arrival at the institution. The overarching goal was to restructure the institution to align with the vision of implementing a uniform center of excellence model across a large, complex, multicollege institution. The entire instructional division was to be restructured, moving from campus deans to districtwide deans.

Given that this was a large multicollege institution, the college's CEO decided to implement a matrix organizational structure. Once all the leadership employment decisions were made, the senior leadership team required all deans; executive directors; associate vice chancellors; and, in some workshops, all chairs to participate in training. In this instance, the level of change that was desired at the institution was so great that all leaders needed to be walking to the same beat to make the reorganization work and accomplish the institution's student success outcome goals. The district launched a year-long midlevel leadership development program. During the year, monthly sessions with assignments took place between meetings. Because the college was moving toward a one-college concept in the matrix structure and leaving the five-college concept behind, scenarios and case studies were important components of the curriculum. The culture encouraged listening solely to the college president with the district policies and procedures taking a secondary role. As a result, walking participants through real change situations was transformational. Implementing a comprehensive transformational change left no room for excuses, and the institution's administration was able to move forward and make positive strides in achieving student outcomes. The professional development series was taken seriously by the campus stakeholders. The professional development academy was an organized leadership development program for midlevel managers. At the end of the leadership academy, the institution hosted a graduation ceremony for the participants, which is a formal program to celebrate their achievements and features a conferral of certificates. See Appendix 4A for an overview of a typical leadership development academy.

Lessons Learned

Developing teams is not a task for the CEO alone. Many midlevel leaders are developing teams as well. Developing good teams is not an art, but a process. Five important leadership lessons are provided in the following section.

First, developing teams takes time. Don't be afraid to take the necessary time to make selection decisions when employing new team members. It is necessary to ensure that candidate skills and values are aligned with the position and with the vision of the college.

Second, when developing midlevel leadership teams, the CEO must be prepared to invest the necessary time and energy. Maxwell (1998) refers to this investment as the law of the lid. It takes time to develop the capacity for people to reach that lid in their leadership roles. According to Maxwell, leadership ability is the lid that defines the leader's overall effectiveness, and the lower the leader's ability to lead, the lower the lid of the leadership ability; the higher the leader's capacity to lead, the higher the lid for the leader's level of accomplishment.

Third, CEOs should make a personal commitment to the selection and development of the leadership team. Again, the goal is to align midlevel leadership teams with the vision of the college. It is important to look for connections to the institution's vision and the candidate's background when the employee is selected for the job. Also, it is critical for senior leaders to consciously connect with midlevel managers. Maxwell (2011) describes five levels of leadership (position, permission, production, people development, and pinnacle). In Maxwell's level of leadership model, level 2 is about the human relationships the leader has built up around him. At level 2, people follow the leader because of the connection and relationship they feel they have with the leader. To be effective, the CEO must find time to make connections with all levels of leadership, including the midlevel leadership.

Fourth, CEOs should create a culture of professional development and ongoing learning, which is aligned with Maxwell's level 4 leadership principle. People need to feel their leaders are making an investment in them, and this occurs best when people development is embedded in the culture of the institution. According to Maxwell, a caring culture is vital to developing a team and to its members' sense of belonging and connection to the college vision.

Fifth, CEOs are generally high achievers. As such, they tend to strive to get things perfect the first time around. However, many factors can cause a leadership development program to not have the expected outcomes or for a team member to leave. Regardless of the situation, CEOs should evaluate and learn from it and then make corrections to inform decisions the next time around.

Final Thoughts

Societal and political issues continue to shape the mission and priorities of comprehensive community colleges. External pressures, including demands for higher levels of accountability from accrediting bodies and state agencies, have created a need for new skill sets in midlevel leadership teams. With dwindling funding support, resource management is a skill that midlevel leaders must have to develop, expand, and sustain programs. Further, with the growing demands of industry and the need to fill the middle-skills gap, college programmatic needs are becoming more expensive and ever changing. Leaders have a responsibility to develop midlevel leaders so they have the competencies to meet these demands.

Leaders in higher education are not in this business for the money; they are committed to the unique mission of the community college. Community college leaders are serving those who may not necessarily see college as a pathway to a livable wage. Community college leaders owe it to the students to develop institutional capacity through the skills of the leadership teams to effectively serve the institutions. The midlevel leadership arm of the institution is critical to ensuring this mission is accomplished. Presidents and boards are encouraged to take the time to invest in midlevel leadership development because the institution, and most important, the students, are worth it.

References

American Association of Community Colleges. (2018). *AACC leadership competencies for community college leaders.* Retrieved from https://www.aacc.nche.edu/wp-content/uploads/2018/11/AACC2018Competencies_111618_FINAL.pdf

Maxwell, J. (1998). *The 21 irrefutable laws of leadership.* Nashville, TN: Thomas Nelson.

Maxwell, J. (2011). *The five levels of leadership: Proven steps to maximize your position.* Nashville, TN: Center Street.

Metropolitan Community College. (2017). *Vision statement.* Retrieved from https://mcckc.edu/what-drives-us/mission.aspx

Leadership Development Academy Program Overview

Program Purpose and Learning Outcomes

The purpose of the academy was to develop a group of community college practitioners at Red, White, and Blue Community College District (RWBCCD) to lead the college in its quest to be a "regional leader in educational programs and services to an ever-changing world" as specified in its mission statement. This customized leadership development program is designed to develop leaders who will sustain the organization and enhance student success and completion.

In drawing from the American Association of Community Colleges' leadership competencies and other practical need-based competencies established by the institution, participants in the academy will be community college practitioners who

- focus on improving the quality of RWBCCD, protecting the long-term health of the organization, promoting the success of all students, and sustaining the RWBCCD mission and future trends;
- sustain people, processes, and information as well as the physical and financial assets to fulfill the mission, vision, and goals of RWBCCD;
- use clear listening, speaking, and writing skills to engage in honest, transparent, open dialogue at all levels of the college and its surrounding community to promote the success of all students and to sustain the RWBCCD mission;
- develop and maintain responsive, cooperative, mutually beneficial, and ethical internal and external relationships that nurture diversity and promote the success of all students and sustain the RWBCCD;
- understand, commit to, and advocate for the mission, vision, and goals of the RWBCCD; and
- focus on student success and completion to enhance the academic health of the institution.

Participants can expect the following:

- Mini case studies written and presented by midlevel community college practitioners
- Facilitated discussions with experienced community college leaders
- Cross-sector and intrasector strategic conversations

Program Design

There are six components of the program:

1. Institute Kick Off and Retreat: The program will begin in September with a three- to five-day interactive retreat designed to set the context for the program through the examination of topics that influence all aspects of daily work at RWBCCD.
2. Focused Seminars: October through April will include full-day seminars one Friday a month on focused topics designed to increase the leadership success of all participants.
3. The Digital Connection: Electronic journals tracking the participants' experiences will be required throughout the year. There is a learning activity attached to each seminar. These learning activities are submitted electronically one week before the next seminar.
4. Capstone Project: The capstone presentation is meant to be a celebration of students' professional accomplishments rather than a defense of their work (scheduled for May).
5. Closing Session/Ceremony: A luncheon forum designed to create an opportunity for participants to showcase their capstone projects for the executive leadership and board. A certificate of completion will be provided to each participant. Institutional or professional development credit is recommended.
6. Professional Growth Plan/Coaching: The participants will create an individual professional growth portfolio to include topics covered throughout the year and creatively respond to a case scenario as a team.

Instructional Modules

Module I: A Unique Higher Education Institution—The American Community College (September 26)
Module II: Me and the Institution—Where Do They Intersect? (September 27)
Module III: Discovering the Leader in Me (October 24)

Module IV: Managing People, Places, and Things (November 14)
Module V: Building a Culture of Student Success and Completion (January–April)

Sample Module Outline

Module III: Discovering the Leader in Me
In this three-part interactive session, participants will learn theoretical perspectives about leadership while identifying their own leadership style. In this process, participants will apply critical elements of leadership to their roles in the institution such as understanding the institutional culture, effective communication, and decision-making in difficult situations. Lecture, group discussions, and case studies will be used to achieve the learning outcomes.

Learning Outcomes
By the end of the session, participants will be able to

- Identify their leadership style
- Describe the institutional culture at the RWBCCD
- Explain the process for deciding the existing culture
- List best practices associated with communicating decisions
- Identify effective communication strategies that enhance collegiality at the RWBCCD
- Develop and implement strategies to resolve difficult situations
- Identify the consequences of the decision in advance of making the hard decisions

Assessment
Participants will be given a post evaluation and extended learning activities to measure the achievement of learning outcomes.

Extended Learning Activities

- Participants will be asked to develop a monthly journal recording situations encountered in the workplace.
- Participants will create a response to the case study given to them highlighting the critical thinking steps they would take to making the decision and discussing the anticipated consequences

- Participants will be asked to develop a professional development portfolio
- Participants will complete required reading

Competencies Addressed

- Communication
- Internal and external relationships
- Sustaining people, processes, and information

After the training and as the transformation of the college unfolded, senior leaders at the institution continued to nurture relationships across silos to discover better solutions to new, emerging problems. Breaking down these organizational barriers was an essential step in broadening networks and empowering midlevel leadership at the college.

5

TEAM LEADERSHIP IN WORKFORCE DEVELOPMENT PRACTICE

James Jacobs

T he idea that an organizational leader can mandate change is a relic of the past; the power of the leader is to persuade others in the organization to initiate and accomplish change. Developing a team approach significantly aids institutional transformation because it encourages staff to work together to achieve college goals. In this chapter, I discuss my experiences as a new president at Macomb Community College in Michigan to point out how leaders can develop and use teams to bring about needed change.

Many community colleges suffer from deeply ingrained divisions that negatively affect their operations. Divisions often exist between occupational and academic areas and college credit and noncredit programs, and a disconnect between college workforce programs and employers is not uncommon. Sometimes it takes significant events to provide the motivation for institutional change. At Macomb Community College, the significant events included my selection as the new president and the effect of an economic recession on its service area.

A team approach to workforce development issues at Macomb Community College was part of an overall institutional change strategy implemented in 2008 with a change in leadership. Prior to 2008, teamwork was not the management operating style at the college. The previous president, who was an extremely talented administrator, operated the college through traditional lines of authority that held individuals accountable for their own areas and reported upward in a traditional hierarchal design to him. There was a President's Council, but the agenda for meetings was set by the president with little input from others. He had been president of the institution for almost 30 years, and most of the senior administration was hired during his tenure, so centralized authority defined operations.

I was an internal candidate and had been at the college for the entire tenure of my predecessor. Although I appreciated the leadership of the former president, I believed there was a need for a different approach to bring the wisdom and talents of many individuals to the issues facing the college. There was also a pragmatic reason for taking this approach. Because I assumed the presidency relatively late in my career, my window of time to make change was relatively short, and it was important not to expend a lot of time or significant effort building my own team through administrative reorganization. I decided to work with the present set of administrators and develop a more collective approach to the issues facing the college.

Even before I was selected as president, I signaled this approach with the following vision statement submitted during the presidential search process:

> I would draw on my skills to create an organizational team from the talented members of the college staff who share my vision and commitment to the college. My goal is to manage the institution through setting goals with measurable outcomes that hold team members accountable for their programs. I would encourage professional growth to catapult our senior college leadership into the forefront of national programs that teach and that contribute to the development of the college as a leader in institutional innovation. I believe in shared institutional leadership success and have demonstrated that I can put that belief into action. (Jacobs, 2007)

New teams were established on many levels of the college organization. The new style of work at the college was based on greater participation of faculty and staff to create cross-functional task forces. This meant a lean, flattened organization with collective decision-making across the organization. Moreover, for the implementation of any change to be successful, it had to start at the very top of the organization, so the President's Council had to become a functional team. To create this team approach, a process of developing positions on key issues through consensus among the vice presidents was initiated. They reported regularly to the college governing board on their activity and were encouraged to use a team approach in the development of their own unit structures and plans.

New teams were created across the college, and in many instances, faculty members were encouraged to participate on the teams. This was not an easy change to implement, given the fact that Macomb Community College operated in a unionized environment. Of the 2,000 employees (full- and part-time), all but 25 were in 1 of the 9 bargaining units. To make sure the union leadership was informed of the key issues affecting the institution, I established a new team with the union presidents and met monthly with them. These regular meetings were designed to inform all the bargaining units of issues faced by the college. Teams were established to handle cross-functional issues such as student recruitment and registration. Other teams worked on specific grants and research opportunities for the institution. The operating belief was that the issues facing the institution were often complex, and issues needed to be examined through a multitude of methods.

Implementing a team approach to organizational change was a process that combined an overall vision with the day-to-day realities of the institution and external events and the willingness of leadership to focus efforts at convincing others of the importance of the change. Although a collaborative approach to decision-making was new to Macomb Community College, many of the college workforce staff members were already familiar with the use of teams. The local economy in Macomb County is dominated by the auto industry, and teamwork was necessary to address the industry's challenges. As a result, many college staff in the workforce area recognized and accepted that the transition to a team approach was a legitimate activity used favorably in industry. These operational changes were not simply nice ideas sprung from the president's head but an approach effectively used by other organizations in the community. The initial decision to flatten the college's organizational structure, especially at the top, allowed for the redistribution of decision-making and power at other levels within the organization. The number of President's Council members was reduced from 10 to 6, and more power was distributed to middle-level administrators.

Although there are lessons from the experiences of team building at Macomb Community College, the approach is not necessarily a model to be implemented precisely at other community colleges. Each college leader needs to forge his or her own approaches to the implementation of teams in the local context faced by the leader. The decision to implement change and determine how to carry it out are always judgments best made on the ground by the leadership involved. Yet it is highly likely that the issues raised in this chapter will emerge as a college moves forward with its implementation of teams. At Macomb Community College, the use of teams became part of an organizational philosophy to drive change from the top down inside the college.

The Context: Changes in Local Workforce Needed

Context matters in understanding any institutional change process. At Macomb Community College, the Great Recession that started in 2007 moved the challenges facing workforce development activities to the forefront. Macomb County is one of the major centers of the American automobile industry in terms of research, design, and production. The rapid decline of the U.S. economy in 2008 significantly influenced auto sales. As a result, there were major industry lay-offs, and two of the large auto companies—General Motors and Chrysler—were forced to declare bankruptcy. By the summer of 2009, the official unemployment rate hovered close to 20% of the workforce. Thousands of laid-off autoworkers streamed to Macomb Community College looking for any programs that could prepare them to reenter the workforce.

The careful distinctions the college had made in the past between credit and noncredit courses were irrelevant to the majority of these workers—they wanted skills to obtain work immediately. The need to respond to this new influx of adult learners provided the college with the opportunity to bring credit and noncredit activities together under one vice president. The merger forced two units of the college into a collaborative arrangement to serve the needs of the new adult learners from the local community. As part of this transition, a new set of teams was developed that cut across the traditional college organization. Teams were established to not only help develop the new unit but also write grant proposals to provide resources for the college to serve credit and noncredit students. The general strategy adopted by the institution was to use grant funding to provide additional resources to advance institutional innovations, which, if successful, would be adopted and sustained in institutional operations.

Implementing this process required new relationships with the local workforce board, and the Michigan Department of Energy, Labor, and Economic Growth implemented a new program titled No Worker Left Behind (O'Gorman, 2009). This program was designed to grant jobless Michiganders two years of free community college education or training, provided they selected an occupation program in demand (Hilliard, 2011). Thus, from the outset, college teams were forced to seek a positive relationship with another public agency. Fortunately, the director of the local workforce board was a staunch supporter of college activities, and he regularly participated in many of the workforce team meetings. He colocated his counselors in the technical counseling area of the college and often met with the college president and other senior leaders to discuss potential projects initiated through resources he controlled from state and federal agencies. As director of the local workforce agency, this individual took the position that working with community colleges maximized his ability to serve the needs of his clients because community college classes and services were considerably less expensive than any of the private training competitors. Although he was not a college employee, his participation in college activities was important because he was able to use his funding sources to stimulate the college to undertake some very creative work.

Special Challenges With Team Building for Workforce Development

Several challenges surfaced during the implementation of the team approach to enhance occupational education. To begin with, implementing a team approach in the workforce development area is particularly complicated because the design, execution, and evaluation of these programs do not rest solely under the control of community colleges. Effective workforce development programs involve the intervention of two major constituencies outside the institution: the employers who will be hiring students from programs or sending their employees to the college for training and the communities that depend on the college to develop appropriate skills for community economic growth objectives. Effective workforce development practice mandates not only consulting with individuals from these sectors to formulate a strategy but also directly involving them in the institutional team-building process. This relationship was further complicated by the impact of public policies on the workforce development process. Federal and state legislation often prescribe many practices used in this area, something that does not occur for most other areas of postsecondary education.

Building teams across education and businesses sectors raised specific issues. First, employers and academics speak different languages, are distrustful of each other, and often do not share the same social vision. Employers are motivated by profits and will support workforce development efforts providing they yield returns for their businesses. Educators support workforce development efforts because they lead to jobs for their students. Finding common ground is sometimes difficult to achieve and maintain in an unstable economy.

Second, the long-term separation of workforce development administration and staff from the rest of the college sometimes made it difficult to achieve organizational change. The career and technical staff members tended to have backgrounds in industry and were less familiar with academic norms and culture. In addition, because of a variety of federal and state programs, a separate occupational leadership structure was created that segregated workforce development staff from the rest of the institution. Yet, for the success of students and for good practices in the workforce area, it was necessary for the institution and the community to bridge these differences and form collaborative efforts. Ultimately, the success of workforce activities depended on whether the college programs were accepted by the business community, so these divisions had to be overcome.

Third, some Macomb Community College–specific issues presented challenges. The college was already well known in the local community and among the staff for its successful workforce development activities. Because workforce development was not a broken system at the college, initiation of a team approach could have been met with the conventional response of if nothing is broken, why change it? Because the staff members in the workforce area had been recruited from local industry or had been at the college for a long time, they were familiar with the community and steeped in the culture of the dominant auto industry. Indeed, many of the internal practices of the college originated from this industry, which had a positive and negative impact. Although some of the staff members were set in the old ways of the auto industry, they were still aware of the changes that were taking place in the business world. Because part of that industry-based change was the increasing use of a team approach, lessons could be drawn from the private sector; at least in the workforce area, administrators and faculty recognized the advantages of a team approach.

Fourth, one of the key distinctions of the workforce development mission in the community college is its consistent need to respond to the economic events external to the institution. Even the best and well-developed program in the workforce area must be altered or terminated if there is no workplace demand for graduates. In some ways adoption of a team approach at Macomb Community College was accelerated by an external event—the Great Recession of 2007. This economic downturn significantly disrupted the community and propelled the workforce development mission into a central priority for the college. The community leadership turned to the college for help, and this provided a strong impetus to embrace change. To quote economist Paul Romer, "A crisis is a terrible thing to waste" (as cited in Rosenthal, 2009, para. 2). The severity of the downturn in the community provided a significant opportunity to introduce many organizational changes, one of which was building teams.

Changing Needs in Workforce Development

Teams in the workforce development area are particularly important because of the substantial evolutions of this mission in the modern community college. The workforce development mission is central to the DNA of the community college, and most of the colleges offer a range of programs designed to give students entry-level work in careers that pay a sustainable wage. Building on this foundation, most colleges offer learning experiences (often on the noncredit side of the institution) to incumbent workers or their employers to advance skills in particular key areas. Finally, leveraging federal and state policy, community colleges developed public training and education programs to prepare unemployed, underemployed, and dislocated workers for work. Indeed, in the absence of a national job training system, American community colleges have emerged as the network of institutions that can promote employment, economic growth, and national competitiveness.

The increasing speed of technological advances that have altered employment in many important sectors of the economy represents another dimension of the workforce development context. In the past 30 years, the application of computer-based technologies, and especially the movement toward implementation of artificial intelligence, has significantly altered employment in all major economic sectors. These advances influenced employment preparation for younger students entering the workforce as well as incumbent workers who may have been displaced. The increasing specialization of knowledge to become competent in any of these occupations means community colleges must devote significant resources to adequately prepare students. Changes in the workplace mean good community colleges will need to bet on their investments in teaching staff, equipment, and organizational behavior to meet the needs of students, employers, and their communities in providing programs. This may mean not only providing incentives for faculty to learn and adapt their programs to technical change but also eliminating many programs that may not be appropriate in the job market of the future. The comprehensive community college will be challenged to offer 50 to 75 different occupational programs that can adequately prepare students to obtain employment. A future community college occupational program may more realistically focus on 6 to 8 programs that are really in the interests of employers and the community (Rothwell, Gerity, & Carraway, 2017).

Given these dimensions of the community college workforce development context, flexibility, collaboration, and responsiveness are vital to the success of any program. However, administrators in workforce development have gone in the opposite direction, in part because of the distinct location and organization of training and education programs in community colleges. Vocational education programs, often staffed with individuals hired to administer federal funds for equipment, staff development, and leadership training, remain disconnected from other educational priorities in community colleges. Further, career programs and pathways at community colleges are often distinct from transfer programs; even their degrees denote the differences with an associate degree for academic programs and an applied associate degree and the one-year technical certificates for occupational programs. An example of this division occurs when mathematics, which is often very important to some technical areas, becomes shop math taught by instructors outside the mathematics faculty.

Finally, the proliferation of noncredit education programs has encouraged large numbers of adults to return to college, but these courses are often isolated from the credit part of the institution. They are rarely considered a part of the core of the institution and tend to be relegated to secondary positions in colleges. In turn, noncredit faculty and staff think of themselves as more effective, creative, and customer driven than the rest of the institution and promote their isolation as a tactic to free them from the bureaucracy of the rest of the college. Simply mandating the merger of the two units under one administrative system would have been ineffective. Team building was effective at Macomb Community College by bringing all aspects of the workforce mission together and bridging the differences between the credit and noncredit programs.

The Process of Team Building

The distinctive workforce development context dictated that team building had to be developed through a multistep process and required a series of teams, each motivated to undertake part of the process of adapting the occupational areas of the college to new workplace realities. At Macomb Community College, a team of administrators was assigned to determine how to increase enrollment of adults in credit career programs. Another team, working with Macomb Community College's early college high school and its recruitment staff, developed greater ties with high school students through an annual event that brought thousands of students and their parents to the campus to discuss careers with employers. The Macomb Community College early college program is a three-year career-focused program in which students participate in an integrated sequence of high school and college courses with no out-of-pocket costs for books, fees, or tuition (Macomb Community College, n.d.).

A particular specialized program at Macomb Community College provides another example of the effectiveness of teamwork. The college had an extremely specialized but highly significant technical program in auto body design. Macomb County is a major design center for manufacturers of original equipment (components that are sold with new vehicles) and many auto suppliers and local companies considered the auto body design program a major source of talent. In the 1990s an associate degree in auto body design from Macomb Community College was one of the entry requirements for employment at General Motors.

However, with employment in the auto industry down 50% in 2008, many of the former design students were out of work. With financial support from the workforce board, the college developed a program for former auto body design students that would give them additional design skills to make them employable in the design of major construction projects such as nuclear power plants or subway systems in the United States and overseas. With these new skills, the designers were able to find work designing nuclear power plants in New Mexico or working on the redesign of London's subway system. Developing and coordinating this effort required a team composed of college employees, the workforce board employees, an employment service firm to help students locate jobs outside the Detroit metropolitan area, and alumni from the program. It was a major innovation and served to return a considerable number of auto body designers to the workforce.

In addition, as part of this project, the team also developed a program that allowed currently unemployed auto body designers access to Macomb Community College's computer-aided design equipment and a refresher course run by people employed in the industry so that they could remain up to date in skills. When auto sales picked up, they were recalled to work. These efforts would not have been possible had not the workforce board director been willing to collaborate with the college staff to design and fund the program.

In general, the teams at Macomb Community College were responsible for the completion of specific projects and then were disbanded when tasks were completed. Although these teams functioned in many divergent areas of college, they were guided by a similar institutional vision. This was to integrate all workforce development programs whether they were credit or noncredit and to embrace a general institutional culture of student success. Student success was based on program completion as well as employment and earnings. Moreover, there was a general effort to link all career preparation to further postsecondary education and the completion of a four-year degree. Senior leadership was responsible for ensuring that this vision was maintained throughout the transformation process.

The first step in the process of integrating all workforce development programs was to end the silos of isolation for career and technical education and noncredit education from the rest of the institution. This goal needed to be the responsibility of the president and senior leaders of the institution because the changes required important organizational cultural shifts. In the workforce area, the process of merging the credit and noncredit workforce programs under one administrative structure was critical. The strategic vision guiding the change was summed up in a simple phrase: "All learning is learning" (Rothwell et al., 2017, p. 54). Any course offerings, whether credit or noncredit, had to have a similar coherence aligned with the brand, or learning character, of Macomb Community College.

Many key details needed to be worked through by the teams: students' ability to transfer between noncredit and credit courses; elimination of competitive courses between credit and noncredit; use of counseling, scholarships, and wraparound services for the noncredit program; and the creation of scholarships and institutional aid for noncredit students. Many of these efforts were piloted with funding provided by receiving a federal Trade Adjustment Assistance Community College and Career Training (TAACCCT; U.S. Department of Labor, n.d.) grant, which permitted the college to create a program to advise noncredit workforce students. The project evaluation described the process in the following statement:

> Under the team-based approach to student support envisioned by the Michigan Consortium for Advanced Manufacturing (M-CAM) colleges, TAACCCT grant-funded college staff members collaborated with permanent college personnel (such as admissions counselors and college career center staff members) and entities external to each college (including employers, economic development agencies, Michigan Works service center staff members, and faith- and community-based organizations) to provide the full spectrum of counseling and support students needed to successfully complete their training and obtain employment. (Social Policy Research Associates, 2017)

This approach not only successfully created a bridge between the two areas but also aided in the development of staff understandings of each other's roles and provided the basis of team building between the units. Merging credit and noncredit units will not be successful if simply done by administrative fiat; it takes significant leadership to explain the reasons for the change and support to make sure that all the details are carried out. For years, the credit and noncredit areas at Macomb Community College maintained their own separate company contact lists, which they jealously guarded. To pool these lists and make them accessible to all was a thorny, complicated problem that took a great deal of effort and has been only partially resolved. The credit and noncredit units had individuals who were previously employed at many of the companies that were clients of the college, and they had personal ties that made it difficult for them to give them up. Some of this had to be resolved on a case-by-case basis. It is hoped that through continued discussion at Macomb Community College, this conflict will disappear as the combined unit continues and individuals are rewarded by how well the entire unit advances as opposed to just the credit or noncredit part of the institution. This minor dispute exposes the importance of leadership's staying the course; once an institutional change is made, it takes some time before actual behaviors of the staff are altered.

The second step of consolidating all workforce development programs was uniting the workforce mission with liberal arts with the goal of ending the separation between the workforce and transfer missions of the institution. Although Macomb Community College's learning unit was organized into separate areas, a detailed examination of student course-taking indicated that many took classes in both areas. Almost as many students in the career and technical majors said their a goal was a four-year degree as did those who concentrated on the liberal arts. Active participation of workforce staff in national initiatives to improve student success rates such as Achieving the Dream (www.achievingthedream.org) and Guided Pathways (American Association of Community Colleges, 2019) brought faculty and administrators from academic and workforce units together. Technical faculty needed to appreciate the students' desire for degrees beyond their own courses and programs.

An important new understanding was that many workforce development programs were not terminal but were another path to achieving a 4-year degree. Many of the workforce programs had articulation relationships with 4-year partner universities to assist students in transferring between institutions. These relationships were further strengthened by the construction of an Advanced Technology Center by Wayne State University, one of the most important transfer institutions for Macomb Community College students. Also, nearly 80% of nursing students wanted to continue their education to obtain a bachelor of science in nursing, and Macomb Community College established an innovative program with Michigan State University for students to achieve the 4-year degree in an accelerated fashion.

In addition, at one of the Macomb Community College campuses the college hosted part of Michigan State's Osteopathic Medical School, and articulation ties developed in health care with many local colleges. These activities made it clear that workforce development was not simply about acquiring skills for people to obtain entry-level work but a means by which students obtain four-year degrees and high-paying jobs that require advanced skills. All these efforts were highlighted during the Macomb Community College faculty development days, and the message was consistent and clear: Advanced technologies in the fields of manufacturing were now requiring four-year degrees for employment.

The consolidation of workforce teams at Macomb Community College was facilitated by several key grants in the career and technical area. A grant from the National Science Foundation for a Center for Advanced Automotive Technology (n.d.) to the college focused on the emergence of autonomous vehicles technology and other areas that all required advanced degrees. This meant that faculty and staff from some of the engineering programs at Wayne State University were participating in grants and programs developed by the college. Their participation assumed that Macomb workforce students would be entering these four-year schools. These actions lessened the bifurcation between continuing with college or obtaining employment. Many students choose to do both, especially as many of the occupation programs required four-year degrees in their fields of study. The recognition of these student goals by faculty and administrators allowed a more nuanced view of student success, which included the career and technical disciplines.

The goal of uniting the transfer and workforce development missions of the institution was also reinforced through changes in the onboarding of all new faculty through a faculty academy. All incoming new faculty were required to participate in this two-year process of initiation and exposure to the institution. In this academy, liberal arts and technical faculty were mixed together. In the second year of the academy, each participant was responsible for presenting a specific research project to the group in a session attended by the senior leadership of the institution. The faculty academy aided the new faculty to understand and appreciate the challenges for liberal arts and technical faculty and served to increase ties between the two groups.

In addition, when a fund for faculty innovation projects that could be used by all full-time faculty was established, many of the projects were initiated by occupational faculty or teams of occupational and liberal arts faculty. For example, a physics instructor teamed up with the childcare program to develop a physics playground for young children. These projects were highlighted during every institutional faculty developmental day so that all faculty saw the integration of learning. Reports on all noncredit activities were a regular part of the agenda for faculty development, which provided another context for breaking down the artificial barriers between the groups. Although not part of any team-building activity, these reports were important to eliminating the split between liberal arts and technical capacities.

The third step of integrating programs and institutional transformation was team-building efforts. These were also supported through the use of new forms of research and data in the career and technical field. Workforce programs have always focused on general data on employment, occupational trends, and wages. Until recently, most of this information was based on national data and wasn't very useful for determining local trends. However, the emergence of the process of *data scraping* from the Internet permitted community colleges to focus on the labor markers in their specific service areas, which can serve to highlight the labor market issues affecting local students. This approach was used in Macomb Community College's teams, and staff found that more than half the new jobs posted in Macomb County required a four-year degree (Macomb Community College, 2012). This finding confirmed the need to link occupational classes with transfer to a four-year program.

Recognition that postsecondary education is an important part of the preparation for the future of most occupations became obvious in the creation of the vision to integrate technical preparation and liberal arts. Students in the technical areas were as interested in obtaining a four-year degree as students in the liberal arts areas. Employers in the auto industry, which in the past hired workers right out of high school, were now calling for college degrees for many of the entry-level positions, such as computer-aided design operators. These external signals made it easy to realize the internal goals of greater collaboration between the workforce and the liberal arts faculty.

Using Teams to Develop the Workforce Mission

The fourth step in the process of institutional transformation was delineating what encompassed workforce development at the college. To have successful programs, it was necessary to have a good working knowledge of the major industries in the community and the impact of technological change among the common skilled groups found in these sectors. This meant establishing continued intelligence gathering and a process for sharing. Because this role was not formally given institutional support, it had to be created using the resources the college obtained through successful competition for grants. For example, the National Science Foundation's (2019) Advanced Technological Education program awarded Macomb Community College a grant to fund a National Center for Advanced Automotive Technology. The program called for the college to develop a curriculum and establish itself as a technical center for new automotive technologies and, as a result, indirectly provided funding for the college to continue efforts to monitor the automotive industry. Another part of the intelligence-gathering process was the initiation by the college of major work in the entrepreneurial arena.

The college established a Center for Innovation and Entrepreneurship, which was open to students and the local community for business development activities. The college participated in the Goldman Sachs 10,000 Small Business grants to learn more about new industry start-ups in many sectors. This knowledge was important in establishing an innovation fund supported by JPMorgan Chase, which targeted support for start-up information technology and manufacturing companies that could apply to the fund for monetary support if they provided employment opportunities for students (Macomb Community College, 2015).

In each of these activities, administrators in the career and technical disciplines were brought together with other administrators to discuss how well the college as a whole was responding to the changing employment needs of the community. In addition, the focus on entrepreneurial work allowed the college to work closely with private innovators who could educate college personnel in the emerging technology needs of businesses and begin to identify programs of support that could be critical to their future growth. One area that emerged from these efforts was the development of a cybersecurity program for the auto and defense manufacturing industry. The college worked in partnership with Wayne State University to establish the program, which was well received in the community.

The need for curriculum reform and program modification emerged from the intelligence-gathering process. Initiated by the college provost's office, the process consisted of a sustained review of all credit programs, resulting in the elimination of some areas and the development of others. The process was led by a team of administrators and faculty who were given access to research data through the institutional research office. The interpretation of the data was the most important part of the process because this encouraged unique perspectives on the same facts. Two specific outcomes from this initiative were extremely useful. The focus on career academies targeted high school students entering the college through either the early college programs or a new statewide apprenticeship program. The creation of the career academies required the college to consolidate some of its specific career and technical programs into broader, more flexible areas that favored the development of multiskilled technicians.

The second outcome was an improvement of the process in which students completed programs that allowed them to transfer to four-year institutions. Macomb Community College participated in a grant-funded collaborative that developed accelerated learning principles to give adults, based on their work experience, a faster process to transfer into four-year degree programs in electrical engineering. In this process, the business advisory boards, formally mandated by most of the programs that receive federal funding support from the Carl D. Perkins Career and Technical Education Act (2006), were supplemented by adding representatives from business associations, the local workforce board, and four-year university faculty who were responsible for the program at their university. The issues raised included not only what industry needed in a technology but also the foundation skills necessary for students to continue a career path in that sector. The Perkins Career and Technical Education Act was first authorized by the federal government in 1984 and reauthorized in 1998, 2006, and 2018. Named for Carl D. Perkins, a long-term congressional representative from Kentucky, the act aims to increase the quality of technical education in the United States by providing grant funding to schools and community colleges.

An important aspect of workforce team implementation was initiation of a team approach for the development of a workforce curriculum with other colleges. In 2013 Macomb Community College was successful in obtaining a TAACCCT grant (U.S. Department of Labor, n.d.) that organized an eight-member community college consortium in the state of Michigan to develop a new curriculum in advanced manufacturing. This was done through teams of instructors from different colleges working together on specific sections of the curriculum (mechatronics, welding, machining). This curriculum development was unique in that each college implemented the curriculum changes even if faculty from another college developed them. In addition, each college gave college credit for the curriculum even if it was earned in another institution. This four-year project resulted in new forms of collaboration in which Macomb Community College staff accepted the work of curriculum teams to transform their programs. Institutional change was being driven through collaboration with other institutions (Social Policy Research Associates, 2017).

The last aspect of institutional transformation at Macomb Community College, now in the process of development, was establishing ties with very specific industry niches, which were determined through the strategic planning process of the institution. Based on a review of the curriculum, the student enrollment in specific career and technical programs, and the context of the broad occupational trends in the region, the college began to make some important priority decisions to focus efforts in three areas: advanced manufacturing, health careers, and information technology. This meant considering employers who regularly hire the students as customers as well as acknowledging them as employers whose knowledge of unfolding trends brings them into close regular contact with the college. Many of these employers were alumni of the college, and their insights were particularly important because they knew the trends in business and industry.

Overcoming Internal Barriers

Although the team-building approach had the support of most staff and the board of trustees, there was some staff resistance to overcome. For example, during the attempts to consolidate the credit and noncredit divisions, there were issues about the development of a single database of companies and contacts; many of the noncredit administrators were reluctant to share these data with their colleagues for fear of losing credit for the relationships they had built. The contacts were often personal, established while the staff member was working at the company or based on a relationship with a program alumnus or former colleague, so these issues had to be worked through. In the end, some data were shared, but it was also recognized that some ties would be kept by individuals who had specific relationships with some companies.

As a faculty-unionized institution, Macomb Community College had to address potential barriers in contract language that primarily defines individual titles and responsibilities in ways that do not easily foster the collaboration necessary for a team approach. For example, the teacher union contracts use area seniority to determine course selection processes. This made scheduling multiskilled programs difficult when faculty members from different areas were brought together. Scheduling assignments along the time lines demanded by the contract was often difficult to implement when companies wanted the training to start immediately. Fortunately, the union leadership was regularly briefed on general college activities, including the vision behind any changes in the organization, and this regular interaction aided the union's understanding and eventual support for much of the process. Without the tacit support of the union leadership, implementation of many aspects of teamwork would have been extremely difficult.

From the very outset, the union leadership was informed of the strategies to reorganize the units and form teams, and if no one suffered job loss or pay decreases, the union leadership was generally supportive. It also helped that increasing numbers of students were registering for classes as the result of the economic downturn, so faculty benefited from the greater compensation the extra classes brought. There were also difficulties with the administrators over titles and authority, but through dialogue and being very clear about the reasons for the development of teams, the administrative union leadership was supportive. A final and important barrier could have been any opposition from the board. However, Macomb Community College's board of trustees was stable over the years, and trustees rarely involved themselves in micromanagement. To their credit, trustees remained supportive of the general reform of the workforce development area initiated by the administration.

To address barriers to implementation at Macomb Community College, I approved a set of guidelines that proved to be much easier to articulate than to practice. The first guideline was being transparent about making changes. Opposition to change typically emerges when individuals feel there are hidden agendas in the process. Leaders must state clearly why the change is needed and remain consistent in all communications. The second critical guideline was that any change had to be introduced with a rationale that would be accepted by the staff. At Macomb Community College, the Great Recession provided a very good external reason to justify some of these changes. Most staff had accepted and internalized the mission of the institution to help the residents get jobs and increase opportunity in the community. If change was based around these principles, as opposed to adopting something because, for example, other colleges were doing it, there would be greater acceptance. The third guideline was that individuals at the institution had to believe that these changes would be long term and permanent.

Too often educational changes are made and then altered or even reversed with little or no explanation or data given to support the decision.

This flavor-of-the-semester culture results in resistance to change because staff members do not think their efforts are being taken seriously. They believe they can wait out the change. Through the actions of the leadership at Macomb Community College, it was clear that any changes in the workforce area were permanent and long term. When everyone recognizes that leadership is serious about change, a serious response from stakeholders results. Reasons for any actions need to be stated and understood by those affected. At Macomb Community College, even if staff did not support some of the activities, the senior leadership team demonstrated a proactive position that anticipated some opposition to the planned changes. But the approach was to work on these issues to find answers and to continue moving ahead in a positive manner. Overcoming barriers should not be a process to assign blame but an understanding that the institutional structure and culture need to change together. The fact that the new Macomb Community College president was an internal selection who was well known to the staff with a strong faculty and administrative union background helped enormously. No one could question his knowledge of the institution or argue that the changes were simply self-serving. So, although there was some opposition, in general it was muted, and most staff did not oppose the changes.

What proved perhaps most important in winning support is that the team strategy did produce results. One of the distinct advantages to any change in the workforce development area of the college is a relatively quick external validation for the success of any initiative: Did the changes bring about more employment and wage growth for the students? During the implementation of the teams, the college undertook many important new initiatives in workforce development. Most significant was the development of a program organized by Michigan authorities called No Worker Left Behind (O'Gorman, 2009). Because Macomb Community College had developed a very positive relationship with its local workforce investment board, it was possible to initiate some very successful innovations to this program. Macomb Community College became one of the leading colleges in implementing the No Worker Left Behind program.

As a result of this effort, the college received recognition from the state, and in July 2009 President Barack Obama came to the college to announce his initial community college program, the American Graduation Initiative (Shear & de Vise, 2009). This validation from the president's visit was unprecedented for the Macomb Community College staff. Because of the strategic significance of Macomb County in presidential elections, as early as 1980 the college regularly hosted presidential campaign candidate visits. Having a sitting U.S. president come to the college because of its workforce activities served to validate the general approach of the college inside the workforce area as well as the entire institution and the broader community (Bailey, 2009).

Conclusion

The introduction of teams was only part of a lengthy process of needed institutional change in the workforce area. In general, community college occupational programs need major revisions as companies continue to implement innovative technologies and reorganize work. This is especially true in manufacturing but is also applicable to other sectors, such as business and health care. As a result, the programs that have attracted students and have been supported by the community because they led to employment need to be significantly renovated or combined in innovative ways with career pathways through four-year institutions. Data from students entering from high school and adults returning to college indicate that they prefer a four-year degree (Wyner, Deane, Jenkins, & Fink, 2016). This means some major changes will be necessary in the community college workforce programs.

Eliminating programs is a lengthy, slow process in which administrators must often wait for faculty retirements to eliminate and redesign many of the specific areas. The effort to increase community college participation with four-year colleges and universities proceeds unevenly as the faculty and department administrators in these institutions react very differently to the articulation agreements with community college programs of study. This is especially true in the workforce area where for years the programs and the staff were often funded and developed through organizational divisions that are very separate from the rest of the institution.

However, as change occurs in the private sector, it produces opportunities for community college workforce efforts. As labor markets tighten, interest increases from many employers in work-based learning activities and in ties to high school programs. However, wages in many of these areas have risen slowly, and employers are finding it difficult to attract younger people to these jobs. They are also reluctant to use their own resources for training activities because they fear the larger and better-paying companies farther up the supply chain will snatch this talent from them. Indeed, the colleges should initiate a more honest discussion of wages and talent for some of these firms. They cannot remain on the low road of human resources and expect to attract talent to their companies. The college can play an important advisory role for employers in some of these efforts, and a team approach to compensation discussions with local employers seems an appropriate response.

Furthermore, the continual evaluation of skills needed in occupational programs will challenge the comprehensive community college approach in the workforce area. To have excellent programs means significant investments in faculty and equipment and regular interactions with the industry. No community college has the resources and the talent to do this with more than a few major areas. The future of successful workforce development programs will depend on choices college administrators make about which programs to invest in and what areas might be discontinued. Implementing this approach will also make the colleges more likely to network with each other.

In that regard, Macomb Community College administrators have learned a great deal about workforce development through the implementation of a team approach to its workforce activities. In the large National Center for Advanced Automotive Technology (n.d.) grant, faculty and administrators from the different colleges established not only a network that allowed sharing the curriculum but also a statewide articulation agreement that allowed any student from one community college to receive full credit from any of the participating community colleges for the courses they took at another institution (Social Policy Research Associates, 2017). This very limited process of institutional collaboration across community college lines may serve as one important remedy to the growing impediment faced by all colleges: In meeting the needs of business, colleges cannot do everything. There is a need for more specialization and deep involvement in specific areas that are vital to local employers and the community. Achieving this level of specialization means giving up the ability to adequately educate students in some of the other areas. Collaboration of institutions around a specifically designed network that allows students ease of transfer may be the next area of career and technical reform. But without the development of teams, it will not be possible.

Although the use of teams in workforce development may vary at different colleges, it's evident that internal and external collaborations are also at the core of any workforce development initiative. Community college leaders must understand that a contemporary strategy for workforce development means establishing and sustaining networks as an essential feature of an integrated workforce development approach for community colleges.

References

American Association of Community Colleges. (2019). *AACC Pathways 2.0*. Retrieved from https://www.aacc.nche.edu/programs/aacc-pathways-project/aacc-pathways-2-0/

Bailey, T. (2009, November). Can community colleges rise to the occasion? *American Prospect*, pp. A18–A20. Retrieved from https://prospect.org/article/can-community-colleges-rise-occasion

Carl D. Perkins Career and Technical Education Act. (2006). Pub. L. 109-270.

Center for Advanced Automotive Technology. (n.d.). *ATE centers*. Retrieved from https://atecenters.org/et/caat/

Hilliard, T. (2011). *Leaving no worker left behind.* Boston, MA: Jobs for the Future.

Jacobs, J. (2007). *Candidate statement to the Board of Trustees of Macomb Community College.* Warren, MI: Macomb Community College.

Macomb Community College. (n.d.). *Early admission for high school students.* Retrieved from https://www.macomb.edu/future-students/hs-counselors/early-admission.html

Macomb Community College. (2012). *The new Macomb County.* Warren, MI: Macomb Community College.

Macomb Community College. (2015). *Report to the community.* Warren, MI: Macomb Community College.

National Science Foundation. (2019). *Advanced technological education.* Retrieved from https://www.nsf.gov/pubs/2018/nsf18571/nsf18571.htm

O'Gorman, K. (2009). Michigan unemployed receive training from 'No Worker Left Behind' program. Retrieved from https://www.aarp.org/work/job-hunting/info-06-2009/michigan_unemployed.html

Rosenthal, J. (2009). A terrible thing to waste. *New York Times Magazine.* Retrieved from https://www.nytimes.com/2009/08/02/magazine/02FOB-onlanguage-t.html

Rothwell, W. J., Gerity, P. E., & Carraway, V. L. (2017). *Community college leaders on workforce development: Opinions, observations and future directions.* Lanham, MD: Rowman & Littlefield.

Shear, M., & de Vise, D. (2009). Obama announces $12 billion community college initiative. *Washington Post.* Retrieved from http://www.washingtonpost.com/wp-dyn/content/article/2009/07/14/AR2009071400819.html

Social Policy Research Associates. (2017). *Evaluation of the Michigan Coalition for Advanced Manufacturing (M-CAM): Final report.* Oakland, CA: Author.

U.S. Department of Labor. (n.d.). *Trade Adjustment Assistance Community College Career Training Grant: Program summary.* Retrieved from https://doleta.gov/taaccct/

Wyner, J., Deane K., Jenkins, D., & Fink, J. (2016). *The transfer playbook: Essential practices for two- and four-year colleges.* Washington DC: The Aspen Institute.

6

TEAM BUILDING THROUGH COLLABORATIVE LEADERSHIP AND STRATEGIC PLANNING

Irving Pressley McPhail

Team leadership cannot be addressed out of context. The role of team leadership in community colleges is to facilitate a group of people working together to accomplish the goals of the institution. In practice, team building requires a leader who empowers others to play substantive roles in planning programs, making decisions about issues of importance to the institution, and creating a vision for the institution's future. This chapter describes the important role of team leadership in a transformational change process using the example of the Community College of Baltimore County (CCBC) from 1998 to 2005. The discussion focuses on team engagement of trustees, administrators, faculty, staff, and students.

Context

When the CCBC began its journey in 1998 toward becoming a consolidated learning-centered institution, the board of trustees collaborated with the new chancellor to create an environment to empower others to move efficiently through the processes of launching new directions and organizational structures for the college. The change process started with the development of a new strategic plan called LearningFIRST, which was designed to create a learning community dedicated to student success. This plan also addressed lingering challenges faced by this recently consolidated single college, multi-campus institution (McPhail, 1999). From the start of the strategic planning process, steps were taken to engage all key stakeholders and build teams to support and sustain the planning effort.

Three Into One: The First Attempt

McPhail and Heacock (1999) and McPhail, Heacock, and Linck (2000) described the cultural and political context that led to the creation of a new single-college, multicampus institution from what were three independent community colleges serving Baltimore County. In 1994 the board of trustees hired a consultant to review the three colleges and recommend changes. The consultant's recommendations led to the introduction of legislation in 1995 to combine the three formerly independent colleges into a multicollege system. A federated system of colleges, the CCCBC, was formed and placed under the direction of a chancellor and supported by a small-system office. Each college retained its name and individual identity but was under the operational control of a central office charged with finding ways for the three institutions to operate more efficiently. Central administrative services, including finance, information technology, and human resources, were the first areas to be consolidated. Instruction and student services were reorganized the following year. Savings were to be achieved by combining and downsizing the support functions of the three colleges. Matrix management, a model giving each college president and many college employees systemwide responsibilities, was implemented in an effort to achieve greater efficiencies.

However, the stresses created by the sheer magnitude of the consolidation, combined with the differing expectations of internal and external constituencies, increased disenchantment and conflict. Arguments over savings to be achieved, distribution of funds, and perceptions of implemented efficiencies led to difficulties in the relationships among the board of trustees, the Baltimore County government, and the system's chancellor. Employees of the colleges, especially the faculty, expressed discontent with the merger. Faculty believed the reorganization lacked direction and was failing to achieve the proposed efficiencies while directly affecting the quality and autonomy of existing programs. These conditions and the environment of distrust that had developed over time eventually led to open conflict (Fisher, 1997).

CCBC: A New Beginning

The culmination of this ongoing conflict was an unprecedented $2.3 million reduction in Baltimore County appropriations for the three colleges in fiscal year 1997. Six months later, the board of trustees terminated the chancellor's employment in a disagreement over institutional policy and appointed an interim chancellor. As a result of the ensuing political chaos, county government officials, state legislators, and some board members sponsored legislation to reorganize the three campuses into a single-college, multicampus institution to be known as the CCBC. Further, the legislation allowed the governor to appoint a chairman for the board of trustees for a three-year term and additional board members. The three previously independent, autonomous colleges became campuses of a larger institution that was expected to operate as a single institution. The board of trustees, under the direction of its new chairman, Francis X. Kelly, a powerful former state legislator, successful entrepreneur, and accomplished chairman of other higher education boards in the state, moved quickly to establish the new college. In February 1998 the board of trustees appointed me, Irving Pressley McPhail, as the founding chancellor of the new CCBC.

On Vision and Leadership: The Board and Chancellor as a Team

I arrived at CCBC with a clear mandate from the board of trustees to complete the consolidation of three campuses into a single college. This required strong collaboration between the board and the chancellor. During this stage, it was important for this board and chief executive officer (CEO) team to build on the work already undertaken in finance, information technology, human resources, instruction, and student services. However, the challenge of reimagining the teaching and learning paradigm at the new institution became the central driving force in my leadership journey (McPhail, 2004). In collaboration with the board, I set out to reinvigorate a dormant strategic planning process from the previous administration by focusing on team building, strategic planning, and creating a more learning-centered college culture.

George Keller (1983), my guru in the theory and practice of academic strategy, cautioned academic leaders about the need to consider critical prestrategic planning requirements in the following:

> But before an institution begins to shape an academic strategy for itself, it should be sure that it is well managed. It needs to tighten up before it tries to reach out and move ahead. It needs to be certain that it has adequate information on which to base decisions. It needs to be sure that there is quality in the teaching, research, and service it is currently providing. And an institution needs to have the best people it can possibly get to carry out its intentions. No baseball team, army, business firm, or university can succeed, no matter how devoted to strategy, without adequate data;

without high quality equipment, programs, and performance; and without talented, dedicated personnel. (p. 122)

Accordingly, I moved aggressively in my first six months in office to review previous planning documents and task force materials; interview key stakeholders among the faculty, staff, and student leadership throughout the institution; update core trends through ongoing environmental scanning; empower existing leaders in the college; and recruit new leadership talent where needed.

The new vision for the college was carefully crafted to include several of the strategic directions recommended in the previous strategic planning activity but reconceptualized in the theory and practice of the learning paradigm and the learning college (Barr & Tagg, 1995; Boggs, 1995; O'Banion, 1997). It was also necessary for me to build consensus for the change agenda by actively engaging key internal and external stakeholders. The environment for change, given the angst over the government-imposed consolidation of the three community colleges and the resulting chaos, was simply not advantageous. At the same time, the board of trustees expected me to advance a vision that the college community would view as worthwhile.

Neumann (1991) and Rowley, Lujan, and Dolence (1997) are among many planning theorists who have emphasized the importance of teams in building and executing the strategic plan. The team must include top administrative leadership and all key stakeholders who are responsible for implementing the plan. Under ideal circumstances, team members become ambassadors for the plan and leaders in driving the college-wide discussions on transformation. This role is especially critical in a tense organizational culture with a history of conflict and pockets of "fighters" and "watchers" who are opposed to any change effort (Carter & Alfred, 2000, pp. 21–23). It is also a reality that community colleges are by definition centers of learning. Faculty ire is often raised by any suggestion that what they are doing in the classroom is not already learning centered.

The Teams and Time Involved

The chancellor's cabinet was designated as the core of the college-wide strategic planning team. Additional members of the team included faculty, staff, and student representatives from the three campuses. The formal planning process was also infused with learning from active professional development activities that were launched on all three campuses and focused on exploring the possibilities of the learning paradigm and the learning college idea. This dynamic model for team learning and execution drove the strategic planning and strategic thinking processes early in the organizational transformation process.

I developed the model for strategic planning, strategic decision-making, strategic thinking, and strategic budgeting and resource allocation that emerged from the work of the strategic planning teams (McPhail, 2012). The planning team created the LearningFIRST strategic plan, which contained a core strategic direction, student learning, and six supporting directions: learning support, learning college, infusing technology, management excellence, embracing diversity, and building community. Subcommittees were established for each core and supporting strategic direction, and time lines were established for completing the work of the subcommittees.

The student learning strategic direction established learning as CCBC's core value and direction. All actions were evaluated and judged based on this proposition. CCBC's goal was to provide a quality, learning-centered education that maximized learning and made students partners in their education. Students were expected to frame and achieve their own goals and develop skills for the twenty-first century.

Learning support provided a comprehensive, responsive system that increased student access to learning opportunities and recognized the student as central to the learning process. The goals for this strategic direction were to increase student retention and success, create seamless instructional and student support services, improve student skills assessment and placement, and increase community access to programs and services.

The learning college direction supported CCBC's transformation into a learning college, promoting innovation, the free exchange of ideas, continuous improvement through organizational learning, and assessment through a comprehensive institutional effectiveness and evaluation system.

Infusing technology advanced the use of technology to enhance student learning and to improve the effectiveness and efficiency of college operations. The college was committed to serving Baltimore County by maintaining its position as the county's primary provider of technology workforce training.

Management excellence demonstrated CCBC's commitment to the efficient and effective use of resources by linking planning and budgeting. This strategy promoted low-cost access to the college by ensuring efficient operations and focusing on generating additional resources.

Embracing diversity established a bold and measurable vision to recruit and retain a diverse faculty, staff, and student community. CCBC accomplished this strategic direction through a myriad of activities, including advancing a learning environment that embraced and valued diversity, infusing diversity into the curriculum, and recognizing and incorporating diverse learning styles.

Finally, building community positioned CCBC as an active and engaged member of the Baltimore County metropolitan area. CCBC took a lead role in workforce training throughout the county and formed partnerships to support economic and community development.

The Integrated Planning Model

A three-tiered planning model ensured that LearningFIRST was implemented. LearningFIRST provided a five-year planning and execution horizon, whereas the operational plans and quarterly review components focused on achieving measurable annual results. This approach required individuals throughout the institution to measure and quantify long-range plans in such areas as strategic enrollment management, technology, and continuing education. The emphasis on yearly action plans, accountability, open communication, and broad-based participation signaled to key internal and external audiences that LearningFIRST was not the education fad du jour or a public relations gimmick, but the heart and soul of CCBC.

Council on Innovation and Student Development: The Ultimate Guiding Coalition

In his widely cited book, *Leading Change*, Kotter (1996) called for a new decision-making process that must be guided by a powerful coalition that can act as a team. He proposed 4 key characteristics as essential to effective guiding coalitions: position power, expertise, credibility, and leadership. At CCBC, the Council on Innovation and Student Learning (CISL) was created to serve as the guiding team charged with driving the journey from the instruction paradigm to the learning paradigm (Barr & Tagg, 1995; Boggs, 1995; O'Banion, 1997). The CISL was composed of 27 members broadly representative of faculty members, classified staff members, students, administrators, and trustees. The CISL had 4 subcommittees: learning outcomes assessment, campus outreach and staff development, learning communities, and learning paradigm topics. The tasks for the CISL team were straightforward:

- serve as a college-wide think tank;
- serve as change agents;
- help frame policies, procedures, and infrastructure needed to become a learning college;
- educate the institution's and campus communities;

- develop a CCBC-specific operational definition of *learning*;
- stimulate development of a college-wide process for experimentation and innovation; and
- document the change process and establish campus-based CISLs at each campus.

Among the accomplishments of the CISL in its first year of operation (1998–1999) were three college-wide teleconferences; an address to the CCBC community by Terry O'Banion, senior league fellow and president emeritus of the League for Innovation in the Community College; a series of learning community seminars; creation of a newsletter, *The CISL Gazette*; and development of a website. In addition, the CISL established pilot LearningFIRST projects on all three campuses, sponsored regularly scheduled staff development opportunities, promoted visits with other learning-centered institutions, and most importantly involved students in the change process. Finally, the CISL devoted considerable energy to faculty development, offering a full day of faculty development activities for the college community. Campus CISL Days, sponsored by the individual campuses, were also held.

The following outcomes deserve further mention because they illustrate in a robust way the power of team building in advancing the learning college idea at the evolving community college: learning outcomes assessment, teachers learning computer skills, and the Closing the Gap Campaign.

Learning Outcomes Assessment

O'Banion (1997) asserted that the learning college succeeds only when improved and expanded learning can be documented for its learners, which leads to the following critical questions:

1. What does this learner know?
2. What can this learner do?

With this principle as its major focus, the faculty-led Learning Outcomes Assessment Committee developed the guide for learning outcomes assessment and classroom learning assessment (CCBC, 1999). The faculty launched a total of 58 assessment projects between 1999 and 2002. Faculty members began to embrace outcomes assessment as a natural, ongoing part of instruction that served multiple purposes. The projects were conducted in a risk-free environment, allowing the focus to remain on curricular changes and teaching and learning improvements versus the results of initial assessments.

Teachers Learning Computer Skills

An essential part of the infusing technology strategic direction in LearningFIRST was professional development for faculty in the application of technology to instruction. The CISL created a program, Teachers Learning Computers in the Learning College, that used faculty members proficient in various software packages and applications to train other faculty members. Each semester, classes and workshops ranging from beginning to advanced applications were held at the college for interested faculty members. In less than two years, more than half of the CCBC faculty had completed classes and applied the skills learned to improve classroom instruction. Building on the success of this program, the CISL organized and executed two virtual academies to train faculty in the development of online classes.

Closing the Gap Campaign

As the culture of evidence continued to evolve at the CCBC, the learning outcomes of students in developmental education were reviewed in 2001 (McKusick & McPhail, 2003) and revealed unacceptable gaps in performance between African American and White students in course pass rates, retention rates, graduation rates, and transfer rates. This evidence stood in sharp contrast to the assertion of the LearningFIRST philosophy at the CCBC that until all learners were successful, the institution had not yet made good on its promise of access and opportunity.

By 2001 the CCBC was actively engaged in the Vanguard Learning Colleges Project (McClenney, 2001), and additional interdisciplinary teams had been formed around the strategic directions of the project. The college had begun to address performance gaps in two intersecting populations of at-promise students: African American students and developmental students. Consistent with the value proposition of the learning paradigm, those with the Closing the Gap Campaign determined early that the college would not seek to fix its students but would work by itself and in tandem with the K–12 public school system to fix itself to better serve the needs of its learners.

The college established strategies focused on five areas: (a) professional development, (b) instruction, (c) academic preparation, (d) student services, and (e) institutional culture. Each of these interrelated areas incorporated learning-centered strategies for closing the gap that directly affected the success of developmental students. CCBC was the first academic institution in the United States to publicly declare its commitment to close the gap in learning outcomes between African American students and White students.

This effort was controversial in the opinion of some internal and external constituents, but the journey was sustained by the CISL, the Vanguard Learning Colleges Project, and other interdisciplinary teams of helpers and dreamers. Along the path, Congressman C. A. "Dutch" Ruppersberger, former Baltimore County executive, secured $300,000 in federal money earmarked for the Closing the Gap Campaign at the CCBC. Clearly, the CISL represented team building and the learning college at its best. This infusion process had a most profound effect on placing learning more firmly at the center of the educational enterprise.

Having presented the case for organizational transformation at the CCBC, several aspects of the transformative team-building process deserve additional comment: professional development, broad-based engagement, and the culture of evidence.

Professional Development and Strategic Planning

The success of the CCBC as a newly configured single-college, multicampus institution was directly dependent on the effectiveness of leadership and teams at all levels at the college. The LearningFIRST strategic plan defined where the CCBC was going and how it would get there. To support the change process, the CCBC offered a variety of leadership, professional development, and team-building opportunities to help faculty, administrators, staff, and students build the skills necessary to fully execute the strategic plan. Professional development was offered in a number of different forms such as leadership retreats, campus and college-wide forums, conferences, seminars and one-on-one coaching. The professional development activities for different stakeholder groups also enabled the CCBC to customize the leadership development even further, to address particular styles of management or needs of a particular unit. Building a leadership team to support the transition from the instruction paradigm to the learning paradigm presented an excellent opportunity for intentional professional development for faculty, staff, administrators, and students.

Broad-Based Engagement

The transformation of the CCBC benefited greatly from the broad-based engagement of key stakeholders. The literature on change suggests that the earlier stakeholders are engaged, the more likely they are to buy into the change process. Engaging stakeholders was important during the planning and implementation phases of the change process.

Because the CCBC's goal was to make the transition from a three-college model to a one-college model, bringing key stakeholders from each campus into the planning process paid off in a more fine-tuned and effective set of core initiatives for the strategic plan. As the implementation of LearningFIRST progressed, the leadership team learned that providing opportunities for input from key stakeholder groups on campus was critical to the implementation of the directions for the strategic plan. Although engagement of all stakeholders is important, it is clear that the engagement of faculty and students was essential in the change process at the CCBC. For example, faculty-led teams provided important insights for initiatives aimed at student success and made a huge difference in implementing institutional change depending on whether they resisted or embraced the work. The CCBC involved full-time and adjunct faculty in the teams engaged in strategic planning efforts. Students were another obvious group the CCBC brought into the institutional change work. Because one direction of the strategic plan was to close achievement gaps, it was important for the planning teams to engage those student groups the CCBC's data documented were doing less well than other learners.

Culture of Evidence

At the CCBC the data were the coin of the realm in driving organizational decision-making. With a firm commitment to building a culture of evidence, a new Division of Technology and Planning was established under the direction of a vice chancellor. The various planning committees used disaggregated data on student learning outcomes to inform decisions that directly affected classroom practices and student support programs and services targeted by the directions of the strategic plan. During the planning and implementation phases of the strategic planning effort, the planning teams recognized the importance of data generation and using data to inform and drive strategic thinking at CCBC. For example, teams used data to help prioritize efforts on what was working and what was not. This data analysis helped the teams set a direct and clear course toward sustainable institutional change across the core and to support strategic directions in LearningFIRST. The integration of information technology and institutional research also provided planning and operational teams with the key data and indicators required to assess student learning outcomes and other indicators of organizational performance.

Conclusion

Strategic planning is the ultimate team sport in academic institutions. Participation, communication, and cooperation at all stages of academic strategy—plan development, plan execution, strategic thinking, and decision-making—give way to organizational buying in and support. The journey from the instruction paradigm to the learning paradigm at CCBC was more than semantic, fraught with peril, and involved significant structural and cultural changes in the institution and the ways that faculty, staff, students, administrators, boards, and external agents related to the institution (Mathis, 2006; McKusick & McPhail, 2003). Engaging a broad coalition of stakeholders in helping to shape the change paid huge dividends for the institution.

The CISL was the guiding team that shepherded a major transformation in teaching and learning at an organizationally complex community college system already reeling from rapid changes in environmental trends; market preferences, perceptions, and directions; and the competitive situation. The CISL was the ultimate test of the power of finding the right people, creating trust, and developing a common goal (Kotter, 1996).

Finally, noted scholars and practitioners in higher education leadership Fisher and Koch (2004) commented on the accomplishments of CCBC from 1998 to 2005 in their study of the entrepreneurial college president:

> The result has been a kaleidoscope of achievement that has garnered national awards and recognition. In virtually every area that counts, CCBC is light-years ahead of where it was before McPhail arrived. Enrollment is up; relations with trustees and public officials are restored; the college has infused technology in and out of the classroom; it has developed a significant presence in online course delivery; it has developed a reputation for sound budgeting and financial management; it has attracted committed new faculty and invigorated veteran faculty with competitive merit salaries; and it launched an impressive Closing the Gap initiative that concentrates upon bridging the black/white learning divide. Amid all this, relations with trustees and public officials are on solid ground, and morale is vastly improved. (p. 132)

In addition, Mathis (2006) provides an in-depth study of the process and results of institutional transformation at CCBC from 1998 through 2005, with a particular focus on the role of team building and organizational learning.

In closing, the successful transition of CCBC from three institutions to a high-performing single institution focused on a new strategic plan was largely because of the work of teams made up of goal-focused individuals with expertise and compatible skills who worked collaboratively to achieve a common goal. Throughout the transformation process, team members (faculty, staff, and administrators) relentlessly pursued excellence through shared vision, open communication, and a strong commitment to the mission of community colleges.

Teams such as the CISL at different levels of the institution made up the backbone of the transformation process. The leadership teams provided guidance and direction appropriate for changing policies and practices. Project teams in academic affairs, student affairs, governance and administration, institutional research, and technology created new programs and services aligned with the future direction of CCBC. Team building and professional development at CCBC were viewed as ongoing processes that helped the teams become cohesive units at all levels of the institution. The team members not only shared expectations for accomplishing group tasks but also trusted and supported each other and respected individual differences. The teams understood and supported the meaning and value of the team's mission and vision for the future of CCBC, and they created a unified institution focused on student learning and closing achievement gaps.

References

Barr, R. B., & Tagg, J. (1995). From teaching to learning: A new paradigm for undergraduate education. *Change: The Magazine of Higher Learning, 27*(6), 12–26.

Boggs, G. R. (1995). The learning paradigm. *Community College Journal, 66*(3), 24–27.

Carter, P., & Alfred, R. (2000). *Making change happen.* Ann Arbor, MI: Consortium for Community College Development, University of Michigan.

Community College of Baltimore County. (1999). *Guide for learning outcomes assessment and classroom learning assessment.* Baltimore, MD: Author.

Fisher, J. L. (1997). *The Community College of Baltimore County review.* Baltimore, MD: Author.

Fisher, J. L., & Koch, J. V. (2004). *The entrepreneurial college president.* Westport, CT: American Council on Education and Praeger.

Keller, G. (1983). *Academic strategy: The management revolution in American higher education.* Baltimore, MD: Johns Hopkins University Press.

Kotter, J. P. (1996). *Leading change.* Cambridge, MA: Harvard Business School Press.

Mathis, M. B. (2006). Institutional transformation and learning at the Community College of Baltimore County (Unpublished doctoral dissertation). University of Texas at Austin.

McClenney, K. (2001). Learning from the learning colleges: Observations along the journey. *Learning Abstracts, 4*(2), 1–2.

McKusick, D., & McPhail, I. P. (2003). Walking the talk: Using learning-centered strategies to close performance gaps. In J. L. Higbee, D. B. Lundell, & I. M. Duranczyk (Eds.), *Multiculturalism in developmental education* (pp. 15–24). Minneapolis, MN: Center for Research on Developmental Education and Urban Literacy.

McPhail, I. P., Heacock, R. C., & Linck, H. F. (2000). LearningFIRST: Creating and leading the learning college. *Community College Journal of Research and Practice, 25*, 17–28.

McPhail, I. P. (2004). Transformation of a college: From teaching to learning. *The Presidency, 7*(3), 28–31.

McPhail, I. P. (2012). Academic strategy and the management of the learning college. In T. O'Banion & C. D. Wilson (Eds.), *Focus on learning: A learning college reader* (pp. 108–117). Phoenix, AZ: League for Innovation in the Community College.

McPhail, I. P. (1999). Launching LearningFIRST at the Community College of Baltimore County. *Learning Abstracts, 2*(6), 1–2.

McPhail, I. P., & Heacock, R. C. (1999). Baltimore County: A college and community in transition. In R. C. Bowen & G. H. Muller (Eds.), *Gateway to democracy: Six urban community college systems* (pp. 75–83). San Francisco, CA: Jossey-Bass.

Neumann, A. (1991). The thinking team: Toward a cognitive model of administrative teamwork in higher education. *Journal of Higher Education, 62*, 485–513.

O'Banion, T. (1997). *A learning college for the 21st century*. Phoenix, AZ: American Council on Education and Oryx Press.

Rowley, D. J., Lujan, H. D., & Dolence, M. G. (1997). *Strategic change in colleges and universities: Planning to survive and prosper*. San Francisco, CA: Jossey-Bass.

7

LEADERSHIP TEAM DEVELOPMENT AND SUCCESSION PLANNING IN TIMES OF CRISIS

Russell Lowery-Hart

American higher education is at a critical point in history. To simply survive, colleges and universities must reinvent themselves to be more effective, efficient, and responsive (Bailey, Jaggars, & Jenkins, 2015). This reformation will require bold and aggressive leadership with unified, action-oriented teams. These kinds of aggressive leadership teams are currently not the norm in higher education. They must be intentionally developed—the future of higher education may depend on it.

New community college leaders frequently encounter issues of administrative complacency and problems that have built up over time. It can be a challenge to change behaviors that have become individualistic and to develop a team orientation to college leadership. This chapter is, in many ways, a case study of how a new first-time president worked to develop his administration into an effective team, how leadership succession planning improved the college, and how a significant financial crisis was overcome. Although the chapter focuses on Amarillo College in Texas, the principles and the lessons learned may apply to any new leader at any community college.

Typically, new college presidents feel honored and thrilled at their appointments. They can also be scared out of their minds even though they might have a clear vision for where they want to lead the college. Sometimes they have the advantage of having been an internal candidate, giving them a deeper understanding of the challenges than most first-time presidents. They usually believe their vision will push their colleges and employees in new, exciting directions. Yet if new presidents were internal candidates, they likely understand that the most critical part of a college reformation might require a completely different approach to how the college leadership team has communicated and functioned. Any new president will not be able to lead the college without first addressing its biggest barrier to change—a dysfunctional leadership team.

At Amarillo College, the president's cabinet was composed of wonderful people who were skilled at their jobs. Still, the cabinet members did not see the cabinet as leading the entire college as a team; instead, the cabinet members saw themselves as individual leaders of specific divisions. The cabinet was full of smart people, but it was not unified in purpose and lacked clarity in direction. Kegan and Laskow Lahey (2009) helped to clarify this leadership challenge, writing about successful organizations and teams of the future. They suggested that successful organizations would be able to unlock human capital by developing talent and teams unified in purpose and built for transformation. Kegan and Laskow Lahey posed the definitive question for a new president. To transform a college, a president should ask, "What can I do to make my setting the most fertile ground in the world for growth of talent" (Kegan & Laskow Lahey, 2009, p. 11) on my leadership team?

College presidents need to clarify their expectations to unify a leadership team to focus on the purpose of leading the college's students to success. Pink (2009) provides a deep understanding of the kind of team that could lead Amarillo College forward. When I became president of Amarillo College, I gave every team member a copy of his book with the hope that it would provide a blueprint for a new approach to leadership, communication, teaming, and performing. The book became the clarion call for the college leadership team. Pink (2009) asserted that the most powerful teams found their "Goldilocks" moment—team plans that are neither too easy nor too hard—where the relational and execution flows were "just right" (p. 168). In a team setting it is difficult to locate and embrace the "Goldilocks moment," and people "often end up doing the jobs they always do because they've proven they can do them well" (p. 168) instead of embracing the bigger picture. Thus, people jettison the more difficult work of creating a dynamic, unified team for the comfort and control of the individual work no matter if the way they do their individual jobs hinders the team and organization as a whole (Pink, 2009)

This pattern of personal comfort over the challenges of the team were most evident in the Amarillo College leadership team, the president's cabinet. The cabinet members were all capable, worthy, and wonderful individuals. Yet the members did not trust each other to do their jobs. This collective group of people saw the purpose of the college solely in the realm of their own job duties. Certainly, this leadership team perspective of privileging self over the collective is not unique to Amarillo College. To transform any college into an effective and responsive organization the president must start with a transformation of the president's cabinet into an effective team.

Pink (2009) described the following ways to bring a Goldilocks philosophy to a team, which became the foundation of the first leadership team meeting when I became president:

- *Begin with a diverse team.* Set up groups so that people can learn from each other. Frequently, team members do not know what each other's roles truly are in the college. Members usually do not understand the diversity of their collective experiences, talents, and job duties. A good start is to simply have the team members express what they think their duties and roles really are.
- *Make your group a no-competition zone.* Pink said that pitting coworkers against each other to spark competition rarely works even though leadership team members are often inherently competitive with each other. Colleague cabinet members are seen as a threat to each other's resources, processes, policies, and even effectiveness. To be effective, leadership teams need to move from competition to collaboration fast.
- *Try task shifting.* To more fully appreciate the role and duties of each team member, Pink suggested task shifting. It is instructive to rethink the duties and jobs of leadership team members based on their skills and talents rather than monolithically looking only at duties tied to specific jobs. This process allows the leadership team members to see the college in a broader perspective and understand their cabinet colleagues more fully.
- *Animate with purpose.* Teams bond over a shared mission and need a common cause. However, the purposes of too many leadership teams are individually driven and not aligned with the broader college needs. (p. 168)

To move a college forward, a new president needs to develop a dynamic, unified, purpose-driven, and task-shifting team. Members must move beyond competition with each other to embrace a broader purpose for the college and community. After reading Pink's (2009) book together, the leadership team at Amarillo College was poised to embrace a new approach to teamwork. To be effective as a team leader, a president must understand that the solutions needed to reinvent a college do not reside in *me* but in *we*.

The beginning of a college presidency should focus on developing a unified leadership team. Amarillo College did not necessarily have one, and the new president believed that he had to act and act fast.

Building a Leadership Team

Bringing in a consultant with expertise in leadership development who can facilitate meetings can help expand perspectives. Amarillo College contracted with a seasoned retired college president who facilitated the leadership team trainings. His assignment was to jump-start the college leadership team and help develop it into an aggressive, action-oriented unit. The decision to contract with the consultant proved to be a pivotal one for the college. A first step in the process was to understand the leadership team and the individuals who composed it.

Get to Know Your Team

At the first facilitated retreat as a leadership team, the consultant distributed the DiSC (Sugerman, Scullard, & Eilhelm, 2011) survey, a personal assessment tool used to improve work productivity, teamwork, leadership, and communication, for the president's cabinet members to complete. The survey results proved to be a tipping point for the leadership team and the college's development. DiSC profiles describe human behavior in various situations, such as how people respond to challenges, how they would influence others, what their preferred pace is, and how they respond to rules and procedures. According to Sugerman et al. (2011), the DiSC model discusses the following reference points:

1. Dominance—direct, strong-willed, and forceful
2. Influence—sociable, talkative, and lively
3. Steadiness—gentle, accommodating, and softhearted
4. Conscientiousness—private, analytical, and logical

The Amarillo College assessment results revealed that the president was placed in the "influence" part of the DiSC, with a focus on relationships, action, and team-oriented work. Almost every other team member was on the opposite side of the DiSC, landing in "conscientiousness," focused on individual, private, and policy-driven work. The discussions of the DiSC results showed that the team was more focused on creating procedures and writing policies designed to control others on the team and in the college than developing relationships and influences to ensure the procedures and policies were effective. Functionally, the Amarillo College leadership team was focused on control and policy, whereas the new president was focused on relationships and action-oriented results. The facilitator noted that the team and its leader were on completely opposite sides of the DiSC. This realization opened a safe way for the team to understand its shared dynamic. The discussions also clarified that the members wanted different things from the team; the president wanted relationships and group efforts, and the team members wanted written procedures and freedom to complete their work privately and in isolation.

Identify Your Team's Foundation Issue

The facilitator pointed out that the individual results and team assessment identified a foundational issue that could keep the team and the college from excelling. The team members not only differed in their approach to the team's work but also fundamentally distrusted each other. According to Kegan and Laskow Lahey (2009), trust is usually the core issue in any team dysfunction, and to address trust, teams must address four elements:

1. Respect for the importance of the other person's role in producing high-quality outcomes;
2. Belief in the other's ability and willingness to fulfill his or her formal role;
3. Care for the other professionally and personally; and
4. Consistency between what people say and what they do. (2009, p. 197)

The assessment at Amarillo College revealed that the president's cabinet was not inclined toward DiSC (Sugerman et al., 2011) relational leadership, and distrust would inhibit any effort to rebuild the college. The president acknowledged the members' different approaches to work and also had to build trust. The facilitated conversations in the first retreat revealed that the team members did not respect each other or even the formal roles they filled. They did not believe in each other's abilities and apparently talked to everyone in the college—except the person in question—about this distrust. Team members had never learned to care about personal relationships because as the DiSC results showed, the leadership team members avoided bringing them into the professional context.

If team members were to trust each other, they had to find something to build their trust. The unifying tool the president used involved listening to the college's students. Using students as agents for leadership and behavior change with an institution can be transformative (Fullan & Scott, 2009).

Leadership team members might not yet be able to agree on their work or their approach to it, but maybe they could agree on what students needed from the college and from its leadership.

Building Trust by Clarifying Purpose

The president asked the leadership team to embrace a culture change for higher education in which student feedback drives decision-making. The process started by asking the college's students what they needed from the college and its leadership team. Using focus groups and surveys, the leadership team asked students to identify what Amarillo College should look and feel like to ensure their success. Student responses dramatically changed the way the leadership team members perceived each other and the college as a whole.

The foundation of the leadership team's culture change was rooted in establishing the college's values. Students actually drafted values to describe their conceptualizion of the ideal institution, and the leadership team then refined and finalized them. These values are devoid of traditional academic buzzwords, but they truly represent the purpose of the college and the commitments and behaviors students desperately needed from it. The Amarillo College values as defined by the students clearly state that students are the college's core purpose. These values could—and would—drive the leadership team's development and reshape the entire institution.

College Values

Students wanted a relational, service-oriented college that displays the following values:

1. Caring through WOW
   - Every student and colleague will say "WOW, you were so helpful, supportive, and open" after an interaction with us.
   - Every student will experience WOW through engaged, learner-centered classroom experiences.
2. Caring through FUN
   - We will find ways to have fun with each other and celebrate each other.
   - We will find ways to make our work fun and effective.
   - We will find ways to provide enriching learning experiences.
3. Caring through INNOVATION

- We will see ourselves as a "roadblock remover" for students and for each other.
- We will always look for ways to help others and improve our processes.
- We will develop and implement original and creative teaching strategies.
4. Caring through FAMILY
- We will find ways to show we care about our students and each other.
- We will readily and effectively share information with each other.
- We will approach our interactions with each other with trust and openness.
- We will put the needs of others before our own.
- We will enhance learning by creating an atmosphere of mutual respect.
5. Caring through YES
- We will think "yes" first and find solutions, rather than stating "no."
- We will be passionate about our jobs and helping each other.
- We will promote critical thinking and problem-solving skills in curricula. (Amarillo College, 2019)

These values were written into every president's cabinet member's job description and then eventually the job description for every employee. The work was difficult and certainly controversial, and not every original cabinet member supported this approach or welcomed the accountability to live these values in his or her work. However, the president was clear that students deserve no less from the college and its employees. The college had to unify itself around the needs of its students, and if leadership team members could all agree to make the values the foundation of its work, trust in each other would follow.

As a result, Amarillo College and its leadership team unified in purpose and built trust through an intentional culture of caring. Whether college employees stationed themselves at key places throughout the college during registration to assist students through the process, greeted students in the parking lot and walked them to their first class, or cared for students' children during a finals week study session, Amarillo College leadership team members and employees cared about and changed the culture of the college and its community.

Creating a culture of caring required careful systems. For Amarillo College, fall and spring leadership team retreats and then college-wide general assemblies were critical. For the first general assembly, the president talked openly to the entire college about the president's cabinet team development. Issues with trust were clearly addressed. The leadership team DiSC (Sugerman et al., 2011) results were provided, and the president talked about the unifying purpose that was created based on students' direction.

The initial general assembly was the first time the new college values that created a unified purpose for the leadership team were shared with the college community. The goal was for the values to create the same unifying purpose for the college that they did for the leadership team. Students were asked to discuss these values and what they meant to them. As an indication of the importance of the values, the college was closed for an entire afternoon for an assembly. During this assembly time, the focus was on understanding the college's students more fully, reviewing the college report card data, and sharing new ideas about how to better serve students and each other.

If one of the leadership team members became so focused on using procedures and policies to control rather than improve, the team would refer the member to the yes value (item 5 in the preceding list). In every situation team members had to find a yes to any impasse, forcing the leadership team members to talk and work with each other. When students faced a barrier in the college, the leadership team could unify around innovation to solve it. The members challenged themselves as a leadership team to build the family with each other that students said they needed as well. When the team worked together on a new process or project, the goal was to wow each other with collaboration. When the work itself became challenging, the team embraced fun with commitments to team development by reading a common book or engaging in a shared activity. (Let's just say some of the team members were better bowlers than others.) To create the effective team the college needed, its leaders had to demonstrate what its students needed most—relationships and service.

Building a Succession Plan as Culture Change

For Amarillo College to reach its full potential, the college itself needed to embrace the same culture change established in the president's cabinet leadership team. A trusted colleague, Don Cameron, president emeritus at Gilford Tech Community College, shared an important lesson about his success in transforming a college culture: Cultural transformation requires intentional succession planning (D. Cameron, personal communication, January, 14, 2016). The succession planning at Amarillo College included three phases of leadership development: academic dean; midmanagement; and all college, representing all parts of the organization.

Phase 1

The first phase of succession planning at Amarillo College focused on deans and others in leadership positions who reported directly to members of the president's cabinet leadership team. This phase included three different sessions over the course of three months. During these sessions, development focused on key issues facing senior leaders. The same facilitator who guided the president's cabinet team through its development guided each of the phases in our succession planning as well. For phase 1, each participant read Kouzes, Posner, and Biech (2010). These participants also completed the DiSC (Sugerman et al., 2011) assessment to develop skills as internal coaches to strengthen those behaviors that produce more effective leadership. Over three months, participants covered the following topics specific to the college and those broadly applicable to higher education in general:

- mission and philosophy of community colleges in America
- building partnerships with business, industry, and the community
- effective communication as an obligation of leadership
- technology's implications for education
- building high-performance work teams
- pathways to improved student access and student success
- becoming an effective leader and competent manager
- developing a positive college culture
- finance and budgeting

These sessions included a variety of presenters from the college as well as external experts.

Phase 2

This phase, which involved middle managers, was critical to the foundation of the college's succession planning. As with phase 1, this second phase took place with three two-day training sessions over the course of three months. Although these topics shared some similarities with phase 1, this phase typically addressed issues central to leading from the middle, such as the following:

- emerging issues facing community colleges
- the courage to lead
- leading change
- leading from the middle

- effective communications
- case studies of success and failure of leadership
- data-based decision-making

These training sessions proved critical to moving the entire college forward. Participants were empowered to lead from their positions and felt supported to improve processes and recommend policy shifts.

Phase 3

To develop the leadership skills necessary for true succession planning, the college president created a President's Leadership Institute (PLI), a decision that proved to be the most critical for shifting the college culture. Employees at every level below the cabinet were invited to apply. The application was simple, with only two questions: What is the greatest challenge you face in your current position? and What is your ultimate career goal? Although the president anticipated that employees would be reluctant to apply, within 72 hours of sending the invitation college-wide, more than a third of the entire college, 230 employees, applied for 30 available slots. Although narrowing the pool was difficult, the president made sure the college was represented in all job types and levels across all divisions. The guiding theme for the leadership program was to encourage participants to understand how their individual roles aligned with the overall values and mission of the college.

The PLI was invited to continue its leadership development by engaging in projects designed to enhance participants' leadership knowledge, skills, and abilities. The participants were assigned to project teams directly connected to the college's culture, goals, and initiatives. The college president identified projects or issues that were important and appropriate. The PLI started with a one-week intensive session and then carried throughout the entire year with monthly meetings. Each PLI class was assigned books to read that dealt with important issues of the year; for example, the inaugural cohort was assigned Achor (2010). The following cohorts were assigned readings specific to their year including Dweck (2006); Brown McNair, Albertine, Cooper, McDonald, and Major (2016); and Bok (2017).

During the monthly sessions, the project teams' work was discussed, but the participants continued to focus on major leadership themes as well. The PLI members had assigned readings as a discussion focus for each session. In the time between monthly sessions, the PLI was divided into project teams and met independently to research and discuss their project topics. The college president stayed engaged with the participants throughout the process.

It is important for the leader to be present to show the importance of the PLI and to develop personal relationships with the participants.

At the end of each PLI, the teams made presentations to the college leadership team to recommend an implementation plan for the initiative they had been studying. Depending on the effectiveness and viability of the plan, teams were invited to make presentations to the elected Amarillo College Board of Regents. The team members' presentations included a description of their research, the resulting data they gathered, the recommendations they developed, and a budget to support their recommendations.

These projects ranged from identifying gaps in student engagement to equity gaps in student performance and changed the landscape of the college physically and organizationally. One group researched student engagement using various data-gathering tools and concluded that the college should change the food and beverage options on campus. The presenters were persuasive, and the college implemented their plan. Another year, the group focused on student poverty barriers. After extensive research, the team recommended that the college should invest in a childcare center. The plan was executed, and the college is now enrolling children of its students.

The goal of the PLI was to build a talented and diverse group of individuals who would be ready to step into key leadership roles as the opportunity was presented while fundamentally changing the direction for and effectiveness of the college in the process.

Impact of Team Development and Succession Planning

The ability to educate large segments of college employees about the challenges facing the college and higher education in general proved to be critical to creating necessary cultural change. The majority of the college employees were trained in leadership at some point and level through the PLI. The president believes that the results of team development and succession planning functionally saved the college and, frankly, his presidency.

No college president welcomes a surprise, especially one that has financial implications. During the first year of his presidency at Amarillo College, the president scheduled a meeting with the college's vice president for business affairs to respond to a series of questions about the budget. Before the president could ask a single question, and even before the vice president was seated, he received stark news. The college budget was going to be far more challenging than the new president could have predicted.

The college had fundamentally budgeted the same levels as the previous decades amid enrollment drops and state funding decreases, perhaps in the hope that state funding would return and enrollments would increase. They never did. Facing this reality, the college's president had to make decisions he was not expecting and felt ill prepared for. He had to cut the budget by 5% while working to increase student enrollment. As the state legislative session came to a close during his first year, college leadership was shocked to receive an unexpected $3.5 million cut in state appropriations. The 5% budget cut was not going to be sufficient. The college leadership eventually offered an early retirement incentive, reorganized the college, and then reduced the employee workforce. All told, the college eliminated 99 positions in the president's first year.

The leadership team was a critical element in defining the core funding issues, identifying the options eventually selected, communicating the situation and options college-wide, and then executing the plan. A unified leadership team with a clear purpose and an eye on the long-term financial health of the college was crucial. This team met, on occasion, multiple times a day. The team was committed to presenting a unified front even if the subsequent decisions created difficulties for specific team members' divisions. The team developed scenarios and role-played communication strategies, practiced presentations for each other before informing the college and community, and even accompanied each other to division meetings during the initial rollout of the financial plan. Most important, the team members listened to each other and to faculty and staff throughout the college. Listening proved to be the most helpful skill because it allowed the team to truly understand how employees were reacting, and it improved communication with the team and the college.

Still, the president believed the only sustainable path forward for the college was committing to the development of the leadership team and of the college employees as a whole. Without the critical intervention with the cabinet team, the college would never have unified behind a clear purpose and built the trust necessary to deal with the financial crisis. Without the three phases of leadership development, the employees would not have been empowered to innovate and problem solve. Equally important, a deep understanding of the issues facing higher education in general would not have been generated. If the new president had failed to develop his leadership team so intentionally and had not trained emerging leaders throughout the college, he believes that Amarillo College would have suffered for decades to come.

Instead, Amarillo College went from significant budget cuts in 2015 to the *Chronicle of Higher Education*'s Great Colleges to Work For in 2018 (Wyatt, 2018). Leadership development and succession planning enabled the college to survive serious financial crises and allowed the president to establish an effective leadership team and lead the college with strong support from employees at every level of the institution.

The president's cabinet leadership team was transformed. Several of the original team members took advantage of the early retirement incentive or moved to other organizations. These events enabled the president to put the college succession plan into action. Two internal candidates, who were intentionally developed and groomed, were hired as vice presidents. Throughout the academic division, PLI graduates advanced into positions of department chair and dean. Throughout the college, employees who were intentionally trained in phase 1, 2, or 3 were tapped to lead at various places in the college.

Leadership at all levels of the college now had a deeper understanding of the reform agenda, the issues facing higher education, best practices in leadership and team development, and how to research and identify emerging needs in the college. College leaders not only received robust training, they were actually charged with evaluating college effectiveness and researching and implementing plans to improve the institution. The results of these efforts are powerful. College employee and faculty feedback is incredibly supportive. The college culture is now defined by caring behaviors for students and each other.

For higher education to meet the significant political, financial, social, and cultural challenges ahead, colleges must change. Leaders must "join a change in behavior with a change in the way we think and feel—and in order to change the way we think and feel, we need to change our mindsets" (Kegan & Laskow Lahey, 2009, p. 222). Amarillo College used team development and succession planning to change the way its employees think and feel about their shared work. In doing so, college leadership created a *change-capable* higher education institution as defined by Fullan and Scott (2009). These organizations

- are undefensive,
- are evidence-based,
- set priorities that are actionable for all employees,
- can make a hard decision,
- make clear who is responsible for what activities,
- acknowledge that all staff members have a role to play,
- are outcomes focused,
- limit bureaucracy and empower employees to act, and
- operate in a responsive, collaborative, team-based, and focused fashion. (p. 76–77)

Although I did not initially appreciate how team development and succession planning could truly transform the college and reshape it as a change-capable institution, I knew the college faced real dangers and needed to ensure that employees understood the challenges and were prepared to overcome them. In addition to accomplishing the president's initial goals, the institution became an example of a turnaround college in the process (Fullan & Scott, 2009)

College leadership was also clear in its belief that training and succession planning activities without measurable actions would be futile and even destructive. As Kegan and Laskow Lahey (2009) noted, training "without action is ultimately as unproductive as action without reflection" (p. 222) and training. The impact on the Amarillo College was dramatic. Student success data showed incredible progress that corresponded with the leadership development and improvement plans.

Critical to any leadership team development, especially in times of crisis, is a strong, trusting relationship with the board of regents. In Amarillo the community voters elected the regents, who were clear in their expectations of the leadership team: Use the budget crisis to become more efficient and effective. The leadership team and regents held a budget retreat in 2015 focused on a 10-year budget scenario with reductions in state funding, declining populations in the region, and enrollment declines. Through this retreat, the leadership team and the regents had a clear understanding of the crisis. Without bold leadership and a willingness to make difficult decisions, the college would suffer. Each regent meeting required updates on the budgeting process and the approach to solving it. Regents attended college presentations for all employees and were supportive of the president and his leadership team, publicly and privately. The final statement during the leadership team and regent retreat was clearly offered by one regent, who told the attendees that to save the college, and even higher education, one must kill the bureaucracy that so often keeps higher education from changing and improving. He was right. As the leaders at Amarillo College developed their team approach to reinventing the college, they found that bureaucracy often impeded improvement and perpetuated itself. The relationship between regents and the leadership team allowed the team to take on significant challenges with confidence because the regents were clear in their support of the college leadership team and the direction it was headed in.

When the leadership development and succession planning efforts started in 2014, the college's student completion and transfer rates were 19% and hovered in the midteens for a decade. In 2017 Amarillo College's completion and transfer rates improved to 45%. The college has a goal of 70% completion and transfer rates by 2020. The college's leadership team believes that student success rates can improve by intentionally building team and leadership development throughout all levels of the organization. According to Bailey et al. (2015),

To develop and sustain an effective model, a college needs a critical mass of faculty and staff excited about the process, ready to collaborate with one another to achieve larger goals, and willing to engage in inquiry, reflection, and improvement. (p. 144)

At Amarillo College the team development and succession-planning model has transformed the institution. It works.

The challenge is now determining how to continue leadership team development and further the succession planning without the urgency of a crisis. Amarillo College is growing, and student success is dramatically increasing. Intentionally developing leaders, from cabinet to frontline staff, when things are going well is surprisingly challenging. Amarillo College made new employee and faculty orientations a full year-long process and plans to expand leadership training. Regents will be more visible in these orientations. Reimagining a college during crisis is frightening and difficult. Yet, the urgency of the crisis allows the acceleration of change. When things improve, the challenge for the president and his leadership team is to maintain the commitment to change and continue the intensity of serving and educating students. The future of Amarillo College is more secure and exciting because the president intentionally developed his leadership team and worked to prepare future college leaders simultaneously. As a result, the college will be able to ensure that even more students complete their degrees and either transfer to a university or find employment with a living wage. The work to reform higher education is difficult and requires true leadership development. The Amarillo College reformation is ongoing. Yet, leadership development has already allowed the college to not only effectively face a significant crisis but also ensure the crisis response would actually improve the college and its outcomes.

References

Achor, S. (2010). *The happiness advantage: The seven principles of positive psychology that fuel success and performance at work.* New York, NY: Crown Business.

Amarillo College. (2019). *Mission and values.* Retrieved from https://www.actx.edu/president/mission-and-values

Bailey, T., Jaggars, S., & Jenkins, D. (2015). *Redesigning America's community colleges: A clear path to student success.* Cambridge, MA: Harvard University Press.

Bok, D. (2017). *The struggle to reform our colleges.* Princeton, NJ: Princeton University Press.

Brown McNair, T., Albertine, S., Cooper, M., McDonald, N., & Major, T. (2016). *Becoming a student-ready college: A new culture of leadership for student success.* San Francisco, CA: Jossey-Bass.

Dweck, C. (2006). *Mindset: The new psychology of success*. New York, NY: Random House.

Fullan, M., & Scott, G. (2009). *Turnaround leadership for higher education*. San Francisco, CA: Jossey-Bass.

Kegan, R., & Laskow Lahey, L. (2009). *Immunity to change*. Boston, MA: Harvard University Press.

Kouzes, J., Posner, B., & Biech, E. (2010). *A coach's guide to developing exemplary leaders*. San Francisco, CA: Pfeiffer.

Pink, D. (2009). *Drive: The surprising truth about what motivates us*. New York, NY: Riverhead.

Sugerman, J., Scullard, M., & Eilhelm, E. (2011). *The 8 dimensions of leadership: DiSC strategies of becoming a better leader*. San Francisco, CA: Berrett-Koehler.

Wyatt, J. (2018, July 16). The *Chronicle of Higher Education* recognizes AC as a "great college to work for" [Web log post]. Retrieved from https://www.actx.edu/blog/id/259

8

TEAM LEADERSHIP IN THE URBAN COMMUNITY COLLEGE

Curtis L. Ivery and Gunder A. Myran

T his chapter examines team leadership, also known as collaborative, distributive, collective, and shared leadership, as an increasingly important role of the urban community college president or chancellor and his or her executive team. Team or collaborative leadership is an essential dimension of an emerging student-centered, design-driven, equity-focused, and team-based model shaped by the unique challenges facing urban community colleges. In an era of rapid and transformational change, community college leaders, especially in urban settings, are engaging student, faculty, staff, and community constituencies in seeking solutions to large-scale, enterprise-level challenges.

Brief History of the Urban Community College

From the beginning of urban community colleges in the 1960s (including start-ups in Cleveland, Dallas, St. Louis, Phoenix, Denver, Miami, Philadelphia, Detroit, and Seattle), early leaders saw the need to design community colleges as instruments for social justice to address the challenges of inner cities and their residents. They were at the forefront of the civil rights movement at local, state, and national levels. In 1966 a group of urban community college representatives met in Dallas, Texas, to discuss their potential to energize change. The report that resulted from this meeting contained this statement: "We accept the challenge of the inner city with all its complexities, its difficult problems and immense costs. The battleground is in the inner city—stay and fight where you are" (Myran, Ivery, Parsons, & Kinsley, 2013, p. 1).

In 1970 a group of African American community college presidents worked to democratize the American Association of Community Colleges (AACC), which to that point had not had a minority person on its board of directors; the first African American member, Malcolm Hurst, was elected that year. During the early 1970s Edmund Gleazer, then the AACC's president, led Project Focus to further democratize the association. A number of administrative groups were incorporated into the AACC structure, including the National Council for Black American Affairs. Another national organization that continues to influence the development of the urban community college today is the RC-2020 (2019), a nonprofit association of the largest community colleges serving urban cities. Member chancellors and presidents hold periodic roundtables to advance the RC-2020's mission, which is to (a) empower a diverse urban population to respond to crisis and renew their communities and (b) constantly challenge and improve services and use partnerships to better serve the students, faculty, and communities of urban and metropolitan regions. Today's urban community college leaders truly stand on the shoulders of those pioneers who came before them. A case in point is Walter Bumphus, the AACC's current president and chief executive officer (CEO) and the first African American to hold that leadership position.

Today urban community colleges are leading efforts to overcome the entrenched and persistent racial, educational, economic, and social inequities that create barriers to individual and economic success. They are embracing new collaborative and team-based approaches to engage all constituencies—students, faculty and staff, as well as community stakeholders—to shape not only the future of their colleges but also the future of the city, region, state, and nation they serve.

Snapshot of the Contemporary Urban Community College

Myran et al. (2013) described the urban community college as serving a large metropolitan region anchored by a major urban hub. Its service area includes a high-density urban center and related neighborhoods, an urban and suburban transition fringe, suburban areas, and limited rural areas. Of the 1,119 public community colleges in the United States, 123 are identified as urban in the largest cities of more than 250,000 residents. They served 2.6 million for-credit students in 2016–2017, 25% of the total enrolled in all public community colleges. About 63% of those attending urban colleges are African American, Latino, Asian, American Indian, and other minorities, compared to 48% across all community colleges and 43% of undergraduates at the 582 public 4-year universities. The largest urban community colleges include Los Angeles Community College District in California, Maricopa County Community Colleges in Arizona, Miami Dade College in Florida, Dallas County Community College District in Texas, and Houston Community College in Texas (National Center for Education Statistics, 2018).

The Milieu of the Urban Community College: The Paradox and Challenge

Pierce (2010) described the paradox of all urban and metropolitan regions: On the one hand, they are centers of racial and economic isolation, poverty, crime, drugs, family disintegration, failed schools, and dashed hopes; on the other hand, they are economic powerhouses, cultural hubs, and drivers of social change. West spoke of a "pathology of despair" (Ivery & Bassett, 2011, p. xii) in our inner cities, yet low-income areas can also be vibrant centers of mutual support, creativity, and entrepreneurship.

The future of the urban community college is deeply interwoven with the future of those disenfranchised and impoverished groups that live in the shadows of our large cities and struggle to overcome the impact of racial isolation and concentrated poverty. For them, the urban community college is the primary—and often the only—gateway to the economic mainstream and social justice. The urban college is called on to provide pathways to career and college success for these underprepared and underserved populations. It serves on the front lines of the ongoing civil rights and social equity struggle to overcome the persistent and entrenched disparities in income, education, and economic opportunity experienced by minority groups. Warren (2017) calls for a fierce commitment to this core mission:

> If urban community colleges were to focus their concerted efforts on the students for whom they are the only gateway for accessing higher education, and truly invest in their communities, their overall enrollment would significantly improve, as would their communities. Instead of competing for the same small group of highly qualified students, urban community colleges need to stay true to their core mission and serve their entire communities with innovative outreach and support structures on multiple levels—interacting with community members, entrepreneurs and businesses, local nonprofit organizations, and government agencies. (para. 18)

If urban community colleges fail to lead the creation of a multiracial democracy in which all citizens "come together across lines of race, religion, class, and gender to collectively unite in support of racial and ethnic equality" (Ivery & Bassett, 2011, p. xcii), they forfeit their most vital and irreplaceable value to society. Team leadership is a powerful way for the executives of an urban community college to engage internal and community stakeholders in shaping the best future for the urban democracy's college.

Team Leadership as a Cultural Shift for Community Colleges

Team or collaborative leadership of the community college represents a cultural shift from viewing leadership as an individual and solitary trait (the hero leader and the leader-follower binary) to viewing it as a shared and collaborative trait among many. Schwarz (2013) describes two organizational leadership mind-sets (the set of core values and assumptions that individuals and groups operate from): the unilateral control mind-set and the mutual learning mind-set. In the traditional hierarchical structure, the unilateral control mind-set, in which authority, knowledge, accountability, and control are invested in the formal leader, tends to prevail. Schwarz advocates a shift to the mutual learning mind-set for all organizations but particularly for those functioning in rapidly changing and complex environments. With the mutual learning mind-set, institutional leadership is invested in cross-functional teams rather than in the formal leaders only. It is based on the values of shared purpose, transparency, curiosity, compassion, informed choice, and shared accountability. The mutual learning mind-set assumes that all team members have knowledge and information, all relevant information will be shared, all members can state their views, differences are opportunities for learning, and all members can contribute to the decisions and recommendations of the team. In the community college setting, the formal leader with a mutual learning mind-set continues to be the ultimate decision maker unless that authority is delegated to the team but acts in a spirit of shared purpose, trust, openness, and mutual respect.

The emergence of a mutual learning mind-set and a collaborative leadership culture are most evident in the work of enterprise-level, cross-functional teams that involve faculty, staff, students (and possibly designers, software developers, consultants, and community representatives) working on complex, difficult, and future-shaping redesign efforts. An excellent example of an enterprise-level redesign project that affects all dimensions of the college is a student success and completion initiative. This college-wide initiative involves transformation of student support services, redesign of developmental education, professional development of faculty and staff, redesign of curriculum, and the use of data-based decision-making and analytics. It comes about through leadership from the chancellor or president, the executive team, and cross-functional teams that engage all constituencies.

An excellent illustration of a team-based student success and completion model in an urban community college is the Achieving the Dream Equity Wheel of Kingsborough Community College (n.d.a) in Brooklyn, New York. The college has been twice recognized as a finalist by the Aspen Institute's College Excellence Program for being "a national pioneer in developing innovative cohort-based models for supporting students with intensive academic and nonacademic supports" (Aspen Institute, 2018). Kingsborough's Accelerated Study in Associates Program is an equity-driven student success and completion initiative that provides clear college and career pathways with a range of student support services including intensive advising, tutoring, and career advising (Kingsborough Community College, n.d.b). Its equity wheel organizes a steering team and four cross-functional teams around the core purpose of increasing student success and completion, which include

- leadership and vision team (steering committee),
- teaching and learning team (faculty professional development, focus on culturally responsive teaching),
- student success team (student support services to meet individual needs),
- data and technology team (for evidence-based decision-making), and
- engagement and communications team (dialogue with internal and community groups).

Other examples of enterprise-level redesign projects include the reinvention of student support services, career education, and college and career readiness programs. In these institutional-level redesign projects, the president or chancellor and executive team members retain their positional authority but within a culture of shared decision-making, collaboration, trust, and teamwork.

Many types of teams have their appropriate and useful place in all community colleges: committees of the governing board, the executive team of the chancellor or president, governance committees, and the teams of academic departments and administrative units. Although these functional teams continue to be an important dimension of governance and decision-making, the emerging collaborative leadership model places more emphasis on cross-functional teams that engage students, faculty and staff, and community constituencies in redesign initiatives that have an impact on all functions of the college and shape its future. According to Holcombe and Kezar (2017),

> Team or shared leadership is characterized by leadership being dispersed across organizations or even across organizational boundaries. ... Different individuals at multiple levels of the organization cross organizational boundaries to exert influence during particular projects or times of change. In higher education, this approach to shared leadership often exists in the form of task forces or committees with members at varying levels of seniority taking on broad, cross-cutting issues such as first-year experience or general education reform. (para. 7)

A college that is collaborative (creating a participative and team-based culture) and enterprising (keen to undertake initiatives of some magnitude, complexity, and risk) is a collaborative enterprise. *Merriam-Webster's* defines *enterprising* as "marked by an independent energetic spirit and by readiness to act" (Enterprising, 2019). In that sense, a community college is certainly an enterprise. Adler, Heckscher, and Prusak (2011) list the following keys to building a collaborative enterprise:

- Defining and building a shared purpose: "Collaborative communities seek a basis for trust and organizational cohesion that is more robust than self-interest, more flexible than tradition, and less ephemeral than the emotional, charismatic appeal of a Steve Jobs, a Larry Page, or a Mark Zuckerberg" (para. 10).
- Cultivating an ethic of contribution: Collaborative communities accord the highest value to people who look beyond their specific roles and advance the common purpose.
- Developing processes that enable people to work together in flexible but disciplined projects: Collaborative communities create protocols for brainstorming, participatory meeting management, decision-making, and other group processes so that a sense of shared purpose is aligned across and within major large-scale interdependent redesign projects.
- Creating an infrastructure in which collaboration is valued and rewarded (participative centralization): Collaborative communities create an authority structure so that the knowledge and skills of multiple leaders are mobilized, valued, and rewarded, and yet the work can be coordinated to apply innovations at scale. There is an ultimate decision-maker, but that leader is expected to push decisions down to the working teams and other leaders to the extent possible.

An excellent example of a collaborative, team-based enterprise is the Alamo Academies, an industry-driven workforce development program of the Alamo Community College District in San Antonio, Texas. Alamo Academies uses a dual enrollment model that enables students to complete their high school diploma while earning college credits in a number of high-demand occupations such as aerospace, information technology, advanced manufacturing, health, and heavy equipment. The program includes a paid summer internship. Graduates earn a beginning salary of about $42,700 per year, and most continue toward an associate degree at one of the Alamo colleges. Seventy-five percent of the 2-year program's graduates are minority students, and 86% are from economically disadvantaged backgrounds. Collaboration between the Alamo Academies and regional businesses is vital to the program's success. Stakeholders include regional chambers of commerce, governmental agencies, manufacturing associations, 67 regional high schools, and more than 100 regional employers. The enterprise benefits graduates as well as businesses and the economy of the San Antonio region (Hu & Bowman, 2016).

Community College Design and Idea Centers

When people hear the word *design*, they typically think of an architect designing a building or an engineer designing a product. They may also think of computational design, the use of metrics, analytics, and big data to understand customer preferences, patterns, and trends. A third type of design being used in community colleges is a human- or student-centered redesign of programs and services in ways that meet the precise needs of those being served.

A number of urban community colleges are establishing design or idea centers to provide human- or student-centered services for their large-scale transformational initiatives. For example, the Design Center of the Wayne County Community College District (WCCCD) in Detroit serves as the hub of the district's innovation and entrepreneurial enterprises. Design staff support leaders by facilitating group solution-seeking processes, leading consultative dialogue sessions that help members of the WCCCD family anticipate the future and design innovative responses, and encouraging student, faculty, and staff innovation and entrepreneurship at all levels. The Collaborative Design Center at Valencia College in Orlando, Florida, provides design services to regional businesses and organizations as well as internal college groups. The center staff provides skilled process design expertise, and exploratory design studios offer a setting for participants to collaborate and bring innovative solutions to light (Valencia College, n.d.). The Idea

Center at Miami Dade College serves as a hub of innovation, creativity, and entrepreneurship for students, the college, and the Miami Dade region. The center sponsors programs to advance innovation across the curriculum, provides coworking spaces for students to generate ideas and accelerate start-ups, and provides other entrepreneur-focused programming for students, businesses, and community groups (Miami Dade College, n.d.).

The Team Leader, Team Members, and Designer Partnership

A key feature of student-centered design is the involvement of a designer who is the architect or facilitator of the processes in which a cross-functional team does its work and designs solutions. The designer may be a member of the team trained for this purpose or a staff member of the design center of a community college (see previous section). The leader of a cross-functional team and the designer form a partnership that enables the team leader to focus on the opportunity or issue being addressed and the development of the team while the designer supports the leader by facilitating the problem-solving process. The designer may use *design-thinking* methods that emphasize collaboration and the iterative engagement of students and other customers solutions will be designed for. That is, there is a focus on walking in the shoes of the customers and engaging them at each step in the problem-solving process so that the ultimate solutions are tailor-made for those being served. The five basic principles of the design-thinking approach to team-centered problem-solving are as follows (Morris & Warman, 2015):

1. Empathize: By working with the end users (students, faculty, or others), the design team creates empathy. The team members immerse themselves and come to deeply understand what is needed. Empathizing with end users is a source of inspiration for designing truly responsive and effective solutions.
2. Define: Framing the problem is the foundation of the design process. With an end-user focus, design team members ask questions about whom they seek to serve, what benefits they seek to convey, and why they are addressing this particular problem.
3. Ideate (sometimes called brainstorming): The design team generates lots of ideas so the best can emerge. It encourages wild ideas, building on the suggestions of others, being visual, going for quantity, and being nonjudgmental.
4. Prototype: The design team develops a possible solution based on the ideation phase and demonstrates it to potential end users. This may involve using storyboarding or other interactive and visual means to

move an idea into a prototype. In this way, the design team and end users can think carefully about the problem, expose the flaws, invite fresh new concepts, and come up with a best solution to be tested.

5. Test: The solution is tested in a live environment. End users experience the solution, their response is observed, and adjustments are made. In this iterative, fail-fast way, designers move toward an ultimate solution.

Creating the Collaborative Enterprise

Urban community college leaders are creating collaborative enterprises that engage students, faculty, and staff, and community constituencies in problem-solving and decision-making processes. They are leading the transition from traditional vertical or hierarchical administrative structures to more horizontal and team-based structures. Among the characteristics of this collaborative enterprise, there is more emphasis on the following:

- Encouraging innovation and entrepreneurship to increase the capacity of the college to adapt to changing community and internal conditions and trends. An entrepreneurial community college has the following characteristics:
  - manages and achieves bold, holistic, and measurable large-scale change that increases student, business, and community success at a sustainable level;
  - nurtures an institutional culture of innovation, collaboration, faculty and staff empowerment and recognition, an openness to enterprise-level change, and a commitment to shared mission, values, vision, and goals;
  - supports purposeful and transformational initiatives to produce sustainable changes at scale and shapes the strategic direction of the college as a whole; and
  - implements large-scale enterprise-level changes that reinvent the student experience; respond to educational, economic, demographic, technological, and cultural changes in the college's service region; and increase the institution's creative capacity to nurture a culture attuned to student success and completion.
- Supporting cross-functional teams working on large-scale institutional change strategies that affect the future of the entire enterprise.
- Designing concepts such as design thinking—borrowing the problem-solving processes of architects and engineers and applying

them to the strategic change of the curriculum, student services, and internal processes.

- Creating value for the end user, whether it is students, businesses, communities, college faculty, or staff. Community colleges have not historically asked the customer value proposition questions, such as, How are they adding value in the lives of those they serve, and how will they measure that added value? How are they deepening their relationships with those they serve? How are they differentiating themselves from their competitors? How are they using this information to redesign programs and services?
- Promoting the college as a primary center for community talent development—opening the door to the economic mainstream for all citizens and particularly for underserved and underprepared populations.
- Being an advocate and leader for social justice: (a) enhancing educational services that empower students and citizens in general to overcome barriers to educational and economic success caused by disparities in income, educational level, and economic opportunities, and (b) addressing community equity issues such as concentrated poverty, racial isolation, mass incarceration, unemployment, lack of mobility, and inadequate education.
- Serving the public good—shaping the college as an educational resource for addressing, in partnership with other community organizations, major community and economic development opportunities and challenges.

Enterprise Examples From the Urban Field

Making the transition to a collaborative enterprise requires long-term, sustained, and persistent leadership by the CEO and his or her executive team. However, as illustrated by the following examples, such enlightened leadership has the potential to produce significant outcomes in the areas of student success and completion, responsiveness to changing community educational needs, and institutional vitality.

Los Angeles Trade-Technical College

Located downtown, the Los Angeles Trade-Technical College (LATTC) serves a population of about 15,000 students, of whom 87% are African American or Latino. LATTC formed a cross-functional team of faculty, staff, and students in 2014 to plan and implement the Pathways to Academic, Career, and Transfer Success (PACTS) initiative in cooperation with the Center for Urban Education at the University of Southern California. The designers of PACTS were determined that race consciousness and equity would be a requisite of this transformational project. LATTC President Larry Frank (2013) stated "visionary and equity-minded leadership, collaboration, and clear communications helped LATTC create a culture of student-focused change among staff at all levels" (p. 3). PACTS has resulted in changes in the way student progress is monitored, new forms of personalized counseling, changes in how faculty members teach and engage with students, new use of student data, and modified administrative roles. Faculty and staff now view their practices through the lens of racial equity. Through the PACTS initiative, LATTC developed career pathways in advanced transportation and manufacturing, applied sciences, construction, maintenance and utilities, design and media arts, health sciences, and literal arts.

Maricopa County Community College District

Maricopa County Community College District is composed of 10 colleges in the Phoenix, Arizona, region, including 5 in urban environments. It serves a diverse population with an increasing percentage of Latino students. During the past 20 years, the district has systematically integrated a commitment to equity for minority populations into its mission, vision, and strategic goals statements (Myran et al., 2013). The district undertook an all-encompassing diversity strategy, which included

- a central diversity advisory committee led by the chancellor;
- diversity coordinator at each college and at the district office; and
- community advisory groups representing each constituency, including Chicanos for Higher Education, Hoop for Learning (support for American Indians), Asian Pacific Islanders Association, Equality Maricopa (supporting lesbian, gay, bisexual, and transgender groups), the Council on Black American Affairs, VOICE (supporting people with disabilities), and the Women's Leadership Group (Myran et al., 2013).

The district launched another major initiative in 2016 to transform its business model by becoming more enterprising and focused on customized workforce education for corporate clients. An initial task force of community members and Maricopa administrators, faculty, and staff produced 42 recommendations for redesign and improvement. In addition to the primary goals of corporate partnerships and enterprise performance, the initiative will transform the student experience with an emphasis on structured or guided college and career pathways. Maricopa has formed a partnership with the

National Center for Inquiry and Improvement to work with cross-functional teams from all 10 Maricopa colleges to bring the massive initiative to scale.

Dallas County Community College District

When leaders of Dallas County Community College District evaluated the forecast that by 2030 the Dallas region would have one million illiterate adults and many jobs would be unfilled because of the lack of skilled workers (Literary Instruction for Texas, 2014), they decided to do something about it. The result was a district-wide study of the student experience led by the district chancellor, the chief strategy officer, the college presidents, and a collaborative leadership team. A large number of faculty and staff teams were trained to conduct structured conversations with students regarding all aspects of their experience at the district. Retreats were held for the governing board and leadership team. The result was the transformation of many college functions that relate to the student experience. In addition, an updated strategy was developed for preparing businesses and communities in the district's service area for success, including initiatives related to poverty and unemployment (Brumbach & Rousey, 2018).

Houston Community College

To transform the transition of public school students to Houston Community College (HCC), HCC launched Priority Student Onboarding, Admissions, and Registration to address the large percentage of junior and senior high school students who were not applying for admission to any college (Brewer & Grays, 2018). Through extensive interactions with students, parents, and school personnel conducted by trained HCC faculty and staff, many processes were streamlined, including adding an automated admissions system, parental information and consent methods, placement testing, career exploration, financial aid and Free Application for Federal Student Aid assistance, advising, and enrollment management. The eventual goal is to achieve agreements with local school districts to provide automatic admission of all high school graduates to HCC unless they opt out to seek admission to another college or university (Brewer & Grays, 2018). In 2017 HCC reported a 39% commitment to attend HCC among graduating high school seniors contacted through the program.

Wayne County Community College District

The Pathways to the Future initiative has been the innovation focus of WCCCD for the past 25 years. Led by Chancellor Curtis L. Ivery, the initiative has progressed through the following major phases:

- Pathways I, the jump-start phase (2002–2008): Immediately following the approval by district voters of a major millage increase that moved WCCCD to financial parity with other Michigan community colleges, the college's leadership embarked on a high-energy and rapid process to jump-start the transformation of programs, services, facilities, equipment, and technology. National community college leaders and local officials were invited to join a WCCCD Blue Ribbon Leadership Task Force to advise the district during this critical jump-start phase. Faculty and staff members served on the New Century Master Plan leadership team, which outlined the strategic direction of the district during this formative phase.
- Pathways II, the leading WCCCD to enduring excellence phase (2008–2015): Building on the success of Pathways I, the second phase concentrated on student success and completion and targeted the elevation of WCCCD's programs and services in ways that could endure in the years ahead. During this period, WCCCD was invited to become an Achieving the Dream partner college and was eventually selected as an Achieving the Dream leader college. Achieving the Dream is a national community college organization focusing on increasing student success rates and closing achievement gaps.
- Pathways III, the designing bold future pathways phase (2016 and into the future): The celebration of the 50th anniversary of WCCCD's founding provides a dramatic platform for launching a number of major initiatives that will shape the future of the district. Included in these initiatives are continuing efforts to increase student success and completion; positioning the district as a leader in community talent and workforce development; expanding diversity, equity, and multiracial initiatives; expanding school and university partnerships, and redesigning technology-enabled instructional processes.

An example of innovations during the current Pathways III period includes the creation of WCCCD's Regional Training Center, which has become a vital part of the Detroit talent pipeline. The center is guided by the Chancellor's Leadership Roundtable, which includes members from business, government, and labor. The center works in partnership with businesses and other community organizations to provide customized programs in areas such as health, construction trades, transportation and logistics, and information technology. A special emphasis is empowering unemployed and low-income adults to secure employment and achieve self-sufficiency.

WCCCD is also a founding member of the Academic Consortium of the American Center for Mobility (ACM). The ACM is located near Detroit on a 500-acre site and is 1 of 10 federally designated proving grounds for developing and testing autonomous vehicles. WCCCD and other members of the consortium are cooperating with the ACM to develop career programs in growing fields such as mobility and connected vehicles, cyber security, information technology, intelligent transportation, and supply-chain management. Washtenaw Community College, in Ann Arbor, Michigan, has created an advanced transportation center and has established offices at the ACM. WCCCD and Washtenaw are both working with the Michigan Economic Development Corporation in a Detroit-based spin-off called edu-mobili-D. This partnership brings the resources of the ACM and Washtenaw Community College into Detroit's urban center and provides programs in high-demand automotive and transportation career fields to WCCCD students.

Another hallmark of WCCCD is its role as an advocate and a leader of social justice. Chancellor Ivery is passionate about empowering disenfranchised and underrepresented groups to overcome barriers to college and career success such as racial and economic isolation, poverty, illiteracy, lack of access to quality education, and limited career opportunities. As a concrete expression of this advocacy for social justice, Ivery and WCCCD's Institute for Social Progress have sponsored a series of national summits on the urban crisis.

This series of urban summits, with stakeholders from the Detroit metropolitan region and around the nation, provide an excellent example of a large-scale, enterprise-wide, and cross-functional initiative sponsored by an urban community college. Each summit attracts educators, governmental officials, economists, journalists, authors, scholars, and other thought leaders who engage in dialogue leading to solutions that can be implemented in Detroit and other urban and metropolitan regions. Known as Detroit Summit III, the third event was held in June 2018 and featured the themes of integration, civic engagement, and educational equity.

Moral Leadership and Social Justice

Wangari Maathai (2004), recipient of the 2004 Nobel Peace Prize for her contribution to sustainable development, democracy, and peace, stated that "in the course of history, there comes a time when humanity is called to shift to a new level of consciousness, to reach a higher moral ground, a time when we have to shed our fear and give hope to one another" (para. 27). The commitment of an urban community college to involve a variety of stakeholders in the struggle for social justice is a commitment of the heart, a commitment to exercise moral authority and leadership. Through leaders and collaborative teams who embrace the ideals of social justice and equality, the ideals of a multiracial democracy can be achieved at the local level and well beyond. To paraphrase the words of John F. Kennedy (1961): The energy, the faith, and devotion we bring to this endeavor will light our nation and all who serve it, and the glow from that fire will truly light the lives of generations to come.

References

Adler, P., Heckscher, C., & Prusak, L. (2011). Building a collaborative enterprise. *Harvard Business Review*, 95–101.

Aspen Institute. (2018). *Announcing the 2019 Aspen Prize for Community College Excellence finalists*. Retrieved from https://www.aspeninstitute.org/blog-posts/announcing-the-2019-aspen-prize-for-community-college-excellence-finalists/

Brewer, A., & Grays, S. (2018, May). Houston Community College's P-SOAR program—streamlined onboarding. Paper presented at the meeting of the American Association of Community Colleges, Dallas, Texas.

Brumbach, M., & Rousey, D. (2018, May). Through the looking glass: Changing the focus of an entire system. Paper presented at the meeting of the American Association of Community Colleges, Dallas, Texas.

Enterprising. (2019). *Merriam-Webster's online dictionary* (11th ed.). Retrieved from https://www.merriam-webster.com/dictionary/enterprising.

Frank, L. (2013). *Pathways, partnerships, and progress: Transforming a community college*. Los Angeles: University of Southern California, Center for Urban Education.

Holcombe, E., & Kezar, A. (2017, May 10). The whys and hows of shared leadership in higher education. *Higher Education Today*. Retrieved from https://www.higheredtoday.org/2017/05/10/whys-hows-shared-leadership-higher-education/

Hu, X., & Bowman, G. (2016). Leading change: A case study of Alamo Academies—an industry-driven workforce partnership program. *Community College Journal of Research and Practice, 40*(7), 632–639.

Ivery, C. L., & Bassett, J. A. (Eds.). (2011). *America's urban crisis and the advent of colorblind politics: Education, incarceration, segregation, and the future of U.S. multiracial democracy*. Lanham, MD: Rowman & Littlefield.

Kennedy, J. F. (1961). Inaugural address. Yale Law School; Lillian Goldman Law Library. Retrieved from https://avalon.law.yale.edu/20th_century/kennedy.asp

Kingsborough Community College. (n.d.a). *KCC's ATD equity wheel: Kingsborough's Achieving the Dream Structure*. Retrieved from http://www.kbcc.cuny.edu/atd/Pages/wheel.aspx

Kingsborough Community College. (n.d.b). *Welcome to CUNY ASAP*. Retrieved from http://www1.cuny.edu/sites/asap/

Literary Instruction for Texas. (2014). *Dallas has a big word problem*. Retrieved from https://lift-texas.org/wp-content/themes/lift_/assets/btt/lift-bend-the-trend.pdf

Maathai, W. (2004). *Wangari Maathai—Nobel lecture*. Retrieved from https://www.nobelprize.org/prizes/peace/2004/maathai/26050-wangari-maathai-nobel-lecture-2004/

Miami Dade College. (n.d.). *The Idea Center at Miami Dade College*. Retrieved from https://theideacenter.co/

Morris, H., & Warman, G. (2015). *Using design thinking in higher education*. Retrieved from https://er.educause.edu/articles/2015/1/using-design-thinking-in-higher-education

Myran, G., Ivery, C. L., Parsons, M. H., & Kinsley, C. (Eds.) (2013). The future of the urban community college: Shaping the pathways to a multiracial democracy. *New Directions for Community Colleges, 162*.

National Center for Education Statistics. (2018). Summary tables for 2016–17: Public 2-year, public 4-year or above, degree-granting not primarily baccalaureate or above; and public 4-year or above, degree-granting primarily baccalaureate or above. Retrieved from https://nces.ed.gov/ipeds/use-the-data

Pierce, F. (2010). *The coming population crash and our planet's surprising future*. Boston, MA: Beacon Press.

RC-2020. (2019). *Welcome to RC-2020*. Retrieved from https://rc2020.org/about-us/

Schwarz, R. (2013). *Smart leaders, smarter teams: How you and your team get unstuck to get results*. San Francisco, CA: Jossey-Bass.

Valencia College. (n.d.). *West Campus Collaborative Design Center*. Retrieved from https://events.valenciacollege.edu/collaborative_design_center#.XRTb43dFw2x

Warren, C. (2017, November, 21). The gentrification of the urban community college. *Inside Higher Ed*. Retrieved from https://www.insidehighered.com/views/2017/11/21/community-colleges-should-stay-true-their-core-essay

9

MULTICOLLEGE
LEADERSHIP TEAMS

Shouan Pan

A ccording to the American Association of Community Colleges (AACC; American Association of Community Colleges, 2018b), there are 1,103 community colleges in the United States. In totality, they boast a rich diversity. Some are single-campus institutions, some are multicampus districts, and still others are multicollege districts. These organically evolved organizations have developed into distinctively different institutions in the way they are organized and governed, creating intriguing differences in culture, identity, leadership, and the processes of decision-making and communication. This chapter explores the unique cultural and structural characteristics of multicollege ecosystems and their implications for leadership teams.

The Evolution of Multiunit Community College Districts

All American community colleges share a common commitment to the mission of providing open-access educational and training programs, but they differ in how they are organized to fulfill that mission. Because America's communities are diverse, the colleges established to serve them become equally distinctive as they grow and change. Gerald (2004) observed that every community college is unique, and no one is quite like another.

Ratcliff (1994) suggested one perspective for the emergence of two-year colleges at the turn of the past century: They were small single-campus colleges focused on a liberal arts education with the goal of transferring students to four-year colleges. Later, during the 1920s and 1930s, the mission shifted to developing a skilled workforce. The post–World War II GI Bill (Servicemen's

Readjustment Act, 1944) and the report by President's Commission on Higher Education (1947) spurred a further expansion in the mission of two-year colleges. The enrollment of veterans, baby boomers, minority, and women students between the 1950s and the 1970s caused the national network of community colleges to explode almost overnight. As a result, new colleges mushroomed across the landscape of America.

To respond to the ever-increasing local demand, many single-campus colleges began to expand their service areas by adding branch campuses at locations convenient to students and responsive to community needs (Jensen, 1984). Rather than opening brand new colleges, it was much easier to gain community and legislative support for creating additional campuses. For single-campus colleges, opening additional centers and off-campus sites was an effective and economical way of taking education to the people and increasing revenue at the same time. Clearly, the emergence of multiunit community colleges not only reflects the innovative and pioneering spirit of the American community college movement but also demonstrates the community college's commitment to social unity, mobility, and equity from the very beginning.

Although most public two-year colleges in the nation are single-college districts, roughly one-third of them are part of multicampus or multicollege institutions (Katsinas & Hardy, 2004). Many of these districts started from humble, makeshift locations in local high schools, churches, or repurposed buildings and eventually grew into large comprehensive institutions serving tens of thousands of students. Kintzer, Jensen, and Hansen (1969) described the creation of multi-institutional systems as a way to "maintain quality with diversity, individualization in spite of numbers, and close community identity within an expanding administrative structure" (p. 1).

Jones (1968) conducted one of the early studies of multiunit junior colleges. In his research, he identified the following levels of developmental sequences: (a) the one college branch model, (b) the one college multicampus model, (c) the multicampus district model, and (d) the multicollege district model. He concluded that the evolution of the multiunit community colleges by and large followed these four developmental stages, starting from a small, very centralized one-college model to a more autonomous, decentralized multicollege model.

According to Jones (1968), the one college branch model at the first stage came about when a college branched out with an off-campus site. Later, as the branch site grew, it expanded to function as a separate but identical campus, the second stage that he called the one college multicampus model. As the new campus matured and grew in student size, programs, and budget, it became more autonomous and independent, requiring separate administrative oversight. At this third stage, two or more full-fledged campuses formed a district with a strong central office granting a minimum amount of local authority to the campuses. Each of these campuses would have its own leadership team. Jones called this the multicampus district model. At the final stage, multicollege districts emerged in metropolitan cities or counties with large territories. Two or more constituent colleges with their own budgets, leadership teams, and set of degree programs became fully operational. They were coordinated by a central district leadership team but loosely connected to each other.

Today, some 50 years later, multi-institution community colleges have not only survived but matured in their size and sophistication. Across the country, many prominent community colleges are part of multicampus or multicollege districts. Together, they share similarities and dissimilarities in important ways. They are similar in that both types of districts have two or more campuses that are overseen by a central district administration, and they share a single board of trustees. They are different in the organization of accreditation, the degree of autonomy, and institutional identity.

In a multicampus district, the campuses are generally accredited as one body by the same accreditation agency. The campuses enjoy a minimal to moderate degree of autonomy, and, as a result, the district shares a clear collective identity. Miami Dade College, Valencia College, Portland Community College, St. Louis Community College, Houston Community College, and Pima Community College are all well-known multicampus districts. All the campuses in these districts, however many there are, share one single accreditation and a degree of autonomy that is far from being independent.

By comparison, the case is very different in multicollege districts like Maricopa County Community Colleges, Dallas County Community Colleges, City Colleges of Chicago, Seattle Colleges, and Contra Costa Community College Districts. Each college in these districts is separately accredited and offers academic programs designed to meet the needs of students and communities according to state laws and governing board policies. In addition, each has a comprehensive leadership team. As a result, individual colleges enjoy a great deal of operational autonomy and identities that often overshadow the district's fuzzy system identity. Kintzer et al. (1969) described the multicampus district as being synonymous with minimum local authority and the multicollege district as being synonymous with maximum local autonomy.

The Interplay Between Organizational Culture and Structure

American community colleges were conceived as mission-driven institutions. The organizational structure—how leadership roles, authority, and responsibilities are assigned, controlled, and coordinated; how decisions are made;

and how information flows through the organization—should be considered first and foremost with its mission in mind. Drucker (1954) observed that

> the starting point of any analysis of organization cannot be a discussion of structure. It must be the analysis of the business. The first question in discussing organization structure must be: what is our business and what should it be? Organization structure must be designed so as to make possible the attainment of the objectives of the business for five, ten, fifteen years hence. (p. 190)

However, the evolutionary paths of how community college districts progressed from a center to a branch campus to a multicampus or a multicollege district suggest that many other factors may have influenced their organizational structure. The stories may be different from one district to another, but researchers (Chang, 1978; Eddy, 2006; Gerald, 2004; Kintzer et al., 1969) found that external and internal factors had a role in shaping the organizational structure of community colleges, particularly the formation of multicampus and multicollege districts. As mentioned earlier, the external factors include local demographic trends, burgeoning enrollment, availability of land, ability to finance, community and legislative support, and workforce demands.

Internal factors, however, are far more complex and deserve special consideration. As with all organizations, community colleges require an organizational structure to carry out teaching and learning, provide leadership and management oversight, and allocate resources. Like other organizations, most community colleges have been organized according to tradition, with management structures at the opposite end of a continuum: the mechanistic, or the hierarchical structure, and the more organic, or networked structure (Burns & Stalker, 1961). The former approach is marked by precise and formal delineations of functions, whereas the latter has fluid and flexible functions and interactions. Like other organizations that face changing expectations, community colleges strive to constantly evolve and innovate. However, more than corporations, community colleges must also contend with robust influences of institutional culture because they are tradition-bound and culture-bound organizations. Academic departments, campuses, or colleges live and breathe culture. *Culture* may be elusive and hard to define, but it is palpable, compelling, and enduring.

Many cultural elements exert influences on the organizational structure and leadership processes in the academy. Two elements, in particular, create significant challenges for community college leaders. The first, from the culture of traditions, is that every college across the country has a set of traditions that dictates how things customarily get done. A new idea must be introduced ever so carefully and gradually, otherwise it is seen as a challenge to long-held beliefs and values. Seymour and Bourgeois (2018) described American colleges and universities as comfort-driven institutions where "we cherish our traditions, our specialness, our shared governance, and our past successes" (p. 99). Constant attention to honoring academic traditions explains why change moves at a glacial speed at colleges and universities.

The second element originates in the culture of independence and autonomy. From the very beginning, colleges and universities were organized along the lines of academic disciplines. Academic specialization and disciplinary boundaries serve to define a differentiated organizational structure: program clusters, departments, divisions, and colleges. The work activities of faculty and staff mostly are carried out in their disciplinary-based units, and there are minimal interactions with colleagues outside their units. Over time, all these units become "isolated pigeonholes with their own subcultures and pockets of power and influence" (Seymour & Bourgeois, 2018, p. 100).

Culture shapes organizational structure, and structure reinforces culture. The quick expansion in the number of multi-institutional districts was possible because they responded to new community demands, but also because the differentiated organizational structure was agreeable with the established culture of the academy. The multicollege districts are fundamentally federated systems in which individual campuses or colleges behave independently of each other. The relationship between the central administration and the campuses or colleges seems to be hierarchical in theory but coordinational in practice. Weick (1976) describes American educational institutions as loosely coupled systems where highly controlled relationships do not exist; constituent units, leadership teams, and employees enjoy a great deal of autonomy. On the one hand, such systems allow easy adaptability to local conditions but, on the other hand, prevent standardization. Consequently, systemwide, large-scale changes are hard to realize; effective and innovative practices are difficult to implement throughout the organization (Meyer, 1975). The we-they thinking and the sibling rivalries have been protracted challenges in community colleges and in multi-institutional districts in particular.

Compared to the case in a multicampus district, the coupling is much looser in a multicollege district, where a district chancellor serves as the chief executive officer (CEO). He or she supervises two or more college presidents assigned to serve as CEOs of the colleges. However, because these colleges are scattered across different parts of a large county or city, each college is more connected to the local community than to the central office. Over time, each college develops its own look and feel and a unique personality. Moreover, colleges in a multicollege district are separately accredited, which is often cited as the legitimate reason to question or resist a decision or a change initiated by the central office. Unfortunately, such an overemphasis on differentiated identity often marginalizes the most important focus on students.

Sometimes students find it difficult to register for courses at another college in the same district because the colleges have different academic requirements or use different registration procedures. Concerns like this likely prompted two governing boards to change the initial multicollege structure to a multicampus structure. For example, the St. Louis Community College District was once a multicollege district made up of the Florissant Valley Community College in Ferguson, Forest Park Community College in St. Louis, and Meramec Community College in Kirkwood. In 1976 the board of trustees authorized renaming the three colleges in a different format: St. Louis Community College–Florissant Valley, St. Louis Community College–Meramec, and St. Louis Community College–South County. According to Henry Shannon, former district chancellor, the move was taken to clarify that the three campuses were part of the same system (H. Shannon, personal communication, July 26, 2018).

A more comprehensive reorganization occurred at the Community College of Baltimore County. The district started with Catonsville Community College and Essex Community College in 1957. Dundalk Community College was added later. In 2005 the district board of trustees hired a new chancellor who had a different vision for the multicollege system. After a year-long assessment, the new chancellor convinced the board to demote the title from chancellor to president and redistribute the work of nine top-level administrators among four vice presidents. In addition, the three college president positions were eliminated and replaced with three midlevel campus administrators who report to a vice president. By flattening the administrative structure, the redesigned college was positioned as a much leaner but more cohesive institution to serve its students and communities (McMenamin, 2006).

It is clear that the culture of traditions, independence, and autonomy, reinforced by a dispersed, loosely coupled structure, makes multicollege districts an unconventional organization with a unique set of dynamics. They tend to be large, reputable systems, but at the same time they can become complex, fragmented, and incohesive. They may be well established, however, their organizational culture and structure have hidden costs.

The Risks of Fragmented Systems

Researchers have been studying the implications of loosely coupled systems laden with traditions. For example, the intention of the George W. Bush administration's No Child Left Behind Act of 2001 was to improve the academic achievement of all students and to close the gap between high- and low-performing groups. Linn, Baker, and Betebenner (2002) noted that because the quality and rigor of assessments of student performance varied significantly from state to state, a meaningful comparison nationally was not possible. Another example is offered by Bailey, Jaggars, and Jenkins (2015). Despite an intense nationwide focus, support by the Obama administration and major foundations, and tremendous institutional efforts, Bailey and colleagues concluded that the completion agenda stalled. Distilling a wealth of data, they urged community college leaders and faculty to reject the traditional model in favor of integration of services and instruction, a model called guided pathways. Christine McPhail (2016), a nationally recognized consultant and scholar on higher education, also warned that continued use of the rigid traditional hierarchical management structure would significantly restrict community colleges from facilitating a fast-moving and effective student success agenda. According to Rittling (2016), "Community college leaders are recognizing that isolated efforts—no matter how well-intentioned—will fail to comprehensively alter the institutional culture if not designed to move to scale from their inception" (para. 3).

More than at any other time, community colleges are juggling the high expectations of taxpayers and elected officials. Colleges are expected to serve and graduate more diverse students with much higher success rates, using more technological tools but with diminishing resources. Doing more with less is the new normal. Ready or not, every community college leadership team is expected to lead and manage in a high-velocity environment. Multicollege leadership teams are especially challenged to rally all employee groups to answer the clarion call of dramatically improving student success rates through well-designed and coherent programs and processes at institutions that have often operated with unaligned policies and practices, disjointed strategies, and fragmented programs. Institutional leaders must be ready to confront unique challenges inherent in a multicollege environment: promoting a unified mission, communicating a consistent message, honoring individual college traditions while strengthening system effectiveness, and streamlining academic and support services programs for students across college boundaries.

Confronting this reality requires a paradigm shift, a change in nothing less than foundational and fundamental assumptions and leadership approaches. As confidence in higher education diminishes, and resources continue to decline, the stakes are high for colleges, and the urgency is real. Although this is a challenge for any college, it is especially difficult for multicollege leadership teams, which must now bring more unity and purposeful focus to multiple institutions operating in a single district.

Community College Leadership Competencies for the New Environment

Fortunately, this leadership work does not have to start from scratch. Much research on organizational development and community college leadership, including the competencies needed by college presidents in organizational and change management, is available to guide this work. The abundant literature is applicable to multicampus and multicollege leadership teams as well as single colleges because leadership principles and leadership competencies are distilled and refined from field-based research with particular consideration of the diverse factors that affect leadership preparation, including different leadership contexts (American Association of Community Colleges, 2005, 2018; Amey & VanDerLinden, 2002; Aspen Institute, 2014; Boggs, 2003; Eddy, 2012; McFarlin, Crittenden, & Ebbers, 1999). Studies that focused on midlevel community college administrators also provide significant value to community college leadership teams (Garza Mitchell & Eddy, 2008; Rosser, 2000; Wallin, 2010).

Between 2003 and 2005, the American Association of Community Colleges' Board of Directors authorized a national study of core leadership skills for twenty-first-century community college leaders. The final report, based on a survey of 95 community college presidents, cited 6 essential leadership competencies, including organizational strategy, resource management, communication, collaboration, community college advocacy, and professionalism (American Association of Community Colleges, 2005). In subsequent years, the board updated the competencies several times. The 2018 edition of the leadership competencies distinguished among those for emergent leaders, those for first-time new presidents, and those for veteran CEOs (American Association of Community Colleges, 2018a).

Similarly, the Aspen Institute and Achieving the Dream (2013) joined forces in studying the looming leadership crisis for community college presidents. Their final report identified five qualities that are common to the most effective community college presidents, regardless of the their context: deep commitment to student access and success; willingness to take significant risks to advance student success; ability to create lasting change within the college; strong, broad, strategic vision for the college and its students, reflected in external partnerships; and capacity to raise and allocate resources in ways aligned to student success. In addition to the leadership skill sets and qualities identified by the AACC (American Association of Community Colleges, 2018a) Achieving the Dream joined with the Aspen Institute to issue a report on competencies that offer multicampus and multicollege leadership teams extremely valuable guides for leadership enhancement (Aspen Institute and Achieving the Dream, 2013).

In today's fast-changing community college environment, effective and visionary leadership matters more than at any time before. To move from a model of loose coupling and segmentation to a model of integration and cohesion, multicollege districts must develop over time cohesive, strong, and high-functioning leadership teams adept at getting separate parts of an organization to work in synergy. Because differentiation tends to be the default mode of operation in multicollege systems, it is particularly important for leadership teams to overcome the old tendency and to learn, adopt, and model new behaviors of working in unison.

Recommendations for High-Performing Multicollege Leadership Teams

Based on comprehensive research and interviews with several highly experienced CEOs of large multicollege districts across the country, I offer several ideas on organizational realignment and cultural renewal for multicollege leadership teams.

Keep the End in Mind

First, multicollege leadership teams must lead and manage with the end in mind. In his popular book, Covey (2003) described seven daily practices for managing one's personal and professional life. Habit 2 is to "begin with the end in mind" (p. 41). It means starting an initiative with a clear idea of the desired goal. This powerful concept is relevant for leadership, sports competition, sales, entrepreneurship, or personal development. Applied to multicollege leadership teams, it means using student success, for example, as the ultimate goal to define, articulate, and focus institutional energy and resources. It encourages beginning each day, each task, and each project with the clear vision of significantly improving the student success rate as the "desired direction and destination, and then continue by flexing your powerful muscles to make things happen" (Covey, 2003, p. 42). Putting student success front and center serves to unify factions and motivate faculty and administrators to transcend internal differences and disagreements that matter little to the best interests of students.

In the complex multicollege enterprise, members of leadership teams can easily become preoccupied with the day-to-day administrative routines that leave little time for asking and answering the questions that are the most critical to system effectiveness. Leading with the end in mind focuses leadership teams and frames strategic and operational discussions across the entire system. It prompts the teams to ask fundamental questions, such as "Why do the colleges exist?" and "Who are the most important people to serve?" Joe May, chancellor of the Dallas County Community College District, said that he and his leadership team spend considerable time asking and answering the question, "Why does it matter?" By focusing on why, his leadership team finds it easier to decide on what. In addition, the chancellor revealed that this leadership approach has helped his team reach consensus on many difficult and controversial decisions (J. May, personal communication, May 16, 2018).

Model Systems Thinking and Behavior

Second, multicollege leadership teams must encourage and model *systems thinking* as defined by Senge (1990): "It is a framework for seeing interrelationships rather than things, for seeing patterns of change rather than static snapshots. Today, systems thinking is needed more than ever because college leaders are becoming overwhelmed by complexity" (p. 59).

The administrative structures of a multicollege district are organized with a sequential or binary logic that reduces a teaching and learning organization into departments, divisions, and colleges. Further, this model assumes that if the goals and objectives of these separate subunits are attended to, and if problems are solved at the subunit level, then the overall mission of the entire district will be achieved.

Although there may be localized successes in the past under this binary model, it is clearly not conducive to achieving systemwide, large-scale change or innovation. On the contrary, many problems stem from this linear thinking. For example, we see confused students falling through the cracks when colleges in a multicollege district use different placement tests or course prerequisites; we hear business partners express frustrations with a multicollege district because they have to jump through different hoops and deal with several people while trying to arrange training programs; and we often discover that a creative solution or innovative program is only available at one of the colleges in a given district because the colleges are in competition for students, resources, and influence and don't readily share any of them.

A multicollege institution, regardless of its size, exists to facilitate student learning. A system that has evolved for administrative convenience or the interest of a particular employee group impedes student learning. Students and community partners have difficulties connecting the dots when the programs and services are unaligned and disjointed. For their sake, multicollege leadership teams must promote *systems thinking* that transcends institutional silos and disciplinary boundaries. Rather than seeing a multicollege district as a set of sister colleges or a collection of programs or courses, the colleges that make up the district and the departments and programs that make up the colleges should be considered a coherent and interrelated system of learning.

In multicollege districts, it is challenging for presidents, vice presidents, deans, and department chairs to practice systems thinking. To many subunit leaders, it may feel unnatural or counterintuitive to promote systems thinking because they are conditioned to champion the interest of their subunits. For this reason, developing a habit of systems thinking in a multicollege system requires intentionality and discipline. Members of a multicollege leadership team, whether senior or midlevel, must learn to adopt generative and expansive thinking rather than reductive and linear thinking.

In addition to providing leadership and management oversight for their colleges and advocating for their institution's needs, college presidents, vice presidents, and department chairs can and should lead across departmental, divisional, and institutional boundaries and embrace their responsibilities for advancing the effectiveness of the whole system. In other words, multicollege leaders will need to exercise a new set of skills: the ability to facilitate effective interactions among interdependent system components; the ability to work simultaneously toward achieving proximal subunit goals and distal system goals; and the ability to use talents, resources, and commitment across the system. Rufus Glasper, the former chancellor of Maricopa Colleges, was deliberate in coaching his 10 college presidents to balance their leadership responsibilities between the entire system and their assigned college. These dual leadership focuses were clearly established as an important performance goal for all 10 presidents. During the annual performance review, college presidents were expected to report on not only accomplishments of their individual colleges but also their leadership contributions to systemwide goals (R. Glasper, personal communication, May 22, 2018).

Practice Integral Leadership

Third, the multicollege leadership teams must learn and practice integral leadership. Integral leaders have cultivated the skill of analyzing and responding to situations from a broad and deep institutional perspective, informed by but not stifled by the past and based on institutional values. It means looking beyond one's unit and embracing comprehensive and sustainable solutions that advance the system's values and goals. Because leaders set the tone, shape the culture, and influence behavior in organizations, deep transformative changes in multicollege districts are possible only if the leaders model the change they want to see. By leading with student success as the end goal and by adopting a systems perspective, members of multicollege leadership teams can provide a new kind of leadership: integral leadership.

Anderson and Adams (2015) described five stages of leadership: egocentric, reactive, creative, integral, and unitive. At the fourth level of leadership development, integral leaders are able to lead amid ambiguity and complexity. They are systemically and community oriented, and their vision is expansive and inclusive of the welfare and effectiveness of the whole system. Recognizing that leadership on all campuses is "nested via the organizational hierarchy" (Eddy, 2006, p. 13), integral leaders become servant leaders for the whole.

The Association of Governing Boards of Universities and Colleges (2006) convened the Task Force on the State of the Presidency in American Higher Education. After completing a year-long study of the contemporary presidency, the task force identified a series of new demands and expectations of college presidents. As a result, the task force urged presidents and governing boards to embrace integral leadership in which the president "exerts a presence that is purposeful and consultative, deliberative yet decisive, and capable of course corrections as new challenges emerge" (p. vii). The task force concluded,

> Leadership of this sort links the president, the faculty, and board together in a well-functioning partnership purposefully devoted to a well-defined, broadly affirmed institutional vision. Such leadership successfully engages the faculty, student leaders, and key external stakeholders in achieving collectively what no single individual or unit can accomplish individually. (p. vii)

Constance Carroll, the long-time chancellor of the San Diego Community College District, best exemplifies integral leadership in her work. As the CEO of the district, she sees herself as a convener, enabler, and developer of an organic leadership team. She uses every opportunity to reinforce shared leadership responsibilities (C. Carroll, personal communication, June 5, 2018). Similarly, Judy Miner, chancellor of the Foothill De Anza Community College District, devotes a great deal of energy to finding resources and removing obstacles for her college presidents. Together she and her executive leadership team invest time in joint decision-making. She believes that by being servant leaders, CEOs can "unleash energy and creativity" of their whole leadership team (J. Miner, personal communication, May 25, 2018).

Enrich Cross-System Communications

Fourth, the multicollege leadership team must work hard at enriching cross-system communications because communication is important to the success of any organization. Developing enriched processes and channels of communication is even more critical to multicollege leadership teams as they endeavor to effect cultural change and organizational renewal.

Paradoxically, however, effective communication is more difficult to achieve in a multicollege environment because communication in this system goes through not only complicated and siloed networks of internal and external constituents but also multiple layers of hierarchies. The multicollege leadership team members need to develop the ability to communicate urgency, build consensus, negotiate a settlement, and motivate actions.

Weick (1982) insisted that the CEO of a loosely coupled organization is chiefly responsible for using multiple tools of communication to articulate those linkages that bind the organization:

> The chief responsibility of an administrator in such a system is to reaffirm and solidify those ties that exist. This can be done by a combination of symbol management, selective centralization, consistent articulation of a common vision, interpretation of diverse actions in terms of common themes, and by the provision of common language in terms of which people can explain their actions in a meaningful way and communicate with one another in similar terms. (p. 676)

In multicollege districts, leadership is nestled among organizational layers; decisions and messages from the governing board and the system chancellor are frequently filtered by the individual college culture (Eddy, 2006). The leadership teams must be aware of and work hard at minimizing conflicting messages. College presidents play a particularly important role in helping their college community embrace change initiatives. How they react to and frame the change affects acceptance by the college community and, ultimately, the outcome of the change. For this reason, the chancellor and college presidents must first work through their differences, if any, before presidents relay their message to their college campuses.

Another critical communication linkage rests with the midlevel managers in the multicollege leadership team. Because of their contact with the faculty and staff on the front line, vice presidents, deans, and executive directors often have a deeper understanding of the cultural realities and political dynamics on college campuses than the executive leadership does. For this reason, they are in a unique position to serve as interpreters and connectors in the communication loop. It behooves the executive leaders of multicollege districts to invest in the leadership development of mid-level managers and be intentional in involving them in major strategic and operational decisions.

Balance Differentiation and Integration

Fifth, the multicollege leadership teams must strive to achieve a satisfactory balance between differentiation and integration. In the complex environments of multicollege districts, there are many structural, cultural, discipline-based, and task-oriented differences that set apart each of the subsystems such as the departments, programs, campuses, and colleges. These differences have always been and will likely always be part of multicollege systems. They help define the identities of each of the subsystems, build internal coherence and team pride, serve institutional functions, and ultimately help achieve their goals and objectives. In other words, the differentiation in multicollege environments serves vital purposes.

In reality, as the environments of multicollege districts become more complex, the pressure and the need for differentiation increases, such as adding specialized functions or responding to new external requirements. Paradoxically, however, as subsystems in the overall multicollege systems become more differentiated, the pressure and the need for integration also increases for reasons of efficiency, effectiveness, and systemwide consistency (Lawrence & Lorsch, 1967). Multicollege leadership teams must learn to work with two antagonistic tendencies and strive to achieve a satisfactory balance between differentiation and integration.

Multicollege executive leadership teams are generally composed of the district chancellor, college presidents, and other senior administrators who make decisions that affect all subsystems across the district. The chancellor and the central leadership team must be service oriented, responsive, and able to make timely and consistent decisions that enable the best teaching and learning on college campuses. Focusing on gatekeeping or controlling along hierarchical lines stifles creative solutions to local issues, encourages distrust, and forces tunnel vision. Balancing responsive support and necessary system control is a difficult but important task that must be well managed by the central office leadership; the CEO of a multicollege district will be well advised to manage the leadership team dynamics very carefully and invest in building team trust and cohesion.

During his tenure as chancellor of Maricopa Community Colleges, Glasper involved his college presidents and vice chancellors in a carefully coordinated review of Kouzes and Posner (2012). During his chancellor's executive council meetings, college presidents were assigned to team up with vice chancellors in leading discussions on different chapters of the book. More than casual readings by a book club, members of this multicollege leadership team engaged in very substantive and purposeful discussions. The activities helped to strengthen connections, appreciation, and trust among the team members (R. Glasper, personal communication, May 22, 2018).

In addition to the critical role played by system chancellors in balancing the push-and-pull for differentiation and integration, other members of the leadership teams have much to contribute as well. In fact, the more leadership provided by college presidents and midlevel administrators toward system integration, the more solid and long-lasting the balance will be (Eddy, 2006).

To cultivate such contributions, the multicollege leadership teams should be intentional in practicing participative decision-making. Shared governance teams and the network of districtwide committees made up of members of the colleges and central district offices will provide the platforms and opportunities for sound decision-making that is informed by diverse viewpoints and perspectives. Controversial decisions, when made jointly by college and district office personnel, that result in budget cuts, reduction in forces, or structural change will help strengthen rather than weaken cross-system unity, thereby reinforcing system integration.

American community colleges are complex and dynamic institutions. Across the nation, they have been widely applauded for broadening access to higher education, providing essential pathways to the middle class, and supporting local communities' economic development. However, there is no lack of criticism of community colleges, especially on the average rates of graduation and transfer to four-year institutions. The public and legislative pressure for greater accountability continues to mount. Facing these realities, more and more community college administrators have come to realize that some of their institutional culture, structure, and practices may serve to impede urgent, necessary changes. Multicollege or multicampus systems must be aware of the real and potential weaknesses and the liabilities of an overly differentiated organizational structure and be intentional in capitalizing on their strengths as integrated systems to best serve students in this new environment. Achieving a lasting transformation in these complex environments requires a reinforcing loop of understanding system strengths and limits, realigning structures, and building new models that serve to achieve systemwide integration without limiting necessary college-based specialization (Lawrence & Lorsch, 1967; Seymour & Bourgeois, 2018).

As community colleges across the country endeavor to dramatically increase student readiness and student completion, multicollege leaders must take on the urgent work of cultural transformation and organizational realignment to optimize student learning and community impact. By focusing on student success, adopting systems thinking, practicing integral leadership, enriching cross-boundary communication, and balancing differentiation and integration, multicollege leadership teams can help their colleges live up to public expectations and ultimately deliver the promise of America's community colleges.

References

American Association of Community Colleges. (2005). *Competencies for community college leaders*. Washington, DC: Author.

American Association of Community Colleges. (2018a). *AACC competencies for community college leaders* (2nd ed.). Washington, DC: Author.

American Association of Community Colleges. (2018b). *Fast facts 2018*. Retrieved from https://www.aacc.nche.edu/research-trends/fast-facts/2018-fast-facts/

Amey, M., & VanDerLinden, K. E. (2002). *Career paths for community colleges leaders* (Research Brief Leadership Series, No. 2, AACC-RB-02-2). Washington, DC: American Association of Community Colleges.

Anderson, R. J., & Adams, W. A. (2015). *Mastering leadership: An integrated framework for breakthrough performance and extraordinary business results*. Hoboken, NJ: Wiley.

Aspen Institute. (2014). *Hiring exceptional community college presidents: Tools for hiring leaders who advance student access and success*. Washington, DC: Author.

Aspen Institute and Achieving the Dream. (2013). *Crisis and opportunity: Aligning the community college residency with student success*. Retrieved from https://www.aspeninstitute.org/publications/crisis-opportunity-aligning-community-college-presidency-student-success/

Association of Governing Boards of Universities and Colleges. (2006). *The leadership imperative: The report of the AGB task force on the state of the residency in American higher education*. Washington, DC: Author.

Bailey, T., Jaggars, S. S., & Jenkins, D. (2015). *Redesigning America's community colleges: A clearer path for student success*. Cambridge, MA: Harvard University Press.

Boggs, G. R. (2003). Leadership context for the twenty-first century. *New Directions for Community Colleges, 2003*(123), 15–25.

Burns, T. E., & Stalker, G. M. (1961). *The management of innovation*. Abstract. Retrieved from https://ssrn.com/abstract=1496187

Chang, N. K. (1978). *Organizational structure in multi-campus community junior colleges/districts*. Retrieved from ERIC database. (ED158795)

Covey, S. R. (2003). *The 7 habits of highly effective people personal workbook*. New York, NY: Touchstone.

Drucker, P. F. (1954). *The practice of management*. New York, NY: Harper & Row.

Eddy, P. L. (2006). Nested leadership: The interpretation of organizational change in a multi-college system. *Community College Journal of Research and Practice, 30*(1), 41–51.

Eddy, P. L. (2012). A holistic perspective of leadership competencies. *New Directions for Community Colleges, 2012*(159), 29–39.

Garza Mitchell, R. L., & Eddy, P. L. (2008). In the middle: Career pathways of midlevel community college leaders. *Community College Journal of Research and Practice, 32*(10), 793–811.

Gerald, G. (2004). *Perspectives of leadership competencies by multi-campus community college leaders* (Doctoral dissertation). Retrieved from https://sdsu-dspace.calstate.edu/bitstream/handle/10211.3/123824/GERALD_sdsu_0220D_10427.pdf?sequence=1

Jensen, A. M. (1984). *Multi-campuses—Twenty years later*. Retrieved from ERIC database. (ED256413)

Jones, M. (1968). *The development of multi-unit junior colleges*. Retrieved from ERIC database. (ED023391)

Katsinas, S. G., & Hardy, D. E. (2004). *Publicly controlled two-year institutions in the United States*. Denton, TX: University of North Texas.

Kintzer, F. C., Jensen, A. M., & Hansen, J. S. (1969). *The multi-institution junior college district*. Retrieved from database. (ED030415)

Kouzes, J. M., & Posner, B. Z. (2012). *The leadership challenge* (5th ed.). San Francisco, CA: Jossey-Bass.

Lawrence, P. R., & Lorsch, J. W. (1967). Differentiation and integration in complex organizations. *Administrative Science Quarterly, 12*(1), 1–47.

Linn, R. L., Baker, E. L., & Betebenner, D. W. (2002, June). *Accountability systems: Implications of requirements of the No Child Left Behind Act of 2001* (CSE Technical Report 567). Los Angeles: University of California.

McFarlin, C. H., Crittenden, B. J., & Ebbers, L. H. (1999). Background factors common among outstanding community college presidents. *Community College Review, 27*(3), 19–32.

McMenamin, J. (2006, November 11). New CCBC president is formally installed. *Baltimore Sun*. Retrieved from http://articles.baltimoresun.com/2006-11-11/news/0611110304_1_administrative-staff-chancellor-community-colleges

McPhail, C. J. (2016, September 22). From tall to matrix: Redefining organizational structures. *Change: The Magazine of Higher Learning, 48*(4), 55–62.

Meyer, J. (1975). *Notes on the structure of educational organizations*. Retrieved from ERIC database. (ED109768)

No Child Left Behind Act of 2001. (2002). Pub. L. 107-110.

President's Commission on Higher Education. (1947). *Higher education for American democracy: A report of the President's Commission on Higher Education.* Washington, DC: U.S. Government Printing Office.

Ratcliff, J. L. (1994). Seven streams in the historical development of the modern American community college. In G. Baker III (Ed.), *A Handbook of the Community College in America* (pp. 3–16). Westport, CT: Greenwood.

Rittling, M. (2016, February 26). Pathways in name only. *Inside Higher Education.* Retrieved from https://www.insidehighered.com/views/2016/02/26/essay-how-use-promising-student-success-strategies-comprehensive-cohesive-way

Rosser, V. J. (2000). Midlevel administrators: What we know. In L. K. Johnsrud & V. J. Rosser (Eds.), *Understanding the work and career paths of midlevel administrators* (pp. 5–13). San Francisco, CA: Jossey-Bass.

Senge, P. M. (1990). *The fifth discipline: The art and practice of the learning organization.* New York, NY: Doubleday.

Servicemen's Readjustment Act. (1944). Pub. L. 346, 78th Congress.

Seymour, D., & Bourgeois, M. (2018). *Institutional effectiveness fieldbook.* Santa Barbara, CA: Olive Press.

Wallin, D. L. (2010). Looking to the future: Change leaders for tomorrow's community colleges. *New Directions for Community Colleges, 2010*(149), 5–12.

Weick, K. E. (1976). Educational organizations as loosely coupled systems. *Administrative Science Quarterly, 21*(1), 1–19.

Weick, K. E. (1982). Administering education in loosely couple schools. *Phi Delta Kappa,* 673–676.

CREATING AND MAINTAINING THE CHIEF EXECUTIVE OFFICER AND GOVERNING BOARD TEAM

Bill McGinnis, Samia Yaqub, and George R. Boggs

Perhaps the most important team for any college is the team of trustees who are elected or appointed to govern the institution and the chief executive officer (CEO) chosen by the board to lead it. How trustees of a college relate to each other and to the CEO and how the CEO relates to the trustees is of great consequence. If those relationships are positive, they set the stage for successful governance and leadership; if they are negative, the college can suffer, and the CEO's efficiency can be hampered (Boggs, 2006).

The CEO-board team regularly deals with the most significant and sometimes difficult issues faced by a college, especially in today's environment of increased accountability. But the team also is called on to deal with the unexpected. For example, in November 2018 at Butte College, the Camp Fire, the deadliest and most destructive wildfire in California history, surrounded the campus and raged across the county (CAL FIRE, 2019). It became clear that the college would need to remain closed for an extended period of time. Many students, faculty, and staff were evacuated and lost their homes and possessions. The situation changed on an hourly basis.

During times such as these, the relationship between a CEO and the board can be put to a test. Crises create fluid and dynamic situations where decisions need to be made quickly, often without complete information. Should a college be closed and for how long? Should a college accept the request by local officials to become an evacuation center? What if doing so infringes on its ability to continue instruction? The CEO needs to be aware of the delineation between his or her authority and that of the board. District policies should outline which decisions can be made at the operational level and which require board approval. For decisions that require board action, the CEO may need to call an emergency meeting to get approval in a timely manner. Most important, increased communication is necessary so that all parties are kept in the loop during a rapidly changing situation. If there is an established relationship of trust between the CEO and the board, then the CEO can quickly make the decisions within his or her authority while keeping the board informed.

Establishing a trusting relationship in the CEO-board team takes time and effort. The team members must know their roles, and communication lines must be well established. All too often, the CEO-board team becomes dysfunctional. According to a survey of California community college presidents, the primary reason CEOs leave their jobs is because of problems with the board-CEO relationship (Cooper, 2016). This chapter starts at the beginning of the CEO-board relationship and outlines the steps a board and CEO can take to ensure a strong and productive team relationship that will foster a climate of success where their institutions can flourish. It also describes pitfalls to avoid and strategies to ensure long-term success.

A *CEO* in this chapter is defined as the top officer who is appointed by and reports to the board of trustees of a community college district. The title could be president of a college, superintendent or president of a single-college district, or chancellor of a multicollege district. The board is composed of the elected or appointed group of trustees responsible for the governance of a community college district, including the appointment of and support for a CEO. The remainder of this chapter describes the steps that are essential for developing and maintaining a strong CEO-board team.

Step 1: Determine Fit in the Selection Process

One of a board's most important responsibilities is selecting the right CEO for its community college or district. Colleges need different types of leaders at different points in their evolution. A visionary change agent may be needed to move forward an institution that is stuck in some way. Or, a leader skilled in transparency and open communication may be needed to build trust on a divided campus. When applying for a presidential position, candidates must be as concerned about fit as the search committee and the board. Too many new presidents have been surprised by financial problems, pending litigation, personnel problems, labor strife, or political issues. If problems must be addressed, does the candidate feel that he or she has the experience and ability to deal with them, and will the board support the president in tackling those difficult issues (Boggs, 2017)?

All too often the board relegates most of the responsibility for recruiting and selecting a CEO to a search committee or an outside search consultant. If a board is unavailable until the final interview, assuming the college will attract the right candidates, its members may find that six months to a year into the new CEO's tenure they cannot figure out what went wrong and move to terminate the employment of the CEO. To avoid the problem of poor fit between institutional needs and a CEO's skills and style, it is important for the board to remain engaged throughout the search process. Prior to the recruitment of a new CEO, the board should meet to discuss the talents it deems necessary for a CEO to be successful at this point in the college's or district's history. The board should include a list of these desired talents in the recruitment materials and attempt to select the candidate who most matches the talents desired by the board. This list of desired skills is in addition to minimum qualifications such as the education and professional experience that are required for the position.

From the candidate's perspective, it is important to do one's homework in reviewing job announcements. Although being invited to interview for a presidency can be a great boost to one's ego, if the position is at an institution that is not a good fit or has significant dysfunctions that the candidate would be reluctant to address, it may be best for him or her to walk away from that particular search process. A candidate should learn everything possible about that institution and its board. There are a number of actions a candidate can take to get information about a position, such as reviewing accreditation reports, board minutes, budget and expenditure reports, and news articles as well as contacting the current CEO of the institution and asking about the board-CEO relationship.

In the selection process, the board should include methods to get broad input on the CEO candidates from the internal college community and representatives of the college district's service area. Being inclusive and allowing constituents to voice their opinions of prospective candidates will help obtain acceptance from these groups for the CEO who is selected. This can be accomplished in a number of ways, including having candidates speak at a public forum at the college and responding to questions approved by the board. The board can allow constituents to submit their recommendations to the board through written feedback on each candidate's public appearance. Candidates can learn about institutional issues from the questions that are asked by constituents at the public forums.

As the board narrows the list of candidates to a small number of finalists, the trustees are well advised to spend informal time at a social event with individual finalists to get to know the candidates in a setting different from the formal interview. Meeting in an informal setting will provide the board with clues about a candidate's communication skills and demeanor. A social meeting can also provide an additional opportunity for the candidates to interact with the trustees and to assess their fit with the institution and local community. CEOs and boards that have not participated in these types of informal gatherings risk creating an environment in which the personalities of the board and the new CEO clash, causing employment and operational problems for the college and a shortened tenure for the CEO.

After deciding on its top candidate, the board should work as a team to seek unity in its public vote on the selection of the CEO. This should occur even if there was not complete consensus during deliberations on the selection of the candidate. A unified public vote sends a message to the candidate, the college community, and the public that the board is unanimous in its support of the new CEO. Likewise, on accepting the appointment, the new CEO should express enthusiasm for the new position. If the public vote is not unanimous or if the candidate is not able to express enthusiasm about joining the college, the odds are against a successful presidency.

Step 2: Develop a Strategic Onboarding Process

Once a new CEO has been selected, creating an environment that fosters the CEO's success and the success of the CEO-board team is of paramount importance. In fact, this should be the primary goal for the board and new CEO. Foremost in this endeavor is building a climate of trust and respect between the board and the new CEO, beginning with drafting the CEO's employment contract. The search consultant or the board's legal counsel can help the board negotiate an employment contract, which should clearly state the terms of employment, including duties, salary, benefits, expense allowances, working conditions, and term of office. It should also include a process for regular performance evaluation and specify the board's role in monitoring performance. CEOs and boards should never agree to any benefit that is not included in writing in the employment agreement (Boggs & Brown, 2007). It is wise for new CEOs to do their own research on provisions for the employment contract. Additional provisions might include auto and housing allowances, additional insurance, relocation expenses, club memberships, assistance with the costs of child care or care of a dependent family member, and even a clause on separation or employment termination. Wallin (2007) has done significant research on the provisions of community college CEO employment contracts.

After the new CEO has completed all the formal employment-related steps, including signing the employment contract, the board should schedule a meeting with the new CEO to discuss board and CEO communication, board goals, the values and mission of the district, the college or district strategic plan, and the board's expectations and goals for the CEO's first year. Including the district's senior leadership team in some initial meetings between the board and the CEO may serve to demonstrate the board's support of the new CEO and can help foster a team approach with the college district's senior leaders. However, the primary purpose of this initial meeting is the development of a relationship between the board and CEO, so care must be taken to communicate this to other senior leaders in the institution. An independent facilitator can help keep the meeting on track and allow the CEO and board chair to participate more fully in the discussion.

From the new CEO's perspective, being accountable to an elected or appointed board of distinct individuals may be a situation that the CEO has not experienced before. Recognizing the time and effort it takes to cultivate trusting relationships between individual trustees and the CEO is critically important. The CEO needs to make it a priority to develop these relationships in tandem with learning to lead a new institution.

Step 3: Provide Mentorship, Support, and Professional Development Activities

A new CEO will need support in learning about the college, its culture, and the characteristics of the board. If the CEO is new to a position of reporting to a board, he or she will have a steep learning curve to master. If the CEO is from another state, he or she will have a host of new regulatory and governance structures to learn as well. The board should encourage a new CEO to choose a mentor or coach to turn to for advice in the first few years on the job. An ideal mentor could be a retired successful CEO from the college district or a seasoned sitting CEO from a neighboring institution. Some states have established formal coaching programs, such as the California Community Colleges's (2016) Institutional Effectiveness Partnership Initiative, a California colleague-helping-colleague collaborative effort to help advance effective practices.

The board should also encourage and support the new CEO's participation in professional development programs offered to new CEOs. Too often new CEOs are reluctant to leave their colleges at such an early stage, or they might be reluctant to spend money on their own professional development. The board should make it a point to discuss the importance of professional development for the new CEO and the CEO-board team. CEOs and boards can check with state community college associations to see what kinds of professional development programs are offered. In California, programs are offered by the University of California Davis's Wheelhouse: The Center for Community College Leadership and Research, the Community College League of California, and the state chancellor's office. Nationally, the American Association of Community Colleges offers professional development programs for new and experienced CEOs through its Presidents Academy. The leadership development programs offered by these associations and institutions provide curricula that develop the skills and tools leaders need to instill an innovation mind-set in their organizations, inspire their college leadership teams to higher levels of performance, and build and maintain a successful CEO-board team.

The board should also help the new CEO learn about the college district and the communities it serves and to build a support network with internal and external stakeholders. The board has the responsibility to introduce the new CEO to the community with a series of meetings or meals with community leaders and to secure invitations to local community events. The board needs to serve as the conduit to the community until the CEO has had an opportunity to make the necessary community connections and is able to meet independently with the external community. This will also allow the trustees to develop a partnership with the CEO and signal to the community the board's support of the new CEO.

Step 4: Foster Strong Individual Team Member Relationships

Bill McGinnis, a contributor to this chapter, has all too often been invited to facilitate a workshop for a board of trustees involved in a situation that developed as a result of a lack of trust between the board and the CEO. In most of these situations, the problem is with a minority of the board and can usually be corrected, but not always. At one college, an individual trustee lacked any trust whatsoever in the CEO. In that case, it was recommended for the trustee to include another trustee in any conversation with the CEO to help improve trust and communication. Such a situation may have been avoided if very early in the new CEO's tenure, each board member had met with the new CEO on an individual and informal basis to discuss each trustee's communication preference, what the trustee could do to help the CEO succeed in the first year, the educational needs of the community, and the trustee's goals and vision for the college district. This is also a great opportunity for the CEO and individual trustees to get to know each other and build mutual trust and respect. Scheduling these individual meetings over a meal creates a more informal and collegial atmosphere.

Individual trustees and the CEO should continue to develop their team through ongoing engagements following the initial meeting, touching base about communication issues (if any), the CEO's progress with district and board goals, and any issues the CEO has that require the board's guidance. The trustee can start the conversation by asking what he or she can do individually to help the CEO succeed and what the full board can do to help the CEO succeed. Such meetings should continue throughout the CEO's tenure with the college district as a means to resolve any communications issues quickly as well as reaffirm the trustee's support of the CEO or to identify any potential problems that the CEO needs to correct before they become major obstacles for the CEO's success. Care needs to be taken to ensure that trustees and CEOs do not abuse these individual meetings to violate open meeting laws or to push an agenda that may not be acceptable to the entire board.

The frequency of informal meetings between the CEO and individual trustees should be determined very early in the first year. Some new CEOs meet monthly with each trustee, while some meet quarterly. In the first year, having frequent informal meetings makes sense to establish trust and understanding. However, the CEO needs to be careful not to establish an expectation of overly frequent individual meetings beyond the first year. For example, if a new CEO reports to a 7-person board, and each trustee expects a biweekly meeting with the CEO, then 14 times a month the CEO is meeting with individual trustees, a schedule that is difficult to maintain. Reasonably scheduled individual meetings are helpful not only as a support mechanism for the CEO but also to provide trustees with the opportunity to gain insights into district participatory governance processes and the development of recommendations the CEO will be making at future board meetings.

Step 5: Create a Communication Road Map

In addition to informal meetings between individual trustees and the new CEO, regular formal touch points are needed between the full board and the CEO to discuss communication, especially throughout the first year. These meetings can be scheduled semiannually or on a quarterly basis. They are important to ensure that the type, style, and amount of communication is working for the board and CEO. A common trustee complaint is either that the CEO does not provide the board with sufficient information or provides way too much information to the point that the board cannot digest all the data. At a board-CEO retreat, details on communication should be covered. For example, how do the trustees want the board agenda and supporting materials to be presented to them—hard copies or electronically? Do the trustees have the ability to use electronic equipment at the board meetings to follow the agenda, or is there enough light in the board room for the trustees who use a paper version of the agenda to read the materials? How detailed should written materials presented to the board be?

Beyond formal board meetings, the CEO and the board should come to an agreement on how often and in what manner regular communication will occur. For example, some CEOs provide weekly e-mail updates to their board; others update their boards on relevant information as it comes available. Most CEOs use e-mail to share information with their boards to ensure consistency and timeliness. One note of caution: When e-mailing the whole board, it is wise to use the blind carbon copy option to minimize the chance of board members replying to all and thus risking interactions that might be a potential violation of any state laws and regulations that require board deliberations to occur in open public meetings. It is also important to remember that e-mail messages on the college server are discoverable in any legal action. See Step 8 (p. 169, this volume) for more on electronic communications.

After the first quarter of employment, the board and the new CEO should meet to discuss any communications issues, any changes needed to board meetings and materials, and any challenges the CEO has in accomplishing the board's goals. Depending on the subjects to be discussed, these meetings may be required to be public. To encourage a frank discussion, the meeting should be held as a closed session of the board if it is legal to do so. Board discussions about CEO performance can usually take place in closed sessions. The goal of such meetings is to foster a relationship of trust and respect. The new CEO must be encouraged to alert the board to any difficulties he or she is having with aspects of the board's practices (i.e., micromanaging, communication difficulties, disruptive board behavior, etc.). The board's responsibility is then to take proactive steps to correct such issues. In addition, the CEO must be open minded and change communication practices, especially if he or she has not previously worked for board members who do not have unlimited time to attend to college business. For example, a CEO prone to writing long discursive e-mails may need to learn to provide information in a short bulleted list.

At the six-month point, the full board should meet with the CEO to discuss progress on board and CEO goals, any unresolved communications issues, progress on attending continuing educational programs for new CEOs, and people in the community the CEO should meet. The board should also offer the CEO the opportunity to identify any board or college issues that need to be addressed for the board and the CEO to be more effective. As this session is a formative evaluation of the CEO, it should be legally permissible for the board to have this discussion in a closed session or at least a separate board meeting other than the board's regular business meeting. In the event of concerns with the CEO's job performance, the board should be sure to informally address those issues at this time and suggest to the CEO steps that may be taken to improve the CEO's job performance. This can be a time for the CEO to discuss privately with the board any personnel issues with senior college leadership. For example, there may be a disconnect between the new CEO and the old guard of vice presidents that becomes apparent after several months into the new CEO's tenure.

Step 6: Identify Goals and Goal Achievement Benchmarks

At the end of the first year, the full board should again meet with the CEO to discuss the CEO's performance and develop a set of board and CEO goals for the next year. This can be part of the board's annual review of the CEO's performance and must be completed in accordance with the district's policy and procedures for such a review. In addition, the CEO should be offered an opportunity to inform the board on how it can best support the CEO's success (training options, changes to communication methods, board practices, etc.), much like the topics at the sixth-month meeting between the board and the CEO. Boards in some districts perform the board's self-evaluation at the same time they evaluate their CEO, to coordinate with the preparation of the district's, the CEO's, and the board's goals for the next year. It is incumbent on the board to openly identify any issues or changes the CEO should make in the next year to be considered successful and to then support the CEO's efforts for change.

Before the first formal evaluation of a new CEO, the board and CEO should discuss what input and how that input will be gathered for the evaluation. This should be spelled out explicitly in the district's evaluation policies and procedures. However, if it is not spelled out, the procedure needs to be discussed and agreed on prior to the evaluation. Some boards seek input from faculty and staff in the district through in-person interviews or in writing. Some boards also seek input from key stakeholders outside the district who interact regularly with the CEO. Other boards choose to evaluate the CEO's performance without external input. Who gives input and in what forms needs to be explicitly agreed on prior to the CEO evaluation. If open input from all constituents is allowed, boards need to be aware that at times when the CEO is implementing change or when the district is in negotiations with a collective bargaining unit, this open input on the CEO's performance may be used by staff as a means to lobby the board directly or convey dissatisfaction about a particular decision. Boards should recognize these dynamics and not become alarmed or react too quickly. Boards should expect CEOs to do what is right and not necessarily what is popular.

Boards also need to be consistent with expectations for a CEO and to refer to CEO goals during the performance appraisal process. Sometimes boards initially ask a new CEO in the first year to focus on making connections in the community and then criticize the CEO for not spending enough time on the college's campus and too much time in the community. This is a balance that most CEOs struggle with, and boards should be careful to measure performance against the goals and not direct the CEO with inconsistent priorities from one year to the next. This bouncing back and forth on priorities is not good for either the CEO or the college.

Board practices during and between board meetings should also support the CEO's performance. The board can disagree with a CEO recommendation, but discussion and voting by the board should occur in a respectful manner. When rejecting the CEO's recommendation, the board should offer an explanation for the difference of opinion and, as much as possible, provide supportive data or reasoning for its decision. In addition, trustees need to communicate with the CEO before a board meeting if they have any questions or suggestions about items on a board agenda. This allows the CEO to provide in advance the information necessary to ensure the board can make the best decisions during the public meeting.

New CEOs should be on the lookout for small victories in their first year to instill confidence in the board that it made a good choice. Some examples could include initiating a new partnership with a local employment agency or taking action on a long-term problem employee. The CEO should remember to share the spotlight with the board by recognizing its contribution to achievements. By doing this, the board is acknowledged for its support and contribution, and the board is more likely to support the CEO in the future.

Step 7: Adhere to the Rule of No Surprises

A few pitfalls can lead to an unsuccessful and frustrating relationship between the board and CEO. Problems most often occur when either the board or CEO is surprised at a public meeting, when communication is inadequate or ineffective, when there is a lack of accountability, when the CEO and trustees are not meeting often enough or too often, and when disruptive trustees are not held in check.

When asked what creates a good CEO-board relationship, trustees and CEOs alike will immediately say there should be no surprises. This works in both directions. A frequent problem encountered by CEOs is when board members surprise the CEO with questions or accusations during a board meeting or in another public setting. Although trustees may insist they are only trying to find out the truth of a matter, the real reason is often to blame or embarrass the CEO rather than to find the real answer to their questions or to seek information. This kind of a problem could be characterized as a trustee attempting to discredit a CEO in the hope of creating enough doubt about the CEO's performance that the board might consider termination of the CEO's employment. In such a situation, the board chair needs to step in to prevent these attempts from occurring by reminding the disruptive trustee that there is a protocol for asking questions and raising concerns before a meeting to allow the CEO ample time to research the issue and provide the full board with an appropriate and knowledgeable response.

The rule to use in such situations is that there should be no surprises by either the trustees or the CEO during or between meetings. A good practice is for trustees to read the board agenda and supporting materials as soon as possible after receiving them and then contact the CEO before the meeting in an agreed-on manner if there are questions. This practice allows the CEO either to provide the information before the meeting or have staff prepare a response to be provided during the meeting. By being prepared, the staff can provide more complete and accurate information to the board. Some CEOs take the initiative to call each trustee individually before the board meeting to ensure that board members have read agendas as well as to provide an opportunity to vet questions ahead of time. To avoid violation of open meeting laws, CEOs must be careful during these calls not to try to influence a trustee's vote outside an authorized public meeting.

There may be times when a trustee is opposed to a proposed action presented by the CEO. In such a case, the trustee should contact the CEO before the meeting to inform the CEO of his or her position and to provide an explanation for it. Again, there should be no surprises. By learning about the trustee's opposition to the action in advance, the CEO may be able to help the trustee craft an alternative proposal or provide reasons for the CEO's recommendation that may change the trustee's position. Or the trustee may be able to convince the CEO to change the recommendation before the board meeting and seek an alternative proposal. Again, the best course of action is to communicate ahead of time and avoid surprises at all costs.

The same holds true for actions by the CEO. The CEO should not surprise the board in public and thus make trustees appear to be uninformed. Information provided to the board needs to be complete and in a form easily understood by the board. The CEO should make sure there are no surprises for the board between or, especially, at board meetings. No one likes to be surprised in public and thus feel ill prepared to properly respond.

No board member wants to open the local newspaper or listen to a newscast and learn that something has gone wrong at the college. Worse, no board member wants to be confronted by a news reporter on live TV about something that she or he is not aware of. The CEO needs to provide alerts plus regular updates on breaking situations that may end up in the news or affect the college's image. This can be a quick text or e-mail to inform the board and provide assistance on how to respond. Sometimes CEOs are tempted to delay informing their boards on developing situations because they do not have complete information. In cases such as this, it is much better to let the board know immediately what is known and that more information will follow. For example, after a stabbing on a community college campus, the CEO immediately e-mailed the board of the occurrence even though he had no details at the time. This CEO knew it was best to share what little information he had rather than to wait until he learned more before informing the board.

Although it may be tempting for a CEO to hide bad news from the board, this can undermine trust. If there is bad news, such as a sudden decline in enrollment, a serious personnel issue, or a compliance report submitted with significant errors, a CEO should get the information out quickly to the board, accompanied by a proposed plan of action. If there is no immediate definitive plan, the CEO should let the board know that staff members are working on one. When the board discovers a mistake or bad news from someone other than the CEO, it damages the confidence and trust the board has in its CEO. Trying to cover up a mistake or bad news will just make the situation worse when it is found out—and it will be found out. With today's social media and hyperconnectedness, it is much more difficult to bury bad news or a problem. Therefore, the CEO should be honest and forthcoming with the board and seek its support to resolve the matter.

Step 8: Create a Plan for Using Electronic Communications and Social Media

The CEO-board team must collaborate to develop an electronic and social media approach that works best for all team members and minimizes legal and public relations risks. Occasionally, one of us has facilitated a board training workshop only to have one or two trustees frequently reading and typing on their cell phone or laptop. This is disruptive to the meeting facilitator, and it also demonstrates a lack of respect toward the CEO and other participating trustees. Trustees and CEOs need to be prudent in their use of social media. Confidential information should not be conveyed to the board or CEO electronically, as such information in most states is a matter of public record; the media or attorneys could request and obtain a copy of such a communication even if generated on a non-district-owned computer or cell phone. If the message passes through the institution's e-mail or phone system, it becomes a public document. Therefore, sensitive or confidential information should be transmitted either in person or by a noninstutional telephone conversation. A good rule of thumb is to assume every e-mail and text sent to the CEO or to board members could be read by the public and should be composed accordingly. CEOs should be careful not to copy a majority of trustees on any sensitive electronic correspondence (e-mails, text messages, etc.) to avoid creating a chain of communication that may violate the state's open meeting laws. Texting among trustees or with the CEO in a public meeting should also be discouraged as it can create trust problems among members of the CEO-board team. There is nothing more disrespectful to a presenter at a board meeting than to watch the trustees tapping on their phones while the speaker is attempting to impart information to the board. In such cases the board chair needs to point out inattention and ask the offender to stop and to apologize to the speaker.

Posting photos or statements on Facebook, Twitter, Instagram, and other social platforms can also be dangerous if not done prudently with forethought on the possible interpretations of such postings. What may seem harmless at the time could be taken the wrong way by others and bring about political problems for the board or the CEO or both. As an example, if a photo of the CEO and some trustees at a cocktail reception during an out-of-town conference is posted on social media, some viewers might protest that the college is using taxpayer's dollars inappropriately. Problems could quickly develop if a trustee or the CEO posted on Facebook about how he or she was working hard to ensure that the board is more fiscally responsible or to try to make a change for students, implying that the CEO or other trustees are opposing or obstructing these efforts.

Although CEOs and individual trustees have freedom of speech, the impact of thoughtless comments can be divisive. Complaining about the actions of the CEO or other trustees on social media undermines trust and respect and will ultimately have an adverse impact on the institution and the CEO-board team's relationship. The team members can quickly lose their trust and respect for each other, and the impact will create a dysfunctional team.

Step 9: Identify the Board's Information Needs

The CEO needs to talk to each of the trustees individually and then follow up with the full board on a regular basis to ensure that the board is receiving the right amount of information and that it is timely enough for the board to understand the issues and make necessary decisions. The CEO needs to understand the communication style of each of the trustees and provide the information to the board in an understandable format. The most successful CEOs continually check in with trustees to make sure meeting agendas and reports are easy to understand and complete enough for the board to make appropriate decisions. Another practice of successful CEOs is to respond to individual trustee questions about board agenda items by e-mailing the response to the whole board. This covers two areas: First, if one trustee has a question about a specific agenda item, it is likely other trustees are curious about it as well, and second, the CEO is ensuring that all board members are receiving the same amount of information.

It is difficult for a CEO to understand the thinking of trustees without periodically discussing issues with them on an individual basis. Although this may not be practical to do before each board meeting, such meetings should be held at least quarterly during the CEO's and trustees' first few years of working together. Even after the team comes to know each other well, periodic meetings should be scheduled throughout the CEO's career with the college. These meetings cultivate mutual trust and respect. They also provide the CEO with a deeper understanding of which issues and topics are important to each board member, allowing CEOs to provide appropriate individual attention. For example, a trustee may be particularly interested in or challenged by the district budget. When it is time for the board to review the tentative budget, the CEO can meet with that trustee prior to the board meeting and discuss any questions or concerns.

If a trustee has identified any issues that may cause the CEO difficulty, the trustee should bring them to the attention of the CEO and be ready to offer some possible solutions. Again, the motivation should be to help the CEO succeed. By identifying potential landmines, the trustee can help the CEO and the CEO-board team—and thus the college—not only look better to the community but also be more successful in service to students. Trustees need to make themselves available to meet with the CEO if requested, as such a request is purposeful and should be respected. The bottom line is that trustees and the CEO need to maintain an open and frank line of communication that respects all parties.

Step 10: Develop a Cadence of Accountability

Although the board needs to provide sufficient support to the CEO and allow the CEO to try innovative methods to improve the institution, the board must also hold the CEO accountable. According to McChesney,

Huling, and Covey (2011) CEOs and boards can find a practical approach to accountability. The authors provide a framework referred to as the Cadence of Accountability and recommend for teams to meet frequently to review progress toward important goals. The CEO-board team should meet on a regular basis to discuss progress on goal achievement and data on student learning and completion rather than getting sidetracked and focusing on day-to-day operational matters.

Sufficient and thorough board policies that provide the authority for the CEO to act while also establishing limits on certain activities are critical to accountability methods. For example, it is difficult for a board to admonish the CEO about expensive or foreign travel charged to the institution if the board has not previously adopted appropriate travel expense criteria. If no board policy addressing CEO travel exists, then the CEO should ask the board for guidance prior to taking business trips out of state or out of the country.

The best mechanism for the board to hold CEOs accountable is through goal setting and evaluation. If a board has not adopted a set of CEO goals for the year or the adopted goals do not directly relate to the CEO's performance, how can the board effectively and honestly measure the CEO's performance at the end of the year?

The board should meet with the CEO specifically to discuss the institution's goals for the coming year. Once the institution's goals are set, specific goals for the CEO and the board that are aligned with and in support of the institution's goals should be developed. In addition, any areas of improvement identified for the board and CEO in the previous year should be addressed. The board cannot find that the CEO has failed to perform as the board desires if the board does not tell the CEO what is expected.

It may be difficult for the CEO to comment publicly on the board's performance or on areas needing improvement. In this case, the CEO should consult with the board chair or a senior trustee on how to bring issues before the board for consideration when discussing the board's self-evaluation and the board's goals for the coming year. A few boards do conduct extensive self-evaluations that include a 360-degree review by the CEO, other administrators, and even some public officials familiar with their work. Another approach to address areas for the CEO-board team that need improvement is to use a visiting accreditation team or consultants to report on the team's performance and make a recommendation for corrective action. Using a neutral professional entity external to the institution can add weight to the concern and more impetus for change.

When the board properly sets meaningful goals that the CEO is not meeting, or if other factors result in unsuitable behavior by the CEO, it is appropriate for the board to take remedial action. However, because of the unique relationship between the CEO and the board, the board may wish to consider having the board chair initially meet with the CEO to informally discuss the issue (assuming immediate disciplinary action or termination is not necessary) and cooperatively develop an improvement plan with goals to resolve the issue. Depending on the nature of the problem, the board may wish to provide the CEO with a specific time period to accomplish those remediation goals. However, if the board thinks immediate disciplinary action is warranted, the board should consult with its legal adviser and the institution's human resources administrator to assure that proper steps are being followed. Most important, the board should meet with the CEO to discuss the issue and to allow the CEO to respond and provide data supporting the CEO's position. Only after the CEO has had an opportunity to be heard and the board has followed the legal and necessary steps should the board proceed with disciplinary action against the CEO. Because steps to discipline the CEO may need to occur in public, it is important for the board to perform due diligence before proceeding. It is extremely difficult for a CEO to lead an institution if the staff and faculty know the CEO lacks the board's trust and support.

Step 11: Develop a Strategy to Identify Team Problems Early

As important as it is for the board to be willing to meet individually with the CEO on a regular basis, the CEO also has to be open to scheduling such meetings and willing to develop an open line of communication with each trustee. A CEO in a large multicollege district was under fire from her board at the end of her first year. It seemed the trustees did not trust the CEO and were uncomfortable with her recommendations made in board meetings. During a meeting between the board and the CEO, it was discovered that the CEO had not spent any time during her first year meeting with any of the trustees on an individual basis. She had not developed an open and frank line of communication or built trust between the board members and herself. Shortly after a session to try to help remedy the situation, the board terminated the CEO's employment. The board was critical of the CEO, but most of the criticism was related to the lack of communication between the parties and could have been overcome had the CEO and individual trustees spent the time getting to know each other.

Occasionally, a CEO will encounter a disruptive or rogue trustee and have a difficult time building a relationship with the trustee or consistently encounter problems at board meetings. O'Banion (2009) has written extensively about problems with rogue trustees and how to deal with them. Often, CEOs cannot solve the situation with a rogue or disruptive trustee by themselves. In such a case, the CEO needs the aid of the board chair and perhaps the remainder of the board as well. Most institutions have a board policy on how to deal with a disruptive trustee, and the CEO will need to support the board chair and seek his or her help in dealing with such a situation. Sometimes a private conversation between the board chair and the disruptive trustee can help resolve the matter. At minimum, they can develop a plan to reduce the disruptions or bad behaviors. If this does not resolve the situation, then the board chair, with guidance from the CEO, will need to take the matter to the full board and seek its support and possible action against the disruptive trustee. The CEO can also suggest to the board chair the possibility of seeking outside assistance to train the board on best practices in hopes of changing the disruptive trustee's behavior. Although the CEO can support the board's attempts to correct the situation, the CEO should not lead the efforts. This is a responsibility of the board itself. If the board fails to act or cannot cure the situation, the CEO may wish to look elsewhere for employment, and the college climate will suffer.

Step 12: Develop Strategies for Long-Term Success

Trustees need to foster an ongoing work environment that will allow the CEO to succeed. Trustees should provide the support necessary to generate trust and to prevent adverse situations from arising. In the first year or two of a new CEO's appointment, when a problem arises the board's role is to help resolve it quickly and to assure the CEO that these are learning experiences and not opportunities for the board to publicly criticize the CEO. The board must hold the CEO accountable but should do so in a professional and supportive manner. Trustees want the best possible CEO for the institution, but boards cannot rely only on the hiring process. Boards need to encourage and expect the CEO to participate in continued professional development. Although this is even more critical for a first-time CEO, seasoned CEOs also need to participate in professional development to remain current in their profession. There are a number of excellent opportunities nationwide, and depending on the institution's budget capabilities, the board needs to insist that the CEO periodically participate in such opportunities. Trustees should also attend conferences and participate in board development activities. Some CEOs include a regular board agenda item on conferences and trainings attended.

During a new CEO's second year, the board and CEO should continue the individual meetings described earlier. The meetings should continue to focus on the same communication and coordination issues as recommended for the CEO's first year in addition to other topics as decided by the CEO and the trustee. These additional topics can relate to new happenings at the college or in the state or nation related to higher education or other topics deemed important by the participants.

The CEO and trustee need to be sure that the communications link between the CEO and the board is working well and that the levels of trust and respect between the board and the CEO are continually improving. The board should also continue to introduce the CEO to community business leaders or other people who are important to the college.

Midway through the CEO's second year, the CEO and board should meet to obtain a progress update on the CEO's and the board's goals to discuss any issues affecting the CEO's successful performance and to identify any potential communication issues. Again, at year's end, the board and CEO should schedule a meeting, similar to the first 12-month meeting, to review annual performance and establish goals for the coming year. Special attention should be paid to board and CEO relations and communications. This recommended calendar of events should continue for the CEO's entire tenure with the district.

If a new trustee is elected or appointed to the board, an effective orientation for this individual is imperative. Changing a single trustee can affect the dynamic of a whole board. This is important for the board and CEO to recognize and handle proactively. A new trustee may be assigned a mentor on the board to meet with throughout the first year. Moreover, the CEO will need to take extra time to establish a relationship with the new trustee through frequent informal meetings. Bringing a new trustee up to speed on the vast array of college programs and services is the CEO's responsibility. The CEO may wish to schedule periodic campus tours to introduce the new trustee to the various programs and services offered by the college. These tours should be scheduled for the whole board but designed with the new trustee in mind. The new trustee should also attend state and regional trustee meetings to gain more knowledge about community college governance.

In addition, it is beneficial for the seasoned CEO to serve as a mentor or an instructor in a professional development program to assist less-tenured CEOs, which will also help keep the seasoned CEO current. As the CEO learns of new programs or new approaches to providing services to students, the board should support the CEO's attempts to introduce new methods or programs. After all, the college is a learning institution and as such needs to model lifelong learning and continued professional development throughout the institution including the administration.

Although the trustees are the community's representatives of the college, it is also important for the CEO to develop and use connections in the community for the benefit of the institution. Initially trustees need to be proactive in introducing a new CEO to community leaders. Thereafter, trustees must listen to community representatives and pass along any concerns and issues from the community leaders to the CEO. Trustees may be better suited than the CEO in understanding the feelings and needs of their community, and trustees need to transmit this information so that the CEO may take any positive action to help the community.

As good as CEOs are in presenting proposals to their boards for the benefit of the community and the district, it is difficult for CEOs to ask for their own pay increases or improvements in their benefits package. The board may wish to consider tying any bonuses or pay increases to the CEO's role in improving certain measures of the institution's performance such as increasing the number of degree completers or the number of transfer students in addition to reviewing salaries and benefits from comparable institutions for a similar position. Once the board and the CEO agree on the compensation measures, the CEO will need time (a year or more) to implement the steps needed to measure the changes in the agreed-on performance measures.

In many cases, CEOs may be contacted as early as 1 or 2 years into their tenure to consider interviewing for a leadership position at another institution. Boards can provide longevity incentives to retain a successful CEO and not have to incur the expenses in time and money to recruit a new leader. One example is a deferred compensation plan that places funds into a trust that the CEO cannot access until after 5 or 6 years of continuous employment. Other incentives include offering funds for professional development opportunities, extended vacations after a minimum term of employment, improved health insurance coverage for the CEO until the age of 65, or increased car and housing allowances. Because of the high cost of housing in some areas of the United States, a board may find it necessary to assist the CEO with housing costs.

If there is sufficient trust and respect between the board and the CEO, it can be helpful for the board to allow the CEO to comment on the board's performance or to make suggestions on how the board may improve. Again, this can only be implemented if the level of respect and trust between the board and the CEO is strong; without strong trust and respect, individual trustees may take exception to the CEO's suggestions or comments and retaliate against the CEO during a performance review. The board can gain helpful insight from the CEO in this process and should encourage such input.

Step 13: Create an Environment for Innovation and Change

Creating change in academic institutions that are slow moving and entrenched in tradition requires tremendous energy to overcome the inertia supported by such customs. CEOs and boards must never underestimate the magnitude of the forces that reinforce the status quo and resist change. The board of trustees' role in support of the CEO to institute change and creative innovation should include communicating a sense of urgency and rationale for the needed changes. Additionally, the board can assist the CEO by participating in a coalition supporting the change, assisting in the development of the vision and strategy focused on the change, supporting the CEO in the change efforts, and adopting changes in policy where needed to support the changes. Finally, once the changes are implemented, the board should evaluate the performance of the institution under the changed program and anchor the new approaches in the culture of the institution, which sends the message that there is no going back to the old ways of doing things.

Practically speaking, the CEO needs to educate the trustees on the need for the changes and how the changes will benefit the students and the institution. Following the board's education, trustees need to become partners with the CEO to justify the changes to the institution and express the need for urgency in adopting the changes. The CEO can help this process by providing opportunities for the board members to support the desired change during their public meetings. Additional opportunities to communicate support include the board's discussion of the institution's strategic plan with goals that support and enable the proposed change and the board's review of the institution's performance to evaluate the impact of the change in the desired area such as student transfer or student retention. Then, if the change is successful, the board can publicly acknowledge the institution's progress during a regular board meeting and celebrate the achievements.

Step 14: Identify CEO-Board Team Landmines and Rewards

It is important to remember that trustees are elected or politically appointed, and the board needs to be able to act on matters that can be viewed as politically acceptable. Although the CEO will best know what items need to be included on the board's agenda, it will be helpful for the CEO to seek the guidance and assistance of the board chair. He or she can advise the CEO on political issues affecting agenda items, how to present them, and how the matter may gain majority support.

Moreover, CEOs should provide opportunities for recognition of the board members for their actions in support of the institution, the students, and the community. CEOs can create a partnership with the board by always including the board in events and always recognizing the members for any major college accomplishments such as groundbreaking events for new buildings and the announcement of new initiatives like a tuition waiver program. CEOs need to remember to share the spotlight and foster the relationship with their boards.

Board members are elected or appointed to represent the community and to lead the institution on a policy level. However, board meetings can be driven by agendas overwhelmed by fiduciary business and without obvious opportunities for the board to lead. A successful CEO needs to look for opportunities to allow the board to lead on matters under its purview, whether by adopting or updating board policies, considering the institution's strategic plan, or discussing the goals of the institution for student success or student access. Not providing the board with opportunities to provide oversight and guidance can result in trustee micromanagement of the board agenda or the operation of the institution.

When a CEO and board have a strong relationship, the institution thrives. This team can provide a model of effective collaborative governance and leadership for the rest of the college. Working effectively together, the board and the CEO are a powerful team that can enhance an educational institution to benefit the students and the community well into the future.

References

Boggs, G. R. (2006). *Handbook on CEO-board relations and responsibilities.* Washington, DC: Community College Press.

Boggs, G. R. (2017, January 4). Breaking up is hard to do. *Inside Higher Ed.* Retrieved from https://www.insidehighered.com/views/2017/01/04/advice-boards-and-presidents-how-avoid-forced-separations-essay

Boggs, G. R., & Brown, J. N. (2007). Foreword. In D. Wallin (Ed.), *The CEO employment contract: A guide for presidents and boards* (2nd ed., pp. vii–x). Washington DC: Community College Press.

CAL FIRE. (2019). *Camp fire incident information.* Retrieved from http://cdfdata.fire.ca.gov/incidents/incidents_details_info?incident_id=2277

California Community Colleges. (2016). Institutional Effectiveness Partnership Initiative. Retrieved from https://iepi.cccco.edu

Cooper, S. (2016). *Tough job if you can keep it: What California community college CEOs say about their challenges and longevity* (Research brief No. 1). Retrieved from https://education.ucdavis.edu/sites/main/files/ucdavis_wheelhouse_tough_job_research_brief.pdf

McChesney, C., Huling, J., & Covey, S. (2011). *The 4 disciplines of execution: Achieving your wildly important goals.* New York, NY: The Free Press.

O'Banion, T. (2009). *The rogue trustee: The elephant in the room.* Chandler, AZ: League for Innovation in the Community College.

Wallin, D. (2007). *The CEO employment contract: A guide for presidents and boards* (2nd ed.). Washington DC: Community College Press.

LEADERSHIP TEAMS AND INSTITUTIONAL TRANSFORMATION

Christine Johnson McPhail

These are extraordinary times for community colleges. These institutions must find better ways to address the needs of students and respond to a growing number of competing external demands. To make these academic institutions viable and sustainable, community college leaders must examine historical practices and policies to identify which ones have worked in the past, leave behind those elements that no longer serve the institution's objectives and needs of its stakeholders, and identify new and different ways to advance the mission of the institution. In sum, community colleges need to undertake a transformational change. Community college leaders must face the fact that managing change has emerged as one of the essential competencies for today's leaders. Although community college leaders are increasingly exposing their employees to change, there appears to be little purposeful training for leadership teams on how to effectively manage the human aspect of the change process.

The need for change in community colleges was called for by the American Association of Community Colleges (2012) because the available evidence revealed many failures. Thus, the association suggested that community colleges must redesign students' educational experiences, reinvent institutional roles, and reset the system to create partnerships and incentives for student and institutional success (American Association of Community Colleges, 2012). This mission was aptly summarized by the association's president and chief executive officer, Walter Bumphus, who said

179

> I intend to work with community college leaders to breathe life into the vision outlined by the Commission, in which students' educational experiences are *redesigned*, institutional roles are *reinvented*, and the system itself has been *reset* to meet the needs of students, their communities, and the nation. (American Association of Community Colleges, 2012)

It is evident that even though many community colleges are struggling to change, work still needs to be done to examine and revise the existing policies and practices. The twenty-first-century educational paradigm calls for new ways of managing colleges and serving their students and other stakeholders. The question is, Are the institutions responding to the needs of students, and how do they know if they are doing this effectively? To move forward with the times, community colleges must let go of the past and identify new ways of serving and supporting their students and the wider community.

Editors George R. Boggs and Christine Johnson McPhail routinely visit community colleges across the United States to observe educators using a variety of strategies and innovations to change the teaching and learning environment at their institutions. Many institutional leaders, however, launched new projects without the benefit of carefully examining the impact of these new efforts on existing programs and on the people affected by the change. In some cases, existing programs had never been evaluated. Institutional leaders cannot determine whether a program is yielding the desired outcomes without conducting a comprehensive evaluation. In fact, Boggs and McPhail found that the way most of the institutions they visited launched and implemented transformational changes was problematic. Challenges with transformational change at some of these colleges are in part because of faulty implementation strategies. In some cases, lack of engagement or commitment by the entire leadership team is to blame. Also, many institutions appear to have no systematic way of launching new programs, and there is no systematic process for assigning responsible parties to project implementation.

Many senior executives are aware of these challenges, and some even worry about them. Yet few seem to have taken the actions necessary to address the problems. When asked what stands in the way of implementing effective transformational change, chief executive officers involved in transformation efforts often say they are concerned about how stakeholders will react to the change. Thus, they are challenged to find innovative ways to motivate the entire leadership team to commit to actively contributing to change implementation. Community college leaders also appear to be struggling with improving the relationships among team members who do not seem to act together in unison and do not work toward the same goal. It is a matter of conventional wisdom that members of collaborative leadership teams usually achieve better results than if the members worked individually, particularly in high-pressure situations or when multiple skill sets are needed.

Much of the work on student success in community college was focused on pilot programs that served small groups of students. The growing focus on scalable student success strategies in the community college reform efforts has compelled the leadership of community colleges to improve collaboration among team members and different organizational units. The new focus should not be a surprise, as most community colleges are recognizing the importance of cross-sectional changes that must take place if the institution is to thrive and remain relevant in the changing educational sector. However, building effective teams requires more than an abstract commitment to teamwork; it must be cultivated by strong leadership from the top. Without cohesive leadership teams, the president risks limiting the extent to which desired goals can be accomplished. In contrast, much can be achieved if the group is organized and willing to strive toward a common goal. Because this can be challenging to achieve in practice, the remainder of this chapter provides six strategies and a case study that can be used to develop teams to be ready to lead transformational change. To implement a transformational change, a leader must first formulate an execution strategy. In the following, I present six useful strategies for developing teams capable of executing transformational change.

Strategy 1: Assessing the Current Situation

It is next to impossible to lead and implement change if the leadership team does not know its institutional data. In the existing situation at most institutions, the needs of the institution must be assessed to identify problems and thus the need to change. Colleges can begin this process by collecting, understanding, and using institutional data as essential steps in driving change. In preparation for any change, the senior leadership team must examine current student data along the continuum of the student experience, from entry to exit. The process must also include gathering and analyzing qualitative data to identify the causes of any deficiencies in student success outcomes and achievement gaps. Leaders can engage their teams in a question-and-answer assessment process. Some of the fundamental issues the president must address with the leadership group, once the problem is identified and the need for a change established, can be identified by addressing the following questions:

1. What outcomes do leaders want to achieve with the proposed change?
2. What issues make it necessary for the college to conduct this change at this time?

3. What evidence or data does the institution have to show how the change has been accomplished?
4. What is the impact of the change? Which groups and individuals are affected by this change, and how will they react to it?
5. Does the institution have the capacity and the resources to make the difference, and what aspects might require external assistance?
6. What vision drives the institution? Where is the institution now, and where do we want the institution to be one, two, and three years after implementing the changes?

Seeking answers to these questions also demonstrates that the president is committed to a consultative communication process that will help collect information to support the reasons for the change. Engaging all members of the leadership team and constituent groups in conversations focused on these six critical questions is essential when launching a transformational change process. The response to each question can be used to guide the change process. At a minimum, the conversation on the questions will create opportunities for others to participate in planning and implementing the steps required to execute a transformational change. It may also avoid some of the resistance to the change process (De Jager, 2001). The analysis of the issues and data emerging from the questions can serve to ignite and empower the team to lead the transformation process. After the leadership team has assessed the data, its members are ready to take action and lead institutional change.

Strategy 2: Developing an Action Plan

Leadership teams that fail to plan for broad-based action often find that their proposed changes do not produce the desired results. Transformational change (e.g., what would result from redesigning academic advising) typically requires institutions to create new structures, practices, and policies. As redesigning by itself is not a change, the implementation of a redesign would result in changes at the college. These changes must be explained to all college stakeholders to validate their engagement. It is also essential to devise an action plan that can be used to share information about the proposed change. An action plan is a way to make sure an organization's vision is transformed into a concrete, practical course of action that will lead to its realization; it describes the way a group will use its strategies to meet its objectives. An action plan consists of a number of action steps or changes to be brought about at the college, which often necessitates additional training and acquisition of new skills. Realizing that some employees do not possess the skillsets required to carry out some of the new work at the college that would arise because of change, some institutions offer professional development training for faculty and midlevel managers. Unit-level managers or supervisors must also be involved so they can understand the change process, which will allow them to correctly lead the change at the unit level.

Strategy 3: Developing an Engagement Plan

Leaders need to think broadly about the internal and external stakeholders who should be involved in launching a change initiative. For this purpose, the senior leadership team must collaborate to design a stakeholder engagement plan for the upcoming change. The engagement plan must cover all the different ways the college leaders currently involve stakeholders in conducting college business as well as any new duties the stakeholders are expected to assume once the change process is implemented. Typically, the term *stakeholders* refers to all individuals and groups invested in the welfare and success of an institution. In the case of community colleges, this includes students, trustees, administrators, teachers, staff members, students, parents, families, community members, local business leaders, and elected officials such as school board members and city officials. Engagement is the strategy college leaders should adopt to involve stakeholders in the change process. The college's engagement plan must describe the ways stakeholders are involved in the change process as well as identify any potential issues with their engagement and commitment to change. Most important, the plan must be clear about giving stakeholders a voice to influence the proposed change.

For example, the engagement plan should explicitly state whether the change initiative would require the involvement of groups outside the college leadership team such as the board of trustees, students, K–16 partners, community organizations, employers, and state and local policymakers. A clear framework should be established for the change process (Chapman, 2002). If the involvement of these groups is required, it is essential to identify the key leadership team members who will be tasked with interacting with the various external stakeholder groups. The president should empower leaders at all levels—up, down, and across the institution—to use their skills and abilities to embrace their roles as change agents.

When a college launches a new initiative, this raises many questions such as, Who will participate? How can we get folks involved? and Who needs to know about the change? Indeed, administrators frequently lament the lack of engagement in transformational change activities. Comments such as "The employees are not actively engaged in the change" or "Where's the accountability?" show that the leadership team has not fulfilled its responsibility as a change manager capable of motivating employees to do their part in carrying out the change process. In some cases, leaders may counter these arguments by claiming they thought the experts said that student success is everyone's responsibility. Although this is certainly true, the responsibility for leading and managing transformational change lies with the senior executive leadership team and institutional administrators. To increase commitment and engagement, the college's leadership team must explain the transformation in a manner that employees understand. The staff members must also be informed about what is taking place and how they can participate in the change process.

Specifically, the leadership team has the responsibility to facilitate and enable change throughout the institution. In many cases, however, the leadership team members are unsure how to act to achieve this aim. As transformational change unfolds from goal setting to implementation, it affects the behavior of administrators at different levels of the organization. Thus, the senior leadership team must develop and enhance leadership at all levels of the institution. Leadership competencies should not be reserved for those at the top of the hierarchy; innovation and responsibility for creative implementation can and should cascade through all levels of the institution. Leaders at all institutional levels can be identified and trained on the change process, which must be aligned with the college's vision and mission. It is the president's responsibility to ensure that all team members understand the team culture and possess the competencies to execute the tasks they are assigned to contribute to the overall purpose of the change.

Strategy 4: Establishing a Team Culture

The president has the responsibility for cultivating a positive team culture. Although there is no quick fix or easy way to launch transformational change at public institutions, it is necessary for the president to focus on the people who will be executing the change (Hiatt & Creasey, 2003). It is essential to empower the leadership team to make change happen. It is evident that a transformational change entails more than merely looking at data and announcing that a change is coming. Transformational organizational culture changes require thoughtful planning and sensitive implementation (Burgess & Connell, 2006). Most important, they necessitate active engagement of the leadership team and the people affected by the changes. To facilitate engagement and gain commitment from all involved, the president is encouraged to collaborate with the team members to establish a team culture that includes values, goals, communication, and clear expectations.

In addition to organizational culture, organizational structures have a significant influence on the capacity of college leaders to implement change.

McPhail (2016) points out that colleges need to change existing organizational structures to implement transformational change. Prior to the latest scrutiny of the reform efforts, a large number of community colleges had remained primarily focused on the strategy-formation aspect of student success. As impressive as these efforts were, merely designing strategies was insufficient; they needed to be adequately implemented to enhance student success. Empirical evidence indicates the presence of a significant gap between the strategies intended to improve student success and the management practices adopted to execute them. This misalignment points to deficiencies in the way the leadership team communicates the vision and drives organizational processes. One can learn a lot about the culture of the leadership team by examining organizational structures and the team's execution processes. To execute transformational change efficiently, team members must understand their roles and responsibilities as well as the expectations of the senior leadership. Teams function well when they are given specific roles and can appreciate how their contributions fit in the overall organization.

Successful leadership teams understand their president's expectations. Although team building is one of the president's most important responsibilities, the day-to-day whirlwind of duties may prevent some presidents from spending time with the team to clearly articulate their expectations. Making team members aware of ongoing expectations is not something that can be achieved in a short time and then forgotten. It is an ongoing organic process that leaders must develop and fully embrace. Implementing change requires an informed leadership team; being fully cognizant of all aspects of the organization will make the leaders more effective in executing their duties. Indeed, in the context of transformational change, leadership team effectiveness remains the critical factor for success. Thus, the president should realize that he or she must rely on each team member, and it is also essential for these individuals to act in unison and work collaboratively. The president must also take the time to build trust and encourage team members to collaborate with each other and share their skill sets and efforts to more effectively attain the institution's goals.

Leaders who are considering launching a transformational change process should ask themselves what the reason for the change is and if the urgency is real. If the transformational change is deemed necessary and urgent, leaders should communicate the message to the leadership team and other stakeholders and ensure they possess the knowledge and skills as well as the commitment needed to become actively engaged in the change process.

Strategy 5: Developing a Communication Plan

Resistance to change is a common concern for leaders. However, leaders sometimes misinterpret the employees' legitimate unease with how the change will affect their roles as resistance. To avoid any confusion and alleviate such concerns when planning to initiate a significant change, it is essential to dedicate some time to developing a communication plan to define who needs to be informed about the change taking place. The leadership team must also decide how often updates are necessary and what information is shared with which stakeholders. The president should work with the leadership team to determine who will take responsibility for communicating the progress of the change. The communication plan is an essential component of the overall change management process. For example, leaders can ask simple questions, such as "What do people need to know?" and "When do they need to know it?" Different stakeholder groups may need different pieces of information based on their role at the college and their function in implementing the change.

There is no place in the communication plan for speculation, as any ambiguities will inevitably result in resistance. Most employees do not set out to resist change, but they will be concerned about how the change will affect their lives. When leadership teams take the time to build a communication plan for the upcoming change and are willing to answer all questions regarding the change process and expected outcomes, most employees will give the process a fair chance to unfold. There are many ways to keep the college community informed about changes taking place on the campus. For example, some college leaders offer information workshops to discuss the change process and address any concerns. Other institutions might organize a series of focus groups or conduct surveys to solicit feedback on the change process. Whatever strategy is adopted, some of the angst about change can be avoided if the leadership team takes responsibility for developing a communication plan. It is the leadership's responsibility to ensure that all frontline supervisors have information about the change process, whether it pertains to adjustments to day-to-day operations or requires a more substantial revision of frameworks and practices.

Being consistent with messages about the change process is essential. The president, in collaboration with the leadership team, must identify the topics to be discussed as well as the level of detail that will be provided to the college community. For example, in some institutions, employees expect face-to-face communication from the president and the leadership team, but in others a college-wide e-mail would suffice. The president must work with the leadership team to establish the best communication mode and should hold the team members accountable for adhering to it. Transformational change requires the leadership team to communicate with all stakeholders and lead and manage the change efforts in a way that ensures employees understand the main reasons for the change, its expected outcomes, and its effects on their jobs and lives. They should also be kept informed throughout the process. It is amazing how many leaders launch change initiatives without communicating to their teams why the change is necessary and how the change will be evaluated. Sometimes presidents are reluctant to share information simply because they have failed to plan ahead and cannot envisage all the necessary steps that would lead to the desired change. They cannot expect others to be supportive of change if they do not know what it entails. The president is encouraged to share all pertinent information, including evaluation findings, with the entire leadership team (see Boggs & McPhail, 2016, chapter 7, for practical ideas about change management). A positive relationship is an essential component of a successful transformational change process. The leadership team must be prepared to manage the communication process, which starts by building awareness of the change and ensuring that stakeholders are kept informed as the change process unfolds. Therefore, the president of the institution must intentionally send the message to the leadership team members that they are responsible for not only creating college-wide awareness of the reasons for change but alsodesigning the ongoing communication messages and ensuring that all stakeholders receive these at the right time. The evaluation of communication and change approach that will be used to keep the college community informed must also be determined.

Strategy 6: Developing an Evaluation Plan

The final task in developing the team responsible for the transformational change management process is establishing the evaluation methods and standards. Evaluation should be a part of the ongoing improvement in the change management process adopted by the institution. Once the best methods for conducting evaluation and review are determined, the associated activities must be precisely defined and need to be embedded in the planning and implementation process.

Many community colleges use key performance indicators to measure and evaluate change. If the indicators are well defined, they can help determine whether and how well elements of an organization are working toward fulfilling the objectives of the change effort. The change process can move forward only if the outcomes of the steps already taken are evaluated objectively and any areas of concern are addressed. If modifications required to effect the desired change are not evaluated during the execution process, it will be difficult for the leadership team to determine whether the college is progressing toward the goal, and the change is producing the desired results. Because today's community college leaders are accustomed to collecting and reporting data, these same practices can extend to information related to the change process. Similarly, active leadership teams routinely conduct evaluations of various organizational procedures and should adopt this same approach to the change process to ensure the project's success.

The first part of this chapter discussed six steps leaders can take to empower teams to execute transformational change. The next section is a case study that shows how the president of Anne Arundel Community College (AACC) successfully engaged her leadership team to launch a transformational change process. This case is also beneficial for examining how a leadership team can empower stakeholders at all levels of the institution to become engaged in implementing the change process. A detailed discussion of AACC's change process illustrates how the strategies mentioned in the first part of the chapter were adopted in executing the transformational change. It is evident that leading change involves constantly making decisions based on evidence, which in turn allows the institutional leaders (and all employees) to move forward and make further decisions.

Case Study: How to Launch Transformational Change

AACC's homepage (Anne Arundel Community College, n.d.) provides an overview of its main campus, which lies 5 miles outside the beautiful historic district of Annapolis, Maryland, and is the third largest community college in the state. Established in 1961, this public 2-year institution serves more than 45,000 degree- and non-degree-seeking students each year in a diverse county with more than half a million residents. Dawn Lindsay, president of AACC, has dedicated more than 25 years of her life and professional career to community colleges. She leads by following the philosophy of servant leadership in the belief that this leadership style yields the best results. Moreover, she is aware that servant leadership requires a strong ethical platform, transparent decision-making, the ability to develop collaborative relationships that are mutually beneficial, a personal commitment to shared governance, and an institutional commitment to student success. The president believes in open-access, high-quality, and diverse educational offerings and recognizes the need to build bridges among and between internal and external constituents. Most important, her mission is to create a college culture that is student centered and responsive to the needs of the community (D. Lindsay, personal communication, August 25, 2018).

Local residents and stakeholders view AACC as the community's college. This is evident in the fact that about 60% of college-bound public high school graduates in Anne Arundel County who enroll in Maryland higher education institutions attend AACC (Anne Arundel Community College, 2019).

In addition, the college serves students with a variety of academic goals, including adults returning to college for retraining and students taking college courses while still in high school. Although the college boasts an outstanding reputation locally and nationally, in recent years a large percentage of its students were not achieving their goals. The data also showed that the longer students remained enrolled at AACC, the less likely they were to complete their program of study. Achievement disparities between students of color and other learners were also evident (Anne Arundel Community College, 2018a).

These issues were not unique to this institution. Indeed, many community colleges across the United States have found that although the traditional mission focusing on access had succeeded in attracting more students to pursue college education, many of them never completed their course of study. Thus, it was necessary to address these achievement disparities, and to attain this aim, AACC joined the Achieving the Dream (ATD) network in 2010. ATD is a comprehensive nongovernmental reform movement for student success (Achieving the Dream, 2019). During the initial years of engagement with ATD, the management of AACC initiated a few top-down pilot programs focusing on new student orientation and registration processes. However, similar to other ATD institutions, the ATD champions at AACC struggled to engage the larger college community in student success efforts aimed at mitigating achievement disparities and promoting equity. The absence of equity outcomes is a major problem in many community colleges. These challenges were further exacerbated by the senior leadership transition, and most of the student success work at the college was at a standstill until Lindsay came on board as president with a new vision for transformational change.

In the process of launching new directions for the college's transformation efforts, Lindsay built on the college's previous student success work—especially the use of data to inform decision-making. As a part of the transformational change initiative at AACC the college used ATD's capacity framework to assess the college's readiness for change. In addition, the college's ATD coaches conducted a world café experience, in which small groups discuss and share their ideas for addressing issues, to engage the college community in conversations about the institution's capacity to sustain student success. The world café methodology is a simple, effective, and flexible format for hosting large-group discussions.

A year into her presidency, Lindsay determined that she needed to get her leadership team fully engaged in the student success efforts. In particular, the team members needed to provide leadership for their teams while also improving collaboration to demonstrate they are united and fully supportive of the student success efforts. To facilitate this process, Lindsay created an action plan with a compelling vision to guide the change process. She also took steps to ensure that the view was inclusive of all student success efforts and included key stakeholders. Recognizing the importance of aligning the change with the college's strategic planning efforts, the president took measures to identify barriers to the change process and the steps she needed to take to overcome obstacles to a college-wide planning process.

To launch the process, the president adopted a cascading leadership methodology (D. Lindsay, personal communication, August 25, 2018). She worked with the leadership team to provide training for all stakeholders engaged in the planning process. In addition, the president and her cabinet established the strategy for implementing the change. They commenced by setting clear goals for the strategic planning process while being mindful of the institutional capacity and culture. Next, the president created a college-wide taskforce to develop the core components of the strategic plan, assigning the responsibility of its implementation to the vice president of learning. The president provided regular updates to the entire college community as the process moved forward.

The following is a brief summary of the actions taken by the president to launch the transformational change efforts:

1. Formed a cross-functional, cross-hierarchical team to guide the development of the registration onboarding initiative
2. Identified facilitators or cofacilitators and other team roles
3. Developed team charters to specify team purpose, goals, and metrics
4. Established a meeting cycle and scheduled meetings
5. Identified milestones or significant short-term performance indicators used to create meaningful feedback on progress and sustain momentum
6. Celebrated and broadly communicated successes, giving credit to the individual contributors
7. Developed a plan for communicating the vision for the change
8. Continuously used evidence to evaluate and refine the change process, from the planning stages through implementation, and to inform decision-making
9. Cultivated a culture of inquiry in the context of the change process
10. Updated the board of trustees about the new strategic plan on a periodic basis. (D. Lindsay, personal communication, August 25, 2018)

As an award-winning and nationally recognized college and ATD institution, AACC intended to continue to promote student success. The president and the leadership team decided that applying for the Pathways Project led by the American Association of Community Colleges was a clear opportunity for the college to focus on course and program completion as its main goal (D. Lindsay, personal communication, August 25, 2018). AACC's leadership team intended to use the high visibility of the Pathways Project to rally the college stakeholders to support student success as this would increase the chances of participation in this renowned project. The leadership team at AACC viewed focusing the mission on student pathways from college entry to progress to course completion as a strategic approach to increasing and improving systems, processes, and policies, with the ultimate goal of ensuring that a greater number of students would graduate from AACC. Although this idea was certainly based on sound reasoning, the college's application to participate in the project was not accepted. The lack of access to the national project was a significant setback, as it meant that the leadership team would not receive national consultations, peer support, or external guidance on the strategies that could be adopted to increase student success.

Persistence

The decision-making process and the eventual application to the Pathways Project had not been easy. College leadership held many meetings campuswide with faculty and staff representatives and constituency groups prior to applying for the project. During the application process, the college leaders seriously embraced broad-based stakeholders' engagement, especially that of the faculty members. The college's entire leadership team remained visible and accessible throughout the process, prompting open communication. At the planning meetings, Lindsay and the vice presidents presented a united front when discussing the urgent need for reform, insisting that everyone's support was needed to undertake the significant work of implementing the project at scale. The constituency groups closely studied readiness criteria and scrutinized the application process. Thus, when the leadership team asked for honest feedback on the proposal, that is what they got. Participants asked some difficult questions, which prompted many frank conversations. This was the first time in recent history that AACC's leadership team solicited feedback at this scale about whether to move forward with such an ambitious initiative. As these decisions were typically made only at the highest levels of the organization, the stakeholders were appreciative of the opportunity to participate and felt more involved in the process.

Nonetheless, the proposed pace and scale of change was daunting, and many individuals expressed significant concerns about the college's ability to do this work. Some faculty members also voiced their reservations regarding the impact of change on instruction and their responsibilities, time commitment, budget implications, compensation, program changes and restructuring, losing local control, and impact on other programs and initiatives, among other issues. Some of the concerns expressed by staff included additional workloads, budget constraints, initiative fatigue, shifting priorities, scale of change, and so on.

Despite all efforts to gain acceptance, AACC was not chosen to join the national project. Knowledgeable of the college's history and pride, Lindsay was disheartened by the rejection and struggled to find a way to inform the college community that its institution was not selected for the national project. Honoring the leadership team's commitment to transparency, and appreciative of the involvement of so many individuals in the consultation meetings, she notified the entire college campus of the application outcome the same day she received the news. However, in this same message Lindsay informed the campus community that she and the vice presidents were committed to the principles espoused by initiative. The valuable groundwork that was laid in completing the application provided evidence confirming an urgent and strong appetite for change at the college.

The Call to Action

Admittedly, not all stakeholders were unhappy about AACC's not being accepted to participate in the Pathways Project. However, even without AACC's participation, Lindsay viewed Guided Pathways as the next major step to move the college forward. Rather than waiting for the next opportunity for AACC to participate in the national network for change, she made the decision that the institution was going to pursue transformational change through a Guided Pathways initiative. The guided pathways model is a strategy for institutional reform designed to strengthen college programs and majors and help students achieve their end goals (Bailey, Jaggars, & Jenkins, 2015).

In a personal communication to the college community, Lindsay announced that given that pathways reforms at community colleges across the country would play a major role in the national college completion agenda, she wanted AACC to move forward with the required work. Thus, soon after receiving the rejection notice from the American Association of Community Colleges, the leadership team regrouped and announced its intention to move forward with the changes required to meet the objectives of the national Guided Pathways movement. Motivated by these clear objectives (American Association of Community Colleges, 2019), Lindsay worked with the vice presidents, deans, and other senior administrators to determine how best to align current initiatives with the goals of the national movement. Moreover, she encouraged team leaders to identify scalable high-impact programs that could support the Guided Pathways efforts at AACC.

By the convocation ceremonies in January 2016, Lindsay was ready to officially invite the college community to focus on designing and implementing structured academic and career pathways for all students. She was convinced that the American Association of Community Colleges' Guided Pathways (2019) was the right strategic approach for the college to undertake to increase course completion, resulting in a greater number of students receiving high-quality academic credentials. From the beginning, the president and the vice presidents made it clear that this work was different from previous pilot interventions launched under ATD. The leadership team explained that Guided Pathways had the potential to lead the college toward a cultural transformation, as it would affect all areas of the college.

To ensure college-wide engagement in launching the project, the leadership team made presentations at the fall 2018 college convocation about the Guided Pathway's effort (D. Lindsay, personal communication, August 25, 2018). The reaction from the audience confirmed a sense of urgency for the college to improve completion rates. Although AACC's completion rates were on par with the national averages, this was no longer deemed acceptable at AACC. Thus, it was time to challenge the status quo and more fully explore and understand the barriers students faced along their academic journeys at the college. The need to make urgent changes that would increase student success was further confirmed by the evidence that AACC was serving an increasingly diverse student population. To support student success and program completion and provide expertise on diversity, equity, and inclusion, the college established a diversity office in 2014, headed by a full-time chief diversity officer. The diversity officer worked closely with the office of institutional research to identify data regarding equity gaps in student outcomes. Although the work of the diversity office staff was yielding results, all stakeholders at the college expressed the desire to stay relevant and innovative. Thus, the AACC leadership team continued to dig deeper into student outcomes at the degree, program, and course levels, revealing some troublesome course completion numbers, which they shared with others to emphasize the need to change.

Finding Aha Moments

Immediately after the January 2016 convocation, the college's leadership team met with stakeholders from all levels of the organization to share its vision for change and introduce Guided Pathways as the college's framework for completion efforts supported by compelling disaggregated data, which was a novel way to report results for most in attendance. Although these data were informative, their main objective was to serve as a catalyst for change. There was some resistance to the magnitude of work that needed to be done, but no one at the institution could argue that the change was unnecessary. In presentations to the campus community, the president and vice presidents showed data on student outcomes to demonstrate the need for the institution to become more student centered as improving student outcomes was the only way to improve student success and program completion. Despite not officially participating in the American Association of Community Colleges' national Guided Pathways initiative, Lindsay and the leadership team used the Guided Pathways project's principles to inform the Guided Pathways work that was launched at AACC.

In all their communications with the stakeholders, the president and the leadership team made sure to remain enthusiastic, and they fully involved stakeholders in the transformational change work. The following key constituency groups participated in the change process:

- Board of trustees: The president and vice presidents conducted a retreat with the board of trustees and presented the Guided Pathways Project as the college's student success and completion agenda. The presentation focused on the use of disaggregated data to show achievement patterns of different student populations, high-impact practices to show best practices at other institutions, and equity strategies to focus on improving outcomes for all learners. The leadership team felt it was critical to develop a shared definition of *equity*, which was fundamental to guiding the work and formulating the new strategic plan. As a member of the ATD network for almost 10 years, the college adopted ATD's statement on equity: Equity is grounded in the principle of fairness. Equity refers to ensuring that each student receives what he or she needs to be successful through the intentional design of the college experience (Achieving the Dream, 2016). In consideration of their role as policymakers, the trustees had questions about the need for a change in the institution's strategic direction. The trustees wanted reassurance that this systematic change was truly necessary and would not have an adverse effect on the college as a whole. In June 2016, the board approved retiring the existing strategic plan a year early and subsequently approved the new strategic plan (Anne Arundel Community College, 2018b). However, this approval came with two accountability requirements: The board had to be updated of the progress in October of each year, and the implementation, rollout, and success of this work accounted for 40% of the overall goals for the president. In making these stipulations, the board sent a clear message that bold change required bold accountability.
- Senior college administrators: The president and vice presidents conducted a retreat and held regular meetings with senior administrators to further the sense of urgency toward building a culture of

completion grounded in evidence-based data. They also conveyed that in decision-making, the equity imperative, commitment to academic excellence, and pathways must be embraced and prioritized, while explaining how all this could inform the new strategic plan.

- Faculty and staff: Numerous meetings and open forums were held over several months with faculty and staff, along with constituency group meetings that were for faculty only or staff only. Open forums were also held at the college's two satellite locations. By shifting the focus from ensuring equitable access to education only to a firm grounding in course and completion outcomes using disaggregated data, the leadership prompted the employees to fully embrace the change. For some, the aha moment came after seeing the actual percentages of students who failed to graduate. Another aha moment related to dual enrollment as one of the fastest growing areas of the college. When data were disaggregated, equity gaps became more evident, prompting lively discussion. (D. Lindsay, personal communication, August 25, 2018)

As the planning process unfolded, most of the college stakeholders embraced the need for change. Throughout this period, Lindsay and the leadership team worked closely with the college teams to ensure that equity was an important aspect of the student success agenda. According to Lindsay, it was essential for the college to develop a shared definition of *equity* mentioned previously. The college used the principles of ATD (Achieving the Dream, 2019) and the American Association of Community Colleges' Pathways Project efforts to enhance the definition of *student success*, moving away from its traditional focus on access and academic excellence, to a broader mission related to completion of degrees, certificates, or workforce credentials of value in the labor market. This revised purpose derived from employees' general shared sense of the community college. Further, data were widely shared to remind all stakeholders of the transformational potential of education in students' lives.

While pursuing these various initiatives, Lindsay never lost sight of the fact that the change process unfolding at the college required a united senior leadership team. Indeed, she expected all senior leadership team members to step up and lead the change in their areas of responsibility. In some cases, to facilitate change, Lindsay had to make difficult decisions, one of which was undertaking a high-level college reorganization to ensure that her executive team was fully supportive and engaged in the difficult work to come.

Engagement Matters

Over the course of many months, during which many more courageous conversations were held, momentum and excitement were building across campus. Although the leadership team remained open to stakeholder input and feedback, Lindsay was mindful of the need to reframe the conversations from a deficit mind-set to one that emphasized a positive approach to leading change. Lindsay emphasized to all faculty and staff the need for big and brave ideas, with allowances for failure or risk taking, while being aware that the things that went well and those that did not should be viewed as learning opportunities.

Engagement Matters: Pathways to Completion (Anne Arundel Community College, 2018b) emerged as the name of the new strategic plan. Most stakeholders believed the term *engagement* was reflective of the current momentum taking place at the college. Indeed, it was evident that engagement permeated every goal and objective at the college. It was also clear that constituent groups were committed to equity and academic excellence, which were the primary goals when examining institutional policies, procedures, and resources to provide all students with the opportunity to progress to degree completion, transfer to a four-year college, or to find a career associated with their degree.

Because the conversations on institutional transformation were gaining so much traction, the president and vice presidents sought approval from the board of trustees to retire the old strategic plan one year early to allow the campus to focus on the new plan rooted in equity and completion. This request was unprecedented and signaled a significant culture shift that would not have been possible without teamwork from college leadership and candid conversations with the board of trustees.

Strongly rooted in evidence from national research and striving to create the ideal conditions for student success with a focus on equity and completion, AACC's major goals reflected four important milestones in the student journey: connection, entry, progress, and completion (American Association of Community Colleges, 2019). Over the course of several meetings, the senior leadership team defined the key objectives that provided the foundation for the college's annual work plan. The objectives of the strategic plan helped in identifying 20 work teams: onboarding, academic plans, fields of interest, reengineering application and registration, website redesign, enrollment, dual enrollment, multiple measures, securing external resources, student planning module, academic advising, career exploration, faculty referral and early alert system, eradicating achievement gaps, gateway course success, developmental education pathways, scaling student achievement and success program, tracking completion, credit on-ramps, and equity.

At first glance, having 20 work teams may appear overwhelming, but the senior leadership team felt that the specific work areas of the teams provided multiple options for stakeholders to be engaged in the change process. In recognition of the importance of a clear structure, the senior leadership team established an oversight committee to coordinate the strategic plan efforts. The leaders of each of the 20 teams were chosen by senior college leadership, and volunteers from around the campus were invited to participate, indicating their first and second team preferences.

Lindsay put out several calls for volunteers to help undertake this transformative work. Pointing to further cultural change, the president and vice presidents made it clear to managers that all staff members were welcome to participate and that they should do everything in their power to facilitate the participation of any employee who wished to be on 1 of the 20 teams. Initially, the senior leadership team expected about 50 volunteers for positions on the various teams. However, the response was overwhelming as almost 300 faculty and staff volunteered to serve on 1 of the 20 teams. Encouraged by such enthusiasm for the upcoming work, Lindsay used the fall 2017 convocation to initiate the college-wide implementation of Engagement Matters. She clearly communicated the significance of the new strategic plan and set the stage for the important teamwork to be undertaken over the course of the academic year. Lindsay also informed the attendees of her bold decision to delay the college opening for the first time so that all faculty and staff could attend the college convocation. This was unprecedented, as convocation had traditionally been centered on faculty. Furthering the call to action, the president and vice presidents reinforced the president's college-wide engagement approach by calling on all divisions of the college to actively work on planning and implementation of the strategic plan. This new strategic plan emerged as a game changer, and everyone's commitment was needed to make it successful.

Initially, some staff members were not enthusiastic about the change and were waiting for all the work to fail or just go away, claiming that Engagement Matters was too big with too many teams and people to manage. Time proved these detractors wrong. The leadership team put structures in place to ensure that all teams were properly supported as they undertook their work. Each of the 20 teams was charged with writing implementation plans over the course of the academic year. The teams were provided with a template that outlined their responsibilities, team membership, important activities to include in consideration of the charge, how success was to be measured, the impact of change on equity, a time line for implementation, and budget. Teams met regularly throughout the fall semester to review the research and best practices on their subject area, hear presentations about current practices, conduct surveys, and reach recommendations. The Engagement Matters Oversight Committee reviewed and approved these recommendations for consideration by the president and vice presidents. The first team report was completed in January 2017, and, by July 2017, all 20 team reports were complete. The work of the 20 teams resulted in 247 recommendations and 362 milestones that sought to fundamentally redesign the student experience by fall 2018. The reports were nothing short of extraordinary. A celebratory event was held in May 2017 to thank all the team members for their hard work.

Show Us the Money

Like most community colleges, AACC has experienced a significant decline in enrollment over the past several years. Securing funding for implementing such broad and transformational changes that were resource intensive required some ingenuity on the part of the president and vice presidents. Still, Lindsay and the leadership team were unified in their commitment to reallocate existing resources and find ways to be more cost efficient to support the highest priority strategic requests in support of student completion and bringing reform initiatives to scale rather than focusing on small pilot programs. Over the past three years, the president worked hard with the leadership team, dedicating countless hours to combing through existing budgets, leaving no stone unturned, to fund more than $2.6 million in essential human resources and technology upgrades necessary to support the implementation of the new strategic plan.

Moving Forward

The leadership team has been very intentional about embedding Engagement Matters into every process and activity undertaken by the college. The president and vice presidents have set annual performance goals directly related to supporting the success of the strategic plan that trickle down to midlevel administrators throughout the college. Lindsay and the leadership team's main priority was to demonstrate transparency, accountability, and alignment. As a result, this is the first time a strategic plan had come to life at AACC in such dramatic fashion as opposed to sitting on a shelf after planning was completed.

The college reached a significant milestone with the launch of a new student experience in fall 2018. During the fall convocation, Lindsay announced new directions for the academic year, focused on helping students progress from entry to exit in the following key areas:

- Fields of interest (metamajors)
- New student orientation
- Academic advising by field of interest
- Updated student success course
- Targeted model courses to address equity gaps in course success
- Lowering textbook costs using open education resources
- New faculty referral system
- New developmental pathways (D. Lindsay, personal communication, August 25, 2018)

The president sent a clear message to the college community that the administration is committed to using college resources to promote success and completion. In addition to the focus on programs and services aimed at promoting student success, it was clear that AACC had invested significant human and fiscal resources toward making the college a data-driven and student-centered institution. New data tools focusing on equity were adopted to shift the culture from simply reporting data after the fact to one where the data spurs action. Enrollment, retention, and completion are now analyzed in real-time, allowing midcourse corrections. To maintain the momentum, weekly meetings are regularly held, allowing college leadership the structured time for reflection on the progress made and on the further courses of action to promote change. Commitment to transparency and widespread access to data allow faculty, staff, and administrators to find a common purpose and a mutual understanding of the critical need to eradicate pervasive equity gaps.

The college has come a long way in a short period of time, but there is still much to do. As this journey progresses toward building a culture of completion over the next several years, the college's leadership team will continue to strive to sustain the transformational change momentum. The president and the senior leadership team have developed a work plan that will lead toward the development of a new strategic plan for 2021–2024, which will include a comprehensive environmental scan aimed at assessing the needs of the diverse learners pursuing qualifications at AACC and build on a college-wide commitment to continuous improvement. A substantial residual benefit of this approach for AACC was identifying leaders in different organizational units.

Examining the transformation that is taking place at AACC, it is evident that broad-based engagement is taking place throughout the college.

Those in key leadership positions see themselves as collectively accountable. Lindsay said,

> We must provide equitable opportunities for our students. Permeating every goal and objective is a commitment to examine institutional policies, procedures and resources providing all students with the opportunity to progress to degree completion, to transfer to a four-year institution, or to find a career associated with their degree for their outcomes and have adopted a mechanism to support each other to achieve the goals of the strategic plan (Anne Arundel Community College, 2018b).

Conclusion

In closing, working as a team to implement transformation involves genuine engagement and collaboration with others. Acknowledging the uniqueness of individuals needs to be balanced with effective teamwork to expedite progress toward institutional success. Leaders should be mindful that even though the change is vital to the institution, the leadership team members must not use their position to impose change on employees. Presidents can empower leadership team members and other employees to find ways to be meaningfully engaged in the change process. Just because College X has implemented a particular project and has received an award for the yielded results does not mean that a leader at another institution can do the same with equally satisfying results. Transformational change does not work that way. Change must be realistic, manageable, and evidence based, and its progress and outcomes must be assessed by adopting measurable performance indicators, which are essential for leading and managing transformational change. In addition to knowing institutional data, presidents are advised to get to know their team members to identify their leadership preferences, strengths, key motivators, and career goals. Presidents are encouraged to include a broad range of stakeholders in the decision-making process where possible. Instead of delegating tasks, the team members should be entrusted with projects and be given autonomy to determine the best solution for each issue they identify. This empowerment will encourage them to cooperate and develop problem-solving skills to lead transformational change (Anne Arundel Community College, n.d.).

References

Achieving the Dream. (2016). *Equity: Achieving the Dream equity statement.* Retrieved from http://www.achievingthedream.org/focus-areas/equity

Achieving the Dream. (2019). *Achieving the Dream's institutional capacity framework and institutional capacity assessment tool.* Retrieved from https://www.achieving-thedream.org/sites/default/files/basic_page/atd_icat_assessment_tool.pdf

American Association of Community Colleges. (2012). *Reclaiming the American dream: A report from the 21st-Century Commission on the Future of Community Colleges.* Retrieved from http://www.aacc.nche.Edu/21stCenturyReport

American Association of Community Colleges. (2019). Pathways project. Retrieved from https://www.aacc.nche.edu/programs/aacc-pathways-project/

Anne Arundel Community College. (2018a). *Instructional research annual report.* Retrieved from https://www.aacc.edu/media/college/leadership/StrategicPlanBro chure_F16_WEB.pdf

Anne Arundel Community College. (2018b). *2017–2020 strategic plan: Engagement matters.* Retrieved from https://www.aacc.edu/media/college/leadership/Strategi cPlanBrochure_F16_WEB.pdf

Anne Arundel Community College. (2019). *Fast facts 2018–2019.* Retrieved from https://www.aacc.nche.edu/?s=fast+facts

Anne Arundel Community College. (n.d.). Home page. Retrieved from https://www.aacc.edu/

Bailey, T., Jaggars, S. S., & Jenkins, D. (2015). *What we know about guided pathways.* New York, NY: Columbia University, Teachers College, Community College Research Center.

Boggs, G. R., & McPhail, C. J. (2016). *Practical leadership in community colleges: Navigating today's challenges.* San Francisco, CA: Jossey Bass.

Burgess, J., & Connell, J. (2006). Temporary work and human resources management: issues, challenges and responses. *Personnel Review, 35*(2), 129–140.

Chapman, J. A. (2002). A framework for transformational change in organizations. *Leadership & Organization Development Journal, 23*(1), 16–25.

De Jager, P. (2001). Resistance to change: A new view of an old problem. *The Futurist, 53*(3), 24–27.

Hiatt, J. M., & Creasey, T. J. (2003). *Change management: The people side of change.* Loveland, CO: Prosci Research.

McPhail, C. (2016). From tall to matrix: Redefining organizational structures. *Change: The Magazine of Higher Learning, 48*(4), 55–62.

12

IN CONCLUSION

The Why and How of Team Leadership

Christine Johnson McPhail and George R. Boggs

Today's community college leaders are faced with significant challenges, ranging from declining budgets to fluctuations in student enrollment to increased accountability for student success to the need to close equity gaps to keeping pace with technology to demands to prepare students for the workforce in a rapidly changing economy. Looking at the future of the community college, its promises and its challenges, colleges will no doubt be operating in a world that is increasingly demanding and at a time that promises to be the most fast-paced and exciting period in the history of the American community college movement. Competent and prepared leadership for the colleges will be essential.

But it is a mistake to think that colleges can be led effectively by a single strong leader who makes all the decisions, no matter how intelligent, charismatic, and skillful that person might be. The future is not about the perfect leader or the outstanding personalities of individual leaders. Rather, it's about continually learning and finding ways to empower leaders at all levels of the institution to create coordinated and extraordinary impact from where they serve in the institution. It is about leadership teams.

Lessons in Team Leadership

Team Leadership in Community Colleges is designed to provide readers with valuable insights from the contributors, experienced leaders who have thought deeply about the effective use of leadership teams. Their contributions show new and different ways of understanding how teams can work in community colleges. These leaders spell out the challenges they faced, the surprises they encountered along the way, and the lessons they learned.

Sinek (2009) encouraged leaders to become more inspired at work and in turn inspire their colleagues and asked a few basic questions: Why are some people and organizations more innovative, more influential, and more profitable than others? Why do some command greater loyalty from customers and employees alike? Even among the successful, why are so few able to repeat their success over and over? Sinek said that successful leaders have similar leadership behaviors; they "start with why." Contributors to this book not only discuss the reasons that drive major issues facing community college leaders but also take the next step and explain how to develop teams to address those issues.

The chapters in this book provided thoughtful insights about the effect of gender differences on the team, the importance of team diversity, ways to deal with employee unions, budget surprises, working with industry representatives, how a new leader can assess a leadership team, how teams can unify a college, how teams can develop and implement a strategic plan, how teams can inspire and support institutional change and improvements, and how teams can build trust throughout an institution.

It is instructive to think about how the leaders who contributed to this book used challenges, opportunities, and surprises to strengthen their teams and to implement needed changes. In chapter 5 Jacobs talks about how pressures created by the Great Recession affected his college. After assuming his presidency, Jacobs had to change the existing leadership culture into one that was more collaborative, transparent, and team focused. Lowery-Hart in chapter 7 describes being surprised by a fiscal emergency in the middle of his work on succession planning and team development. Lowery-Hart had to transform a team that was individually focused to one that worked together toward a college-wide vision.

In the case study in chapter 11, Dawn Lindsay, president at Anne Arundel Community College, describes how she launched a transformational change initiative at her college. Although she was disappointed that her college was not selected for the American Association of Community Colleges' Guided Pathways Project, she used that situation to launch a transformational strategic planning process. However challenging these issues were to the contributors, they were not viewed as obstacles as much as motivation to strengthen leadership teams and improve the institutions.

Several of the contributors describe their work to build teams as new chief executive officers (CEOs; presidents or chancellors). In chapter 3, Giovannini discusses his experiences as chancellor coming into a new community college district that had an existing leadership team. In chapter 6, Irving Pressley McPhail recounts being called on to create a team to develop and implement a strategic plan to unify three separate colleges into the

Community College of Baltimore County and to focus the institution on improvements in student learning outcomes.

In chapter 1, Boggs discusses how the leader's communications and expectations must be clear, and they must be aligned with the leader's own behavior and actions. He explains how people pay attention to what leaders do perhaps even more than what they say, so leaders need to model the behavior they expect from others.

Is team leadership different in a multicollege or multicampus district? Pan provides some insights in chapter 9 on how these structures developed, the dynamics of the relationships between often competing campuses and a central college or district office, and how experienced leaders have made effective use of team leadership in these complex administrative units. Do female leaders use different team-building and leadership strategies from those male leaders use? Eddy, Hartman, and Liu report on the findings of a 2015 and 2016 national survey in chapter 2 to determine the influence of gender in team leadership. In chapter 8, Ivery and Myron explore how team leadership can be effective to meet the unique challenges of urban community colleges, describing innovative redesign initiatives to improve student success and completion.

Christine Johnson McPhail suggests in chapter 11 that for community colleges to implement transformational changes, the institution must first formulate an execution strategy. Managers of professional sports teams understand the importance of a game plan, and McPhail suggests that this same notion (strategy) can be used by community college leadership teams to launch transformational change. She discusses six useful strategies for developing teams that will be capable of executing transformational change.

One of the most visible and important teams for any college governs the institution—the CEO-board team. In chapter 10 McGinnis, Yaqub, and Boggs list the steps that can be taken to build and maintain a strong team at the governance level that can set a positive tone for the whole institution. Developing governance and executive leadership teams is a good start, but in chapter 4 Beatty also points out the importance of developing a midlevel college leadership team, and she describes how a develop-your-own development program using the leadership competencies developed by the American Association of Community Colleges can provide the framework.

Common Threads

Readers will find that many of the contributors refer to the same principles and practices. Several mention the importance of a unifying vision for the future of the college and a shared mission that is continually expressed by team members. Leadership teams described in the chapters benefitted from clear and consistent expectations for the team and its members. Effective and ongoing communication is pointed out again and again as being critical to team functioning. Persistence through challenge is a common leadership characteristic for successful teams. Decisions and plans have to be evidence based, outcomes focused, transparent, and in alignment with the college mission, vision, and values. Team members adhere to a rule of no surprises. Getting to know team members professionally and personally is cited as a way to develop and maintain an effective team.

The value of ongoing professional development is also pointed out by several contributors. Although much can be gained from conference attendance and participation in association leadership development programs, the contributors discuss what they are doing to develop their own leaders. Professional development activities include president's leadership institutes, midlevel leader training, and the use of established leadership competencies. Contributors mention books assigned to team members to read and discuss together. We have observed that successful teams also use simulations as an effective form of professional development. Using the simulation process, team members are able to discuss how the team would handle challenges before they materialize at the college.

The philosophy governing leadership development has changed. In the past it was thought that preparing college presidents was all that was necessary. Trustees just had to hire the best one they could find to lead their institution. Today we know that leadership must be developed at all levels of the institution, and development of leadership teams is critical.

Looking Ahead

In the future, community colleges will encounter more changes more quickly than any previous generation of community colleges, and this change, driven in part by technology, will be more demanding on leaders, and leadership responsibilities will be more distributed than most can imagine. These were the issues that prompted us and our contributors to write this book. The contributors share a broad range of perspectives on team leadership in community colleges, showing new and different ways of understanding how teams can work in community colleges.

In Bailey, Smith Jaggars, and Jenkins's (2015) evidence-based guide for community college practitioners, they argued that two-year colleges can substantially increase their rates of student success if their administrators are willing to rethink the ways they organize programs of study, support services, and instruction. The significant changes called for can only be accomplished through the work of effective leadership teams charged with carrying out the redesign of programs and structures to promote student success and sustain the mission of community colleges. Community college teams will need to use data to inform decision-making at all levels of the institution. Although leadership teams will use data analytics, how the data are used and handled will be in the hands of all key stakeholders.

In today's community college, leadership teams must learn how to effectively involve a wide variety of stakeholders. Many colleges are struggling with the basics of stakeholder engagement and how they should appropriately respond to increasing pressure. Some leaders struggle to include stakeholder engagement in their strategic plan activities, and some have difficulty building internal support, awareness, and interest. The struggle is in part because of the absence of stakeholder engagement training in the leadership development curriculum for community college administrators. According to the American Association of Community Colleges (2018), which included stakeholder engagement as a leadership competency, community college leaders must be able to demonstrate skills to mobilize internal and external stakeholders to support the mission and goals of the community.

Community college leadership teams will be challenged by the rapid evolution of technology. With the prevalence of social media, internal and external stakeholders will be able to exercise more power than at any other time in the history of community colleges. Leadership teams must have the skill sets to respond appropriately and to protect the privacy and security of stakeholders. The data available to leadership teams through technology are also available to dissenters and have an abundance of information about the business of the college and its employees, all warehoused for the appropriate time to use. Managing this type of information is another competency that must be mastered by community college leadership teams. This abundance and availability of information has never been in the hands of college leadership teams before, and there is always the potential for misuse of the information. Community college leaders and their teams will need to develop policies and practices to handle technology and social media.

The rate of change in community colleges will continue to accelerate. If anything, internal and external demands for change will probably increase over the next decade. Community college leadership teams will be presented with unexpected challenges and wonderful opportunities driven by the interests of students, legislative mandates, and competitors.

Typically, community colleges are burdened with layers of bureaucratic structures, systems, polices, and cultures that may interfere with expedient responses to transformational change. If community college leadership teams do not possess the leadership skills needed to respond to change, the institutions will be at risk of stagnation. In today's community college, teamwork is essential to move the institution forward. In the current environment, even the most talented chief executive officer won't have the skills or sufficient time to handle all the demands and technological information; trained leadership teams are essential. The chief executive officer needs the support of other team members to communicate important decisions to internal and external stakeholders, and the purpose of this book is to assist these leaders, and others throughout the organization, to build and develop effective leadership teams.

References

American Association of Community Colleges. (2018). *AACC leadership competencies for community college leaders* (3rd ed.). Washington, DC: AACC Press.

Bailey, T. R., Smith Jaggars, S., & Jenkins, D. (2015). *Redesigning America's community colleges: A clearer path to student success.* Cambridge, MA: Harvard University Press.

Sinek, S. (2009). *Start with why: How great leaders inspire everyone to take action.* New York, NY: Penguin.

Editors

George R. Boggs is president and chief executive officer emeritus of the American Association of Community Colleges and superintendent and president emeritus of Palomar College in San Marcos, California. He is a professor in the community college leadership program at San Diego State University, and he is chairman of the board of directors of Phi Theta Kappa International Honor Society.

Christine Johnson McPhail is the managing principal for the McPhail Group, a higher education consulting firm; former president of Cypress College; emerita professor of higher education; and founder of the Community College Leadership Program at Morgan State University. She is a recipient of the 2018 Diverse Champion Award from the magazine *Diverse: Issues in Higher Education.*

Contributors

Kimberly Beatty is chancellor and chief executive officer of Metropolitan Community College in Kansas City, Missouri. She has a 30-year career in higher education as an adjunct and associate professor in English and has held progressive leadership positions in community colleges across the nation. Her passion for access, equity, and completion have led to research interests in students and administrators who seek to pursue an education or career in community colleges.

Pamela L. Eddy is a professor of higher education and department chair of educational policy, planning, and leadership at the College of William & Mary in Williamsburg, Virginia. She is also a faculty fellow in the College of William & Mary's Center for Innovation in Learning Design. Her research interests focus on community college leadership, faculty development, and gender.

Eugene Giovannini is chancellor of the Tarrant County College District in Fort Worth, Texas. He is the founding president of Maricopa Corporate College in Scottsdale, Arizona. He also served as president of GateWay Community College in Phoenix, Arizona, for 11 years, where he led the creation of the Center for Entrepreneurial Innovation. He is a former board chair of the National Association for Community College Entrepreneurship.

Catherine Hartman is a doctoral candidate in the program in higher education leadership at the University of Texas at Austin. Her research focuses on community college student success, student transfer from community colleges to four-year schools, and linguistically diverse students in higher education.

Curtis L. Ivery has served as the chancellor of the Wayne County Community College District in Michigan for 24 years. Prior to becoming the chief executive officer of the district, he served in executive positions at community colleges in Texas and Arkansas. He served as the director of human resources in the cabinet of former President Bill Clinton when he was the governor of Arkansas. Ivery is an authority on the urban community college and the urban crisis and is a passionate advocate for racial equity. He is the author of a number of books and a sponsor of a series of national summits. He has a special place in his heart for young adults and children and has written, with his daughter, a series of books containing inspirational messages for these age groups.

James Jacobs is president emeritus of Macomb Community College in Michigan. He is currently a research affiliate at the Community College Research Center, Teachers College, Columbia University, and a lecturer at the University of Michigan School of Education.

Eric Liu is a third-year doctoral student at the College of William & Mary School of Education. His research interests include educational policy, planning, and leadership.

Russell Lowery-Hart is president of Amarillo College and president of the Panhandle Twenty/20 consortium for the top 26 counties in the Texas panhandle. He is past chair of the Texas Higher Education Coordinating Board's Undergraduate Advisory Committee.

Bill McGinnis has been a trustee for the Butte-Glenn Community College District since 1992. He is a board member of the California Educational Facilities Authority and past president of the Community College League of California. He has conducted workshops for many governing boards and has served on several community college advisory committees and accreditation teams.

Irving Pressley McPhail is founder and chief strategy officer at the McPhail Group, a higher education consulting firm. He is president and chief executive officer emeritus of the National Action Council for Minorities in Engineering, founding chancellor emeritus of The Community College of Baltimore County, president emeritus of St. Louis Community College at Florissant Valley, and president emeritus of LeMoyne-Owen College. He is a member of the board of directors of the Society of Manufacturing Engineers (SME) Education Foundation, the 50K Coalition Advisory Board, the University of Michigan School of Engineering Diversity, Equity, Inclusion Advisory Council, and an at-large member of the Cornell Mosaic.

Gunder A. Myran was named president emeritus of Washtenaw Community College in Michigan after serving as the college's chief executive officer for 23 years. Prior to his tenure there, he was a professor in the Community College Leadership Program at Michigan State University. He is the president of Myran and Associates, a consulting firm, and is the senior consultant to the chancellor of the Wayne County Community College District. He is a member of the board of directors and faculty of the doctorate program in community college leadership at Ferris State University. He received the Association of American Community Colleges leadership award in 2014.

Eloy Ortiz Oakley has been chancellor of the California Community Colleges since December 2016. He is a University of California regent and served as superintendent and president of the Long Beach Community College District in California. He is a board member for the California Chamber of Commerce and the College Futures Foundation.

Shouan Pan serves as chancellor and chief executive officer of Seattle Colleges in Washington. During his 27 years in higher education, he has taught as a full- and part-time faculty member and served in several other executive positions in community colleges, including president, provost, executive dean, and dean. As an immigrant, he is passionate about changing the future of the underprivileged.

Samia Yaqub is the superintendent and president of the Butte-Glenn Community College District. She has worked at Butte College for more than 30 years, including 15 years teaching English as a second language and developmental reading and writing. She received her doctorate in education with an emphasis on community college leadership from Oregon State

University. Her research interests include leadership development, student equity, and diversity. She won the Dissertation of the Year award in 2011 from the Research and Planning Group for her dissertation titled *Latina Student Perceptions of Learning Communities.*

INDEX

Practical Wisdom

Thinking Differently About College and University Governance

Peter D. Eckel and Cathy A. Trower

Foreword by Richard Chait

"Treating governance as a learning process and drawing from personal experiences working with public and private institutions, Eckel and Trower challenge trustees and administrators to think more intentionally about the work of the board, while providing well-informed and astute practical guidance for powerful learning to drive higher performance."—**Sabah Randhawa**, *President, Western Washington University*

"*Practical Wisdom* is a must-read on trusteeship and governance. Eckel and Trower have written a clear, smart, and example-laden book to help college and university presidents and their boards of trustees work effectively together to advance their institutions and address the challenges that confront them. If you are looking for the best how-to manual on college and university governance, this is it!" — **Isiaah Crawford**, *President, University of Puget Sound*

22883 Quicksilver Drive
Sterling, VA 20166-2019   Subscribe to our e-mail alerts: www.Styluspub.com

ELAINE P. MAIMON

LEADING ACADEMIC CHANGE

Vision, Strategy, Transformation

Foreword by CAROL GEARY SCHNEIDER

Leading Academic Change

Vision, Strategy, Transformation

Elaine P. Maimon

Foreword by Carol Geary Schneider

"One of America's best university presidents has written a brilliant book that will surely inspire and instruct other educational leaders. Each page overflows with eloquence, wisdom, evidence, and powerful examples. This book is perhaps Maimon's most significant gift to higher education. Anyone interested in transformation must read it." — **Shaun R. Harper**, *Clifford and Betty Allen Professor, University of Southern California Rossier School of Education*

"This book is an indispensable resource for those committed to improving their institutions in the interest of student success."— **Muriel A. Howard**, *American Association of State Colleges and Universities (AASCU)*

(Continues on preceding page)

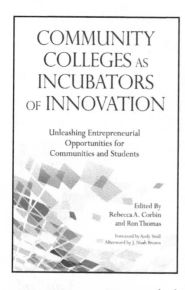

Community Colleges as Incubators of Innovation

Unleashing Entrepreneurial Opportunities for Communities and Students

Edited by Rebecca A. Corbin and Ron Thomas

Foreword by Andy Stoll

Afterword by J. Noah Brown

"Our nation's system of community colleges is a vital resource, and I'd urge anyone concerned about the future of our country to read *Community Colleges as Incubators of Innovation*. The book offers a tapestry of case studies describing the inspiring innovations of community colleges that are determined to equip students of all ages with the 'entrepreneurial-ness' needed in careers spanning business, academia, public policy, or social services. As these community colleges reimagine their role, they're leading the way in providing students with compelling and cost-effective paths to fulfilling lives in an oh-so-dynamic world."— ***Ted Dintersmith***, *Author*, What School Could Be

"Entrepreneurial thinking has the power to facilitate transformational change within our colleges, and this book captures the essence of not only how it can but also why it should. Whether energizing educators to seek innovative curriculum designs, or creating partnerships to better address complex workforce issues in the twenty-first century, the contributors make it clear that the entrepreneurial college is the new standard of excellence." — ***Edward Massey***, *President, Indian River State College*

(Continues on preceding page)